*Paradigms, Thought,
and Language*

Paradigms, Thought, and Language

Ivana Marková
Department of Psychology
University of Stirling

1807 JW 1982
175 YEARS OF PUBLISHING

JOHN WILEY & SONS
Chichester · New York · Brisbane · Toronto · Singapore

Library of Congress Cataloging in Publication Data:
Marková, Ivana.
  Paradigms, thought, and language.

  1. Languages—Philosophy.   2. Thought and thinking.
3. Cartesian linguistics.   4. Phenomenology.
I. Title.
P106.M35   121   81-22022
                               AACR2
ISBN 0 471 10196 6

British Library Cataloguing in Publication Data:
Marková, Ivana
  Paradigms, thought, and language.
  1. Psychology
  I. Title
  150   BF145

  ISBN 0 471 10196 6

Typeset by Inforum Ltd, Portsmouth
Printed at Pitman Press Ltd., Bath

*To my mother
and
to the memory of my father*

Contents

Preface xi

Chapter 1   Presuppositions and Paradigms 1
1.1   The prison of presuppositions 1
1.2   Paradigms 2
1.3   Presuppositions and generalizations in science 3
1.4   Science and philosophy 4
1.5   The collapse of paradigms 5
1.6   The Cartesian and Hegelian frameworks for the study of
       thought and language 6

PART I   THE CARTESIAN PARADIGM FOR THE STUDY OF
            THOUGHT AND LANGUAGE

Chapter 2   The Individual in the Cartesian Paradigm 13
2.1   Introduction 13
2.2   *Cogito, ergo sum* 15
2.3   The Cogito, consciousness, and reflection 17
2.4   The world-of-consciousness and the world-in-itself 20
2.5   Knowledge is certainty 21
2.6   Intuition and deduction 22
2.7   Conclusion 23

**Chapter 3   The Standard of Knowledge is External: The Case of
            Deductive Reasoning** 24
3.1   The laws of thought 24
3.2   Propositional logic 27
3.3   Syllogisms and conditional problems 29
3.4   Encoding and error 33
3.5   Compartmentalization and error 36
3.6   The logical calculus as a yardstick 38
3.7   Conclusion 40

**Chapter 4   The Static and Predetermined Nature of Ideas,
            Concepts, and Internal Representations** 41

4.1   The innate ideas of the rationalists 41

4.2   The Chomskyan revolution 43

4.3   The solution of Locke 45

4.4   The ideas and concepts of the empiricists 46

4.5   The meanings of words 49

4.6   Kant's *a priori* modes of knowledge 52

4.7   Kant and internal representations 54

**Chapter 5   The Passivity of the Knower in the Acquisition of
            Knowledge** 60

5.1   The views of the Cartesian philosophers 60

5.2   The picture theory 63

5.3   One-way information-processing systems 66

5.4   The filter model 68

5.5   Neisser's position: perception changes the perceiver 70

5.6   The limits of capacity in one-way systems 72

5.7   Minds and computers 73

5.8   The algorithmic nature of cognitive processes 75

5.9   The separation of cognition from its embodiment 77

Chapter 6   Mechanisms, Causes, and Effects 80

6.1   The world as a rational system 80

6.2   Hierarchical structures in cognitive psychology 82

6.3   Invariants and homogeneous time 89

6.4   Causes and effects 92

6.5   Purposeful action 93

6.6   Purposeful explanation in information-processing 95

6.7   Mechanisms and organisms 97

**PART II   THE HEGELIAN FRAMEWORK FOR THE STUDY OF
            THOUGHT AND LANGUAGE**

Chapter 7   The Individual in the Hegelian Framework 103

7.1   Introduction 103

7.2   Expression is the realization of the individual 104

7.3   Expression and consciousness 106

7.4   The world-for-consciousness and the world-in-itself 108

7.5   Phenomenal knowledge 112

**Chapter 8   The Development of Consciousness in Hegel's
            Phenomenology of Mind** 116

8.1   Consciousness: sense-certainty 117

8.2   Universals, particulars, and individuals 120

8.3   Consciousness: perception 124

8.4   Consciousness: understanding 126

8.5 Self-consciousness 127
8.6 Master and slave 129
8.7 Man's search for recognition.................................... 132
8.8 Creativity and activity in the acquisition of knowledge..............135
8.9 Conclusion..138

Chapter 9 The Interactive Nature of Mind.......................... 140
9.1 A conversation of gestures..................................... 140
9.2 Synchrony and reciprocity in mother–infant interaction........... 145
9.3 Intersubjectivity has to be taken for granted in order to be achieved 149
9.4 Intersubjectivity in child development......................... 154
9.5 Intersubjectivity in adult communication.................... 159

Chapter 10 The Activity of the Knower in the Acquisition of Knowledge 162
10.1 The laws of thought in the Hegelian framework 162
10.2 Formal logic and Hegelian logic in psychology 166
10.3 The nature of language and concepts 169
10.4 The reflexive nature of thought 173
10.5 The mind as a dynamic whole 174
10.6 Knowledge is acquired through a 'circle returning within itself' 178

Chapter 11 Paradigms and Scientific Method in Psychology 184
11.1 Cartesian and Hegelian science 184
11.2 Theory-ladenness and the neutrality of scientific observation 188
11.3 Research methods in psychology 193
11.4 Universals, particulars, and research methods in psychology 196
11.5 Not a conclusion 203

Notes... 204

References... 205

Index.. 218

Preface

My thoughts on the subject of this book have been developing over the years since my studies of philosophy and psychology at Charles University in Prague where I was introduced to Hegel's work. In 1973–74, during my sabbatical leave at the Department of Psychology, University of Oslo, I was particularly stimulated by seminars on language and communication led by Professor Rommetveit and by invaluable discussions with him on the subject of thought and language.

I should like to thank Colin Wright of the Department of Philosophy, University of Exeter, for his generous help at all stages of writing this book: for endless discussions and criticism of my ideas, for pointing me to many important bibliographical sources, and particularly for reading and commenting upon numerous drafts and correcting my English.

I am also very grateful to Iain Macfarlane, to Professor Charles Taylor, to Professor Rob Farr and to Professor Ragnar Rommetveit for reading and commenting on the manuscript.

I should also like to thank the people, publishers, and institutions who have permitted me to reproduce previously published material.

My children, Ivana and Pavel, have helped me in their own ways by encouraging me to continue and they prepared the index.

November 1981   I. MARKOVÁ

CHAPTER 1

Presuppositions and Paradigms

1.1 The prison of presuppositions

The world into which we are born is a social world and its continuity is secured through the relative stability of our norms, beliefs, and routines. Having been born into such a world and having adopted these norms, beliefs, and routines through the process of socialization, we become quite oblivious to their existence; we also become oblivious to the *presuppositions* on which they are based. For example, in social interaction the baby soon takes it for granted that his smile produces a smile on the face of his mother, and that certain kinds of vocalizations on his part evoke certain types of reactions on the part of his parents. He learns rules of communication, patterns of interchanges, and comes to anticipate such interchanges. He begins to respond to cues given by other people and gets upset when his expectations are not met. Gradually, the child adopts more complex beliefs derived from the beliefs of his parents and other authorities, some of which he subscribes to without questioning while others he accepts with reservation.

The beliefs to which the child subscribes without questioning are usually those that are universally accepted by the social community in which he lives, and those the alternatives to which he has no opportunity to consider. In fact, some ways of cognizing and believing, such as prejudging, stereotyping, and religious and political believing, are often so deeply rooted in our social realities that even the suggestion of an alternative way of seeing the social world may provoke violent reactions. It is only when our presuppositions concerning our social realities are broken that we become aware of their existence and then may even feel threatened. For example, when we see or hear what other people see and hear, we take it for granted that our eyes and ears provide us with a 'correct' picture of the world and function properly. It is only when we realize that others do not share our sensory experiences that we start to question the veracity of our own senses. It is when responses from others constantly fail to correspond to our expectations that we start examining the

1

2

very foundations of our interpersonal communication. It is when our pre-suppositions concerning our apprehension of the social world are not shared with others that we may even question our sanity. We can thus say that the absolute necessity of securing stability and order in forming our concepts and acquiring beliefs makes us prisoners of what we take for granted; since we cannot question presuppositions of which we are totally unaware, we are also unaware that there may be alternative ways of perceiving, believing, and cognizing.

Different social realities provide different experiences. They lead to different ways of seeing the world and consequently lead to different beliefs concerning our apprehension of the world. Hanson (1958)[1] argues that, in fact, all our perception is theory-laden, that is, it is based on our previous knowledge and experience. Such knowledge and experience determine what we focus on when perceiving individual objects.

The role of a temporary or more permanent mental set is, of course, well known in psychology. Leeper's classic figure of a young girl or an old woman, the effect of context on the meaning of a sentence (Rommetveit, 1974), and the perception of a bad outcome of an action as caused either intentionally or by chance (Aydin and Marková, 1979), all point to the theory-laden nature of perception. They also point to the effect of our unquestioned presuppositions upon our apprehension of the world.

1.2 Paradigms

Kuhn (1962) maintains that even such complex creations as scientific theories are shaped by existing presuppositions concerning the nature of the world, and therefore by the way we see the world. A universally accepted set of such presuppositions Kuhn terms a paradigm. A pre-paradigmatic science is characterized by the existence of a number of competing schools of thought springing from different philosophies. In a paradigmatic science it is the philosophical view and associated framework of some outstanding scientific achievement that determines future progress in that particular field. For example, before Newton there was no single generally accepted view concerning the nature of light.

Instead there were a number of competing schools and sub-schools, most of them espousing one variant or another of Epicurean, Aristotelian, or Platonic theory. One group took light to be particles emanating from material bodies; for another it was a modification of the medium that intervened between the body and the eye; still another explained light in terms of an interaction of the medium with an emanation from the eye; and there were other combinations and modifications besides. (Kuhn, 1962, p. 12)[2]

All of these schools asserted that their particular theories were the correct ones and had the greatest explanatory power. Although all of them made contributions to the concepts, methods, and understanding of light, it was not until Newton that a single theory was accepted by the whole scientific community and an actual paradigm became established.

Another example of the effect of different schools of thought upon scientific investigation offered by Kuhn, was the discovery of the pendulum by Galileo in the sixteenth century. All the knowledge necessary for the discovery of the pendulum was available to Aristotle, but because of their different conceptual frameworks Aristotle and Galileo noticed different things when looking at a stone swinging on a rope. The Aristotelian mind conceives fall as the motion of a heavy body to its natural place at the centre of the universe. Hence it focuses on such categories as the weight of the stone, the height from which it falls, and the time required for it to achieve rest; thus the Aristotelian mind sees *constrained fall*. Galileo's mind, on the other hand, works within the conceptual framework of Neoplatonism. It is directed towards the circular form of the motion and so to the concepts underlying it such as the radius of the circle, angular displacement, and time per swing: thus the Galilean mind sees a *pendulum*.

In principle it should be possible to change from one framework to another but this is not usually easy and may even prove to be psychologically impossible. While perhaps we can enforce upon ourselves a Gestalt switch when looking at an ambiguous picture such as Leeper's and see the young girl instead of the old woman, in the case of scientific paradigms it is more difficult because of their complexity and our unconscious commitment to underlying philosophical presuppositions.

We may say that because we are so familiar with our basic presuppositions, we do not, in fact, know them—like the hunter who is said 'not to know the mountains because he is right in them. He has to be up in the air to see the whole range of the undulations' (Suzuki, 1950, p. 46). This, however, is not easily achieved if the 'mountains' are very high, as they are in the case of scientific paradigms.

1.3 Presuppositions and generalizations in science

Our innocence with respect to our existing presuppositions in scientific research is associated with several potential dangers. First, being unaware of our presuppositions, we are unable to reflect upon them and consequently to consider alternatives to the adopted ways of thinking and researching. Secondly, we are liable to make unjustified generalizations across different subjects. Problems of the latter type worried William Whewell, an eminent nineteenth century mineralogist, and historian and philosopher of science. Whewell was concerned with the appropriateness of differing fundamental ideas for different sciences. He argued that specific sciences should have their own specific ideas rather than that they should borrow their ideas from other, though related sciences. Only specific ideas secure progress in science.

Each science has for its basis a different class of Ideas; and the steps which constitute the progress of one science can never be made by employing the Ideas of another kind of science. No genuine advance could ever be obtained in Mechanics by applying to the subject the Ideas of Space and Time merely:- no advance in Chemistry, by the use of mere Mechanical Conceptions:- no discovery in Physiology, by referring facts to mere

Chemical and Mechanical Principles. Mechanics must involve the Conception of *Force*:- Chemistry, the Conception of *Elementary Composition*:- Physiology, the Conception of *Vital Powers*. Each science must advance by means of its *appropriate* Conceptions. Each has its own field, which extends as far as its principles can be applied. (Whewell, *The Philosophy of the Inductive Sciences*, Vol. II, pp. 18–19)

Judged by today's knowledge, this quotation from Whewell may seem rather naive, but its gist remains valid. The successful use of a certain conceptual framework in a certain subject may lead to a strong temptation to import it into other subjects without reflecting on its appropriateness. The view that a framework suitable for the physical sciences is also suited to psychology, and consequently that the subject matters of psychologists and physicists differ 'only in the nature of the phenomena they choose to study—the behaviour of human beings rather than physical objects' (Evans, 1977, p. 341), is still shared by some psychologists.

Moreover, just as the conceptual frameworks and hence the subject matters of the various sciences differ essentially from one another, so do the problems they throw up and the methods that must be applied in attempting to solve them: as Northrop (1947) pointed out, there is no *a priori* and therefore universal method for scientific inquiry. But again there is the temptation to generalize from an established science to a newer one. In his *History of Psychology*, Brett (1912–21) emphasizes that one of Kant's legacies to psychology is his contention that any science is based both on empirical and mathematical description. This heritage of Newtonian practice, with its mathematical prescriptionism, affected the whole tradition of psychology: 'It introduced the craze for measurement in psychology and reinforced the yearning for scientific respectability amongst psychologists which had started with Hume's *Treatise*' (Brett, 1912–21, p. 533). Similarly, while for Descartes the subject-matters of psychology and the physical sciences were totally different in kind, their methods were presumably the same, both being based on deduction from first principles. And this was certainly so for Hume, the purpose of the first book of the *Treatise* being to *study physical method in order to establish psychological method*.

1.4 Science and philosophy

It was in 1840 that Whewell proclaimed that progress in natural philosophy had reached the stage at which it should be called a *science*. By asserting that natural philosophy *is* a science, Whewell in effect also issued an official proclamation of the divorce between natural philosophy and 'non-natural' philosophy, i.e. between a philosophy that used empirical methods to obtain knowledge and one that did not. An unofficial separation between the two had already been in existence for some two or three hundred years, since the birth of the scientific paradigms based on the discoveries of the sixteenth and seventeenth centuries.

Psychology only naturalized itself among the experimental sciences towards the end of the last century, and it was only then that it announced its amicable divorce from philosophy and became the science of the mind (Fodor, 1972).

But as Fodor points out, love affairs with philosophy have continued despite the official proclamation of the divorce in the textbooks. But what is more worrying, Fodor tells us, is that psychology is now unaware of this continuing love affair, and while officially it claims independence, 'philosophy in psychology books tend[s] to go underground, living the life of implicit assumptions and the unstated methodological postulates' (Fodor, 1972, p. 83). Moreover, psychologists have not only been unable to stop doing philosophy but they have been doing it badly. A classical example, Fodor claims, is Vygotsky's work. Just like the philosophical empiricists, Vygotsky takes it for granted that the child's acquisition of a concept is dependent on the isolation of sensory invariants, such as *big*, *round*, or *blue*. Having such isolated invariants, the child is supposed to learn which objects do and which do not exhibit such invariants. But such an approach is unjustified and 'Vygotsky is driven to his conclusions less by his data than by some quite unreasonable philosophical convictions about what it is to think abstractly, logically, maturely, and so on' (Fodor, 1972, p. 92).

Fodor, of course, is quite right in saying that psychologists are unaware that they still rely on a number of epistemological preconceptions that are part and parcel of various schools of philosophical thought. But this problem is not specific to psychology. The natural science of the seventeenth century was 'an essential part of a philosophical paradigm initiated by Descartes and developed at the same time as Newtonian dynamics' (Kuhn, 1962, p. 120). What happened was that, having accepted certain of the philosophical assumptions of Cartesianism, the newly developing natural science bred on them but then progressed much quicker than the maternal philosophy. One day, then, there seemed to be no connection between them. Scientific thought was far ahead of philosophical speculation and those engaged in such scientific activities ceased to be aware that their observations had been based on certain philosophical views: instead, they proclaimed their complete independence from philosophy.

1.5 The collapse of paradigms

It thus seems that it is both conceptually and psychologically impossible to develop a scientific framework that owes nothing to philosophical preconceptions concerning the nature of the world and the nature of man, and nothing to epistemological assumptions. But there are times when it becomes necessary to stand back and attempt to unravel one's presuppositions. This does not occur in what Kuhn (1962) calls the period of 'normal science', that is after the paradigm has been formulated. During that stage, science simply carries out the task of developing new theories and establishing new facts within the framework of the paradigm, and of 'puzzle-solving', that is of fitting new facts into the paradigm. At this time there is no reason to question one's presuppositions because the science is thriving and progress and human ingenuity seem to be unending. It is only when anomalies begin to accumulate that one begins to wonder what has gone wrong.

First attempts to solve the problem of cases that seemingly will not fit are nevertheless made within the existing paradigm. But as more cases are found that resist explanation, the paradigm finally collapses and a new one arises to initiate the same journey through the stage of normal science.

A collapsed paradigm cannot be repaired since it also signifies the collapse of existing philosophical presuppositions. Thus, the newly emerging paradigm cannot be understood in terms of the old. Kuhn, analysing the reasons for the paradigmatic switch from Newtonian to Einsteinian mechanics, points out that it was mainly due to the unsuccessful attempt to fit new knowledge concerning complex phenomena into the existing conceptual framework that the Newtonian paradigm collapsed. But while it was these newly discovered complex phenomena that caused the eventual breakdown of the existing paradigm, it still seemed to apply to relatively simple phenomena. Thus the general opinion was that relativistic dynamics had not shown Newtonian dynamics to be entirely mistaken: Newton's equations were simply a special case of Einstein's more general formulae, and on a terrestrial scale, and at velocities small compared to the velocity of light, its predictions were accurate to within experimental error. Kuhn argues, however, against this position. Newton's equations may be identical *in form* to a limiting case of Einstein's equations, but they do not have the same meaning:

. . . the physical referents of these Einsteinian concepts [space, time, and mass] are by no means identical with those of the Newtonian concepts that bear the same name. (Newtonian mass is conserved; Einsteinian is convertible with energy. Only at low relative velocities may the two be measured in the same way, and even then they must not be conceived to be the same). (Kuhn, 1962, p. 101)

A new paradigm is incommensurable with the old not only because the basic presuppositions have been replaced but also because the *whole field of science* and the *problems* to which it gave rise have been redefined. What may be considered problematic in one paradigm may be not only non-problematic but even nonsensical with respect to another paradigm.

1.6 The Cartesian and Hegelian frameworks for the study of thought and language

The main concerns of this book are the basic presuppositions, and their consequences for research in the psychology of thought and language, of two different philosophical frameworks, the Cartesian and the Hegelian. In some ways it would be more appropriate to talk about the conceptual frameworks of the seventeenth and nineteenth centuries, rather than to attach particular names to them. In discussing these traditions, we shall be concerned more with the *Zeitgeist* than with the work of any individuals. It is likely that many psychologists have never read even a single sentence from the work of the philosopher whose name is attached to the tradition within which they operate. By attaching names to them, we only acknowledge that Descartes or Hegel formulated the ideas of the *Zeitgeist* more distinctly and more profoundly than anybody else.

By the Cartesian tradition I do not mean simply the philosophy of Descartes and his disciples; by the Cartesian tradition I mean the mainstream of philosophy that stemmed from Descartes and culminated in Kant, whether it leaned towards rationalism or empiricism, or towards a reconciliation of the two. Kant has been called by many the philosopher of revolution. He not only represented the culmination of the Cartesian tradition, but also became the spring of knowledge for German romantic philosophy, thus providing the life blood for an alternative philosophical tradition.

As for rationalism and empiricism, most of the accounts of the history of psychology have presented them as two mutually opposing and competing schools of thought, leading to mentalism on the one hand and to associationism and behaviourism on the other. In this book, however, we shall not be concerned with the contradictions between rationalism and empiricism. Rather, we shall be concerned with the seventeenth century philosophical tradition, the features of which, whether common to rationalism and empiricism, or specific to only one of them, have had a profound influence on the presuppositions of the study of thought and language in psychology.

This does not mean, of course, that there are no differences between the effects of rationalism and empiricism. But however important the differences in their effects, I do not consider them to be as important as their underlying *similarities* and *convergences*. In fact, it has been because of the prevailing tendencies to focus on their differences that philosophy and psychology have become blind to their common features, and that it has often been forgotten that they both derive from the same seventeenth century Cartesian philosophy. It is only when we contrast rationalism and empiricism with the nineteenth century Hegelian philosophy that the close relationship between the former two becomes apparent.

In discussing the Hegelian tradition, I have deliberately avoided references to the philosophies that have emerged from Hegelianism, namely phenomenology, existentialism, Marxism, and symbolic interactionism. The reason for this omission is that although all of them have provided a wealth of ideas ranging from art to literature and even to science, none of them has actually surpassed Hegel or contributed any new fundamental concepts that are not already implied by Hegel. In spite of their stimulating and new ways of conceiving objects, they have not led to the development of any scientific concepts or scientific questions. Although such authors as Merleau-Ponty, Sartre, Husserl, and others are most rewarding to read and lay bare the enormous complexity of human existence, their ideas do not lead to clearly definable concepts that can be applied to the problems of science.

In what follows I shall commonly be concerned with what I shall call the *frameworks* of these two philosophical traditions. By the term 'framework' I mean a set of presuppositions concerning the nature of the knower, the known, and the mutual relationships between these two. Because the Cartesian trad-

Table 1.1

The Cartesian framework	The Heglian framework
1. The nature of the mind is individualistic	1. The nature of the mind is social
2. The mind is static and passive in the acquisition of knowledge	2. The mind is dynamic and active in the acquisition of knowledge
3. Knowledge is aquired through algorithms	3. Knowledge is acquired through a 'circle returning within itself'
4. The criterion of knowledge is external	4. The criterion of knowledge is internal

ition won for itself almost universal acceptance in the West, I shall often, following Kuhn, refer to its framework as the Cartesian paradigm. The Hegelian tradition, on the other hand, has as yet gained only limited recognition, and its framework cannot, therefore, properly be described in this way.

The differences between the Cartesian and Hegelian traditions discussed in this book can be represented by the sets of presuppositions shown in Table 1.1. No doubt it would be possible to define the differences between the two traditions in terms of other sets of presuppositions, and, of course, there are a number of other important differences between them that are not mentioned in this book. However, since it is necessary to start somewhere, I have chosen those issues which, to my mind, are the most important. For the purpose of discussing these issues, I had intended Parts I and II of the book to have the same structure. However, I was not able to achieve this because some issues that appeared to be of fundamental importance in the Cartesian framework were less important in the Hegelian framework and vice versa. In consequence, although the structures of Parts I and II have a basic correspondence to one another, they do not correspond in detail. Moreover, since a message of a fundamental kind can only be successfully communicated by presenting it and arguing for it in a somewhat rigid and dogmatic manner, I have in most cases categorized philosophers and psychologists as either Cartesian or Hegelian. This does not mean, of course, that they can all properly be slotted into one or other of these without remainder. Nor is it true that science develops in a neat and orderly way, that concepts are precisely defined from the beginning, or that the history of science follows a straight line. The conceptual frameworks of research workers are not tidy showrooms where everything is in place. It may well be that a researcher accepts the presupposition that the mind is individualistic while at the same time holding that the mind is dynamic; or that the criterion of knowledge is external while claiming that the mind is active in the acquisition of knowledge; and so on. The empirical examples used in this book are extreme cases that fit conveniently into the one or the other tradition, and so illustrate them.

It is therefore important to bear in mind that most psychologists and philo-

Figure 1.1.   Duck-rabbit picture

sophers do not operate within clear conceptual frameworks. What they perceive are not exclusively either ducks or rabbits (Figure 1.1) but rather hybrids of the two with one predominating. But that this is so only becomes apparent if they come face to face with problems which are radically insoluble in terms of their existing concepts and methods. It is only then that their fundamental presuppositions become questioned. However, questioning of fundamental presuppositions and acceptance of alternative ideas do not happen simply because problems formulated in the existing paradigm become insoluble. Discussing the difficulty of changing people's ideas, Kuhn refers to the disappointing experience of Charles Darwin and Max Planck:

Darwin, in a particularly perceptive passage at the end of his *Origin of Species*, wrote: '. . . I by no means expect to convince experienced naturalists whose minds are stocked with a multitude of facts all viewed, during a long course of years, from a point of view directly opposite to mine . . . [B]ut I look with confidence to the future,—to young and rising naturalists, who will be able to view both sides of the question with impartiality.' And Max Planck, surveying his own career in his *Scientific Autobiography*, sadly remarked that 'a new scientific truth does not triumph by convincing its opponents and making them see the light, but rather because its opponents eventually die, and a new generation grows up that is familiar with it.' (Kuhn, 1962, p. 150)

PART I

The Cartesian Paradigm for the Study of Thought and Language

The Cartesian principles, for instance, are very suitable for application to mechanism, but for nothing further; their representation of other manifestations in the world, such as those of vegetable and animal nature, are insufficient, and hence uninteresting. (Hegel, *History of Philosophy*, I)

CHAPTER 2

The Individual in the Cartesian Paradigm

2.1 Introduction

Humanism and the Renaissance proclaimed the break with mediaeval thought mainly through the rediscovery of the *individual* and his *self*. It is the opinion of some historians of philosophy, however, that the outburst of the Renaissance interest in the individual was made possible only as a consequence of the enormous concentration of human intellectual energy in the academic institutions of the Middle Ages.

The world of mediaeval man was theocentric. The human being conceived himself as a creature of God and submitted himself to what he saw as the power of God revealed through His redemption of man from his sins. The character of his life on this Earth was supposed to earn a person a passport to either eternal bliss or eternal damnation; to achieve the former, a human being concentrated on disciplining himself with the aid of ascetic practices supervised by the Church. The activities of people in the Middle Ages were to a great extent determined and coordinated by the feudal system functioning through the guilds and syndicates, and through the Church. Berdyaev (1936) points out that it was monasticism and chivalry that contributed most towards the strengthening and disciplining of the human personality in feudal society. The mediaeval knights and monks were preoccupied with preserving the ordered structure of the feudal system and the Church, shutting themselves up in their mediaeval castles and monasteries and using their 'spiritual and physical armour' to fight against the 'disrupting forces of the external world' (Berdyaev, 1936, p. 125).

However, innovations gradually worked their way through the system. As early as in the twelfth century some people were suggesting that more attention should be given to the study of physical and human nature. Conducive to such views were reformations within the political and economic system, mechanical inventions, and technological and geographic expansion. These innovations were incompatible with the tradition which concentrated human energy in the work of the academic institutions of the Middle Ages, as well as with belief in divine reward or punishment after death. The incompatibility of the strictness of Christian dogma with the rapidly developing changes in the life of the individual gradually led to transformations in the thinking of the individual as expressed in philosophical writings. The authority of the Church thus became weakened by progress in society.

While in mediaeval philosophical thought the ultimate responsibility for the destiny of a human being was given to God, Humanism and the Renaissance elevated the importance of the individual by emphasizing his intellectual abilities and the power of his mind. A number of Renaissance writers and philosophers became preoccupied with the idea of the dignity of man. Initially, their attempts were shy and modest, such as that of Ficino who asserted man's superiority over animals in the variety of his arts and skills but for whom 'The Soul of man, . . . in that part in which it is mind, is the last among the minds of the higher, cosmic souls and thinks only in a passive way' (Ficino, *Opera Omnia*, p. 387). But his later compatriot and one of the most remarkable philosophers of the Renaissance, Pico della Mirandola, put man right in the centre of the world:

I have placed thee at the center of the world, that from there thou mayest more conveniently look around and see whatsoever is in the world. Neither heavenly nor earthly, neither mortal nor immortal have We made thee. Thou, like a judge appointed for being honorable, art the molder and maker of thyself; thou mayest sculpt thyself into whatever shape thou dost prefer. (Pico della Mirandola, *On the Dignity of Man*, p.5).

Several important themes representing the *Zeitgeist* of Renaissance thought and foreshadowing future developments are to be found in Pico's *On the Dignity of Man*: First, man, placed in the centre of the world, is a *microcosm in the centre of macrocosm*. The conception of man as a microcosm is common to a number of Renaissance writers such as Nicholas of Cusa, Campanella, Agrippa, and Fludd. Man as a microcosm mirrors and unites in himself the terrestrial world, the world of the heavenly bodies and the spiritual world. Cassirer (1942, p. 320) points out that the idea of man as a microcosm uniting in himself the whole world is very ancient and has its origin in mythical thinking in various cultures. Pico, however, in contrast to other philosophers, is not concerned with man's one-ness with the rest of nature. Instead, he stresses man's *distinction* from it, and in particular that unlike the rest of creation he forms his own moral character. He is what he makes of himself and decides his own destiny. In Pico, God says to Adam that in creating him He did not give him any fixed abode or any peculiar gift, but instead He gave him free will and free judgement to act as he chooses. Thus, Pico's man is the 'molder and maker' of himself, and it is in this sense that a human being is more like the Creator himself, and different from the rest of the inhabitants of the earth.

Secondly, Pico della Mirandola emphasizes *man's unlimited freedom to choose* his way of life. It is moral freedom that man possesses, and it is up to him to decide whether to 'grow downwards into the lower natures which are brute' or to 'grow upwards from thy soul's reason into the higher natures which are divine' (Pico della Mirandola, *On the Dignity of Man*, p.5). It is man himself who sets his goal. The idea that the primary aim of human life is moral action is also to be found in Pomponazzi who was concerned that man should realize himself through activity rather than through passive contemplation (Pomponazzi, *On Immortality*, p. 350ff). Thus, practical or operative intellect, practical inventions, travel, and economic growth all validated the idea that the ultimate purpose of human life and the dignity of man were to be found in moral action and creativity. This active involvement gradually became more important than the belief in passive contemplation of earlier philosophers.

2.2 *Cogito, ergo sum*

However, it was Descartes' glorification of the *I* that finally became the point of departure for modern psychology. For Descartes, the *I* was more than just an acting microcosm, possessing free will. Descartes' *I* was, in the first instance, the result of an intensive effort *to find rock-bottom certainty* in the face of the radical scepticism that was prevalent at the time. Berdyaev (1936) has pointed out that the individualism of the Renaissance and Humanism brought man to the limit of his ability to withstand the uncertainty and loneliness into which the Renaissance and Humanism threw him. While, on the one hand, man was elevated to the centre of the universe, affirmed himself, and created his own world, he was, on the other hand, weakened by being 'the flesh and blood of the natural world' and thus losing his self-concept as made in the image of God. As a *natural* being, man had to share the limitation of the natural world; the responsibility for deciding right and wrong was now his.

For Descartes more than for anyone else, this newly obtained freedom and the scepticism to which it led was the source of a deep personal crisis and doubt as to what was true, whether truth could be discovered, and how to re-establish certainty for man: 'I wished to give myself entirely to the search after Truth' (Descartes, *Discourse on Method*, p. 101); and the method of critical doubt and the attitude of distrust towards everything we think led him to question first the evidence of the senses, and then in turn the sciences of physics and astronomy, and even mathematics, but eventually enabled him to turn the tables on scepticism. Having doubted everything in the world and having assured himself that there was nothing about *the world* taken by itself that could be treated as certain and therefore true, Descartes went on to ask himself whether there was anything certain about *himself*, whether at least he himself was *something*? But he had already denied the trustworthiness of his senses, and his body was part of the physical world. That did not seem to leave very much. But his *doubting* could not be questioned and doubting was a *form of thinking*. This would provide him with some purchase in his quest:

> . . . afterwards I noticed that whilst I thus wished to think all things false, it was absolutely essential that the 'I' who thought this should be somewhat, and remarking that this truth '*I think, therefore I am*' was so certain and so assured that all the most extravagant suppositions brought forward by the sceptics were incapable of shaking it, I came to the

conclusion that I could receive it without scruple as the first principle of the Philosophy for which I was seeking. (Descartes, *Discourse on Method*, p. 101)

The rock-bottom certainty Descartes was looking for he found in his own existence as a *thinking thing*: 'I am, I exist, is necessarily true each time that I pronounce it, or that I mentally conceive it' (Descartes, *Meditations*, p. 150). And the process of thinking presupposes existence of the self because 'it is certain that no thought can exist apart from a thing that thinks; no activity, no accident can be without a substance in which to exist' (Descartes, *Objections III and Replies*, p. 64). It was from the *I* that Descartes derived the true principles of philosophy. As the existence of the individual became the first principle, the highest point in the hierarchy, it was implied that God and the outside world only took second place. Paul Valéry comments on Descartes' individualism:

Never before him had any philosopher so deliberately displayed himself upon the stage of his own thought, showing himself off, daring to use the first personal pronoun throughout whole pages. And never, as Descartes above all did . . . had any philosopher so gone out of his way to convey to us the details of his mental debates and inward workings, . . . that least personal of *Me's* which must be the same in all men, the universal in each of us. (Valéry, 1948, p. 17)

The use of the first personal pronoun, the 'I' in Descartes' philosophy, was not a matter of grammatical expediency; nor was it an attempt to continue and complete the humanistic tradition of the Renaissance, or an exuberant celebration of the achievements of the seventeenth century mind. Rather, it was a direct consequence of the first principle of philosophy. Descartes presented the *Discourse on Method* in the form of an autobiography, showing the path of thinking and doubting he had followed, and by which he had finally reached the truth that it is the *I* that is the starting point of knowledge and certainty. But in the *Meditations*, as Beck (1965) shows, Descartes plays the role of the leader of a retreat. While in the *Discourse* we read how Descartes himself arrived at the truth, in the *Meditations* one is actually expected to go through the same exercise of the search after truth and arrive at the same conclusions for oneself.

The emphasis on the uniqueness of the individual culminated with Leibniz, who was born fifty years after Descartes. According to Leibniz the universe is constituted of totally isolated or 'windowless' individual substances or monads. All inanimate objects are divisible into these simple substances or souls, which are themselves indivisible, not because they are too small, but because souls do not occupy space. Their existence is given logically: 'there must be simple substances, since there are compounds; for a compound is nothing but a collection or *aggregatum* of simple things' and these things or monads 'are the real atoms of nature' (Leibniz, *Monadology*, pp. 217–18). The human soul itself is a monad and differs from an animal or plant soul by the quality of perception. Each monad represents from its particular point of view the whole universe; in other words, each monad is a living mirror of the universe; each, however, differs in the clarity of its perceptions from all other monads so that no two monads are exactly the same. Each of them is a unique unrepeatable individual which contains within itself its own history and future. This history and future is the history and future of the world seen from its own point of view. The history of each monad unfolds progressively with time somewhat after the manner of a cine film:

The present is big with the future, the future might be read in the past, the distant is expressed in the near. (Leibniz, *Principles of Nature and Grace*, p. 419)

And through each monad we can know the beauty of the universe. Monads retain their absolute individuality, but only by being totally independent of one another, without contact or interaction, so that they cannot influence or produce any change in each other: they are indeed totally 'windowless'. Although there is no interaction between the monads, the universe is synchronized by a harmony between the monads pre-established by God: though there is no relationship between the monads, the inner changes and developments within each of them are pre-arranged in such a way that they synchronize with the developments and changes within all the other monads.

This profound individualism of the Cartesian philosophy later became one of the unquestioned presuppositions of psychology as it was emerging from philosophy. The majority of the main issues to which psychology has addressed itself have been concerned with the isolated individual rather than with the individual as a member of a particular social group. In fact, Kenny (1973, pp. 113–28) has pointed out that it was through the Cogito that the assumption of *the priority of the self's privacy over the public* was introduced into philosophy and then into psychology. The notion of the priority of privacy over the public is to be taken in the epistemological sense. One's certainty is the certainty of one's clear and distinct ideas, and all other certainties concerning oneself or the external world are to be derived from it. Thus, it was through the Cogito that the interest in subjectivity, consciousness, and reflection arose. And since the notions of *consciousness* and *reflection* in the Cartesian tradition are sharply different from the notions of *consciousness* and *reflexion*[3] in the Hegelian tradition, we shall consider the former pair in some detail.

2.3 The Cogito, consciousness, and reflection

Sir William Hamilton (1870) pointed out that the modern usage of the word 'consciousness' was introduced into philosophy and psychology by Descartes: before Descartes 'this word was used almost exclusively in the ethical sense expressed by our term *"conscience"* ' (Hamilton, *Lectures on Metaphysics and Logic*, p. 196). In contrast to previous usages of the word, for Descartes consciousness was an inseparable characteristic of the Cogito. Kenny (1968) maintains, however, that although in all Descartes' writings consciousness is never separable from thought, there is, nevertheless, an ambiguity concerning the relationship between the two. Sometimes consciousness appears to be something that accompanies thought: 'Being conscious of our thoughts at the time when we are thinking them is not the same as remembering them afterwards' (Descartes, Letter for [Arnauld], 29th July, 1648, p. 235). On other occasions consciousness appears to be identical with thought: 'To be conscious is assuredly to think and to reflect upon one's thought' (Descartes, Interview with Burman, 16th April, 1648, p.149). But whichever of the two interpretations we take, it is obvious that when we talk about thought we also talk about consciousness, and vice versa.

Concerning the notion of 'reflection', here again it appears that it was probably Descartes and then Locke who used it first in the sense of being conscious of one's own thought. It was implied, therefore, that none of the notions, *thought*, *consciousness* and *reflection*, had a meaning independent of the others. Indeed, in *Objections VII and Replies* Descartes argued that because it was impossible to be conscious without reflecting upon what one is conscious of, the attempt to introduce the notion of reflection in addition to that of consciousness was redundant: it would lead to an infinite regress, for our awareness, that we are aware that we are aware that we are aware, does not differ from our awareness that we are aware, or, indeed, from our first awareness (Descartes, *Objections VII and Replies*, p. 343).

For Locke, just as for Descartes, consciousness is inseparable from thinking. But Locke, in contrast to Descartes, does not simply acknowledge that we become aware that we become aware. It is the inseparability of consciousness from thought that makes one a *self* and thus distinguishes human beings from other existences. And because one is conscious not only of one's present but also of one's past, one has a feeling of *personal identity*:

And as far as this consciousness can be extended backwards to any past action or thought, so far reaches the identity of that *person*: it is the same *self* now it was then, and it is by the same *self* with this present one that now reflects on it, that that action was done (Locke, *Essay*, II, xxvii, 9).

It is the *identity of consciousness* implied by the comparison of his present self and his past self that makes a person yesterday and a person today one and the same person. This means that in the case of a mental disorder or brain injury in which a person is unable to keep track of his past mental operations and actions, we must say not only that he has lost his memory but that he has lost his self-identity, because he is unable to unify the self that he is now with any self that might have existed yesterday.

The continuity of the past with the present, therefore, is preserved through a train of ideas succeeding one another in reflection. It is a continuity of discrete states of consciousness recorded in the mind like impressions made on a block of wax.

Although the above discussion provides only a sketch of the notions of Cartesian subjectivity, some important features are already beginning to emerge. One's certainty starts with *being in a state* of consciousness (or thought). This state appears to be a *necessary condition* of one's acting or doing. Let us take Descartes' example to explain this issue. If one says 'I walk, therefore I am' or 'I see, therefore I am', the conclusion to one's existence is certain only if one is referring to the *consciousness of performing* or *seeming to perform* the action of walking or seeing; however, if one only meant the action instead of the consciousness of it, one's existence would not be absolutely certain because one can walk or see without knowing it, as occurs in sleep-walking. Thus, the *assertion* 'I walk' means the same as 'I am conscious of walking', and consequently, 'I walk, therefore I am' means 'I am conscious of walking, therefore I am' (Descartes, *Principles*, p. 222). The priority of consciousness and thought over action makes Cartesian man a thinker rather than an actor or a doer. And this is how the psychology that developed from the Cartesian paradigm conceived of man too.

But what about a baby? Is he unconscious because he may not be aware of pushing his legs or lifting his arms? How do we come to have consciousness? Descartes does not get into difficulties in explaining:

I had good reason to assert that the human soul is always conscious (*cogitare*) in any circumstances—even in a mother's womb. (Descartes, Letter to ?, p. 266)

This does not mean, of course, that 'an infant's mind meditates on metaphysical truths in its mother's womb' (*ibid.*) But 'it has in itself the ideas of God, the self, and all "self-evident" truths, in the same way as grown men have them when they are not attending to them' (*ibid.*) Thought and consciousness were given to a human being in their dispositional forms (cf. Chapter 4). In other words, thought and consciousness were characteristics of the human mind as such, rather than being characteristics which a person developed later in his life. Consequently, thought and consciousness were *static* rather than dynamic and unfolding qualities of the mind. We must not forget, though, that the concept of development as we know it today is the product of the nineteenth century and that seventeenth century philosophy was absolutely unaware of it.

Reflection in the Cartesian paradigm has a *contemplative* and *meditative* nature: the knower is the 'looker-on' on his past self, he finds himself in the mirror of the past and thus recognizes that his past self and his present self form a continuity. In the process of reflection, the knower recognizes himself rather than creates himself. We shall see in Chapter 4 that consciousness and thought too have a *contemplative* nature: the knower passively accepts ideas either from 'inside' or 'outside' the mind in order to secure the truth of his knowledge.

These peculiar features of Cartesian subjectivity had essential epistemological consequences. First, they led to the separation of the 'world-of-consciousness' from the 'world-in-itself'. Secondly, they led to the identification of knowledge and certainty. Let us briefly consider these two effects.

2.4 The world-of-consciousness and the world-in-itself

By proclaiming 'I think, therefore I am', Descartes gave 'thinking thing' its own position in the world, independently of *everything material* including its own body. He thus separated consciousness from the rest of the world. The separation of consciousness from everything not conscious is known as *Cartesian dualism*: the mind is thinking and unextended substance, body is unthinking and extended substance. The mind and the body are two independent entities, the mind exercising intellectual activities, the body being governed by mechanical laws.

The Cogito does not claim that the self is conscious of *objects in the world*, all it claims is that the self is conscious of the contents and the operations of the mind, that is of perceptions, and doubting, willing, understanding, feeling, desiring, and so on. The existence of objects in the outside world can only be deduced from the contents of the mind with the help of these operations.

This position led to two important consequences. For all philosophers of the Cartesian paradigm (except for Kant), the separation of the subject and object was complete and the inner world was epistemologically prior to the outer world. Descartes, Locke, and Hume all found the contents of the mind to be directly or intuitively certain. The outside world was mediated through *ideas* for Descartes and Locke. These ideas constituted the world-of-consciousness. The real world, the world-in-itself, could be *inferred* according to Descartes and Locke, was *identified with the world-of-consciousness* by Berkeley, but *remained unknown and impenetrable* for Hume and Kant (for details, see Chapter 5). What had happened is obvious: belief in the existence of the world as it presents itself to the senses was gradually substituted by scepticism, because consciousness is never certain whether, or to what extent, the world-of-consciousness corresponds to the world-in-itself.

The second consequence of the separation of consciousness from the rest of the world was pointed out by Hegel (see also Chapter 7). In order to carry out any kind of exploration, philosophy needs a *standard* as to what counts and does not count as knowledge. Such a standard determines 'whether something is right or wrong on the basis of the resulting agreement or disagreement of the things examined' with the standard (Hegel, *Phenomenology*, p. 52). Having a standard, of course, is a useful practice in everyday life: education aims at achieving certain standards and examinations testify as to whether candidates have reached them; driving tests are supposed to ensure that prospective drivers have obtained standards that will preclude them from causing accidents, and so on. Having a publicly accepted standard enables one to assess the quantity or quality of a thing or performance, with the performance that is accepted as perfect as the standard.

The aim of the Cartesian theory of knowledge is to identify what is *certain* because what is certain is also true. The standard of knowledge is certainty.

2.5 Knowledge is certainty

Descartes' proclamation '*I think, therefore I am*' gave rise to a modern, individualistically centred theory of knowledge, both about the external world and about the self. The most obvious question to ask is what is so distinctive about the proposition, '*Cogito, ergo sum*', that it not only became the first principle of philosophy, but also that through it epistemology was put right at the centre of philosophical interest.

We have already pointed out that the distinguishing feature of the Cogito was its *certainty*. Knowledge starts with the I who thinks because it is the most certain thing that the Cartesian individual can have in the world.

The search for certainty is also an essential part of Locke's epistemology. Thus, in the introduction to the *Essay*, Locke says that his purpose is to enquire into the origin, certainty, and extent of human knowledge (Locke, *Essay*, I, i, 2). And in a letter to Stillingfleet he says:

For with me, to know and be certain, is the same thing; what I know, that I am certain of and what I am certain of, that I know. What reaches to knowledge, I think may be called certainty; and what comes short of certainty, I think cannot be called knowledge. (Locke, *Reply to the Lord Bishop of Worcester*, p. 145)

The search for certainty and the search after truth became the essence of the whole programme of philosophy. For all the philosophers of the Cartesian paradigm, the search for knowledge was the search for certainty. It was in the belief that this sort of certainty had been achieved in the natural philosophies that in 1840 William Whewell pronounced them sciences.

The Cogito is not only the first principle of knowledge. It also provides the criteria by which knowledge is acquired. One is assured that one has knowledge in the case of the Cogito through its perception as something perfectly clear and distinct. For it is utterly impossible, because of the non-deceptive character of God, to suppose that anything perceived with such clarity and distinctness could be other than as it is perceived. And because this could not be the case if it were possible for anything so perceived to be false, Descartes makes the generalization that everything that we perceive (or conceive) clearly and distinctly is true:

Certainly in this first knowledge there is nothing that assures me of its truth, excepting the clear and distinct perception of that which I state, which would not indeed suffice to assure me that what I say is true, if it could ever happen that a thing which I conceived so clearly and distinctly could be false; and accordingly it seems to me that already I can establish as a general rule that all things which I perceive very clearly and very distinctly are true. (Descartes, *Meditations*, p. 158)

The standard for Descartes is certainty—the impossibility of something not being the case—and certainty is arrived at either directly through *intuition*, or indirectly through *deduction*, which is itself made up of a series of intuitive steps (Descartes, *Rules*, pp. 7–8). Thus for Descartes the rationalist notion of truth is based upon certain static elements that can be isolated by clear and distinct perception.

2.6 Intuition and deduction

Knowledge is based upon intuition, the immediate apprehension of clear and distinct ideas. Intuition according to Descartes 'springs from the light of reason alone' and 'is the undoubting conception of an unclouded and attentive mind' (Descartes, *Rules*, p. 7). We shall note later that the mind has two faculties: understanding, which is the passivity of the mind, and judgement, which is the activity of the mind. By understanding alone we neither accept nor reject, neither assert nor deny; we merely apprehend the ideas of things as to which we can form a judgement (Descartes, *Meditations*, p. 174). And because intuition is immediate understanding without any judgement, the result of intuition cannot be knowledge but only material for knowledge. However, we may say that psychologically it may be impossible to intuit something without also accepting it as true, that is, without judging. Some ideas are so clear and perspicuous that we immediately accept them because psychologically we are unable to resist their acceptance, that is, we affirm them to be true:

I could not prevent myself from believing that a thing I so clearly conceived was true: not that I found myself compelled to do so by some external cause, but simply because from great clearness in my mind there followed a great inclination of my will; and I believed this with so much the greater freedom or spontaneity as I possessed the less indifference towards it. (Descartes, *Meditations*, p. 176)

Thus we see that, practically, intuition is immediately followed by judgement which is controlled by the will.

For Locke, likewise, the purest and simplest knowledge, which is of the agreement and disagreement of ideas, is obtained through intuition, which is immediate and irresistible.

Such kinds of truth, the mind perceives . . . by bare *intuition*, without the intervention of any other *idea*; and this kind of knowledge is the clearest and most certain that human frailty is capable of. This part of knowledge is irresistible and, like bright sunshine, forces itself immediately to be perceived . . . It is on this *intuition* that depends all the certainty and evidence of all our knowledge, which certainty everyone finds to be so great that he cannot imagine, and therefore cannot require, a greater. (Locke, *Essay*, IV, ii, 1)

Both for Descartes and for Locke, ideas are thus only materials for knowledge while true knowledge starts with *propositions*.

The simplest propositions, Descartes pointed out, can be intuited. For example, one can see intuitively that $2 + 2 = 4$. This truth is grasped in its totality and at a single time. More complex propositions are *deduced*.

By 'deduction' Descartes means inferring from true and known principles by the step-by-step succession of elementary thoughts, where each further step is firmly based on the previous step (Descartes, *Rules*, p. 8). For example, we can intuit the identity of A and B, and B and C, and from these deduce the identity of A and C. Thus, deduction relies upon a present intuition and the memory of a chain of previous intuitions. Locke, similarly, has demonstration, which is not so clear and bright as in intuitive knowledge, but is 'like a face reflected by several mirrors one to another' (Locke, *Essay*, IV, ii, 4–6).

Intuition and deduction are the only operations of the mind that can provide us with certain knowledge, and as Descartes points out 'the mind should admit no others. All the rest should be rejected as suspect of error and dangerous' (Descartes, *Rules*, p. 8).

By means of pure deduction the mind can formulate complex mathematical and logical systems as well as the laws of nature. Such deductive systems are supposed to be certain and therefore true, independently of time and space; they are a-temporal and immutable. Consequently, although originally produced by the mind, such systems, once formulated, appear to have obtained their independence of the mind. Indeed, they become *external standards* by means of which the mind's performance can be tested.

2.7 Conclusion

We have thus set the stage for the rest of Part I of this book.

The Cartesian interest in the study of the individual and his subjectivity started with the '*Cogito, ergo sum*'. For Descartes, not only was the mind everything that thinks, but also everything that thinks was a mind. This carried the implication that the mind would eventually do nothing but think. This position was reinforced by the assumption of the priority of thought and consciousness over action. Thought, consciousness, and reflection all had a meditative and contemplative nature. Therefore, Cartesian man was a thinker rather than an actor, and thought and consciousness were static rather than developing characteristics of the human mind. Interaction between the thinking subject and the rest of the world was not considered by the Cartesian paradigm. The mind was concerned only with those objects of which it could obtain certain and indubitable knowledge, and such knowledge could be arrived at only through intuition and deduction. The formal systems so established could then serve as immutable external standards by which the mind's performance could be evaluated.

These Cartesian presuppositions have also become the unquestioned assumptions of modern cognitive and behaviouristic psychology. In the four chapters that follow, we shall discuss these presuppositions with reference to the study of thought and language.

CHAPTER 3

The Standard of Knowledge is External: The Case of Deductive Reasoning

3.1 The laws of thought

One of the consequences of the separation of thought (consciousness) from the rest of the world is the problem of how to establish that one can know something that lies outside consciousness: in other words, it appears necessary to establish some principles or methods that would enable consciousness to discover that it does or does not have objective knowledge.

Attempts to establish methods by which consciousness can discover the first principles or axioms of knowledge go back to Aristotle. He maintained that, in general, principles of knowledge need demonstration and proof in order to *be* principles. Only the *first* principles are so basic that they do not need any demonstration, and human beings know them intuitively through immediate apprehension. They are not only the first principles of knowledge but the first principles of all our *reasoning*, and have become known as the *laws of thought*.

These laws of thought are the following: *the law of identity*, stating that everything is what it is; *the law of non-contradiction*, which claims that a thing cannot both be something and not be that thing at the same time; and the *law of excluded middle*, which states that a thing either has a property or does not have that property, and there is no third possibility. For Aristotle these laws of thought had *metaphysical* or *ontological* significance, that is, they were the very conditions of existence. It is exactly because of their very basic nature that there are no proofs available for their correctness: there are no proofs available for the nature of existence itself. The most important of all these principles is the principle of non-contradiction, which is the ultimate common belief from which all other axioms are derived (Aristotle, *Metaphysica*, Book Γ.3 1005ᵦ and Book B.2 996ᵦ).

For Aristotle, formal logic, the laws of thought, and the laws of existence were all mutually related. The conclusions derived from the laws of logic were just the same as those derived from the laws of thought; and the laws of thought, being the conditions of existence itself, were always operating in reality. Thus, to obtain scientific knowledge it is not enough to reason correctly from true and primary premises. The conclusions obtained from reasoning must not only be *logically* correct, but they must also be homogeneous with the basic *facts* of science (Aristotle, *Analytica Posteriora*, 76ₐ, 26–30). So it would seem that we can conclude that, since the laws of thought are the *sine qua non* of existence as such, they are also the *sine qua non* of human reasoning and acting. If they are disobeyed, that is, if a human being contradicts himself, for example both believing and disbelieving something at the same time, then a conflict arises for him and if it proceeds too far and for long enough then his very existence is threatened and his destruction as a living organism will eventually follow.

This Aristotelian conception, according to which the laws of thought and reality were mutually related, was rejected by the Cartesian paradigm. The Aristotelian naive realism, which maintained the unity of thought and reality, was replaced by the scepticism which was implicit in Descartes and explicit in his followers. The result was that the unity of thought and reality broke down.

Kant's laws of thought were purely *formal*. For Kant the laws of thought were the principles of *pure general logic*. Pure general logic is an *a priori* science, and therefore the laws of thought are *a priori* principles of the mind (cf. Section 4.6) and are universal and necessary. They are the laws by which the understanding employs itself, so that they constitute the *sine qua non* of any understanding (Kant, *Critique of Pure Reason*, B 76). Pure general logic, because it is a formal science, ignores all the differences in the objects of understanding, i.e. in content, and the laws hold universally whatever the nature of those objects:

As general logic, it abstracts from all content of the knowledge of understanding and from all differences in its objects, and deals with nothing but mere form of thought. (Kant, *Critique of Pure Reason*, A 54)

Among the laws or forms of thought (Kant uses 'laws' and 'forms' of thought interchangeably), the most important principle is, as for Aristotle, the law of non-contradiction. It is a universal criterion of all truths, though a negative one: 'It holds of knowledge, merely as knowledge in general, irrespective of content' (Kant, *Critique of Pure Reason*, A 151). 'Irrespective of content', however, does not mean 'apart from any content'. Indeed, it would be a mistake to interpret Kant as ignoring content. One of the most famous of Kant's sayings is that *'thoughts without content* are empty' and 'intuitions without concepts are blind' (Kant, *Critique of Pure Reason*, A 51). For Kant, as for Aristotle, the form of thought can no more be empirically abstracted from its content than the shape of a statue can be empirically separated from the stone out of which it is formed. And although all the laws of logic are *a priori*, that is independent of all experience (Kant, *Logic*, p. 12ff), they are discovered by an individual through his empirical experience using understanding and reason.

The laws of thought, as the subject matter of pure general logic and therefore true *a priori*, cannot be investigated empirically. In order to clarify his point,

Kant compares pure general logic with pure ethics. Pure ethics, containing only the necessary moral laws of free will in general, is not concerned with general laws under the limitations of various psychological states, feelings, inclinations, and passions. Such subjects are the concern of applied ethics which, like applied logic, can never be a true science, since it depends on psychological and other empirical factors. The laws of pure logic and pure ethics are immutable: we can intuit them but cannot explore them in any empirical way, and therefore cannot explore them psychologically.

George Boole, one of the founders of modern logic, entitled one of his basic works *An Investigation of the Laws of Thought* (1854). His aim in this book was 'to investigate the fundamental laws of those operations of the mind by which reasoning is performed', to express such operations in symbolic language, and on these laws to build up a science of mind (*ibid.*, p. 3). He had previously realized, and had elaborated the idea in his *Mathematical Analysis of Logic* (1847), that there is an analogy between the principles of logic and ordinary algebra, in particular between the logic of classes and ordinary algebra. Thus, using a suitable system of symbols for classes, such as *1* for a universal class, *0* for an empty class, *x* for a class x and *1 –x* for its complement, he showed that simple algebraic operations, such as addition and multiplication, are applicable in the logic of classes. In *The Investigation of the Laws of Thought* Boole demonstrated that such a correspondence between algebra and logical principles is not due to any decision to assign such a correspondence between these two disciplines, but arises 'because the ultimate laws of thought render that mode possible' (Boole, *Investigation*, p. 11). The laws of thought are mathematical in their form and can be expressed as rules for operations with symbols interpretable as either numerical or logical. The discovery of an analogy between the logic of classes and ordinary algebra led Boole to seek such an analogy also in other parts of logic.

Some authors have maintained that Boole believed that he was 'dealing with laws of thought in some psychological sense' or that he was 'making some psychological claims' concerning the laws of thought (Kneale and Kneale, 1962; Osherson, 1975). It is difficult, however, to see any evidence in Boole's work to justify such claims. It seems to me that Boole refers to the psychological aspects of the laws of thought only with respect to reasoning errors. But Boole, like Kant, was not actually interested in reasoning errors because their origin 'lies beyond the province of science to determine' (Boole, *Investigation*, p. 408).

Although neither Kant nor Boole was concerned with the psychological significance of the laws of thought, their influence on the psychology of deductive reasoning has been tremendous: it has raised the question of the relationship between logic and psychology and also led to the investigation of the precise role of the laws of thought in deductive reasoning. However, in contrast to Kant, psychologists have attempted to investigate the laws of thought *empirically*, and *apart from content*, or at least with content so insignificant, ambiguous or irrelevant that it supposedly does not interfere with pure reasoning. The assumption that there can be such a thing as pure deduction unaffected by psychological factors has, of course, its roots in Descartes' method of deduction from first principles. This assumption was reinforced by the new developments in symbolic logic at the end of the nineteenth century, those in propositional logic having a particular influence on studies in the psychology of reasoning.

3.2 Propositional logic

Kant pointed out that Aristotelian logic based on the syllogism was a completed system to which nothing could be added (cf. p. 31). The development of symbolic logic in the nineteenth century, associated with the names of Boole, Jevons, De Morgan, and in particular Frege and Russell, proceeded along different lines from what the Aristotelian system would allow. We shall not go into this new development in any detail, but for our purpose the following points are important. First, Frege ignored the Aristotelian distinction between the subject and predicate of a proposition and, instead, treated propositions as elementary units. Secondly, he could, as a consequence, replace the whole proposition by a *propositional variable*, such as p or q. Propositional variables can stand for any proposition in the same way that x or y in algebra stand for any number. Single propositions can be related together by *logical connectives* such as '$\rightarrow$', '&', 'v', '$-$', and so on, in order to form complex propositions. Such complex propositions can be subjected to formal operations in accordance with precisely formulated logical rules. The logical connectives '$\rightarrow$', '&', 'v', and '$-$' are translated into natural language as 'implies', 'and', 'or', and 'not', respectively. Thus, using propositional variables and logical connectives, natural language can be formalized and detective stories or novels rewritten in the propositional calculus. The laws of thought take the following forms in the propositional calculus:

Law of identity: $P \equiv P$
Law of non-contradiction: $-(P \ \& \ -P)$
Law of excluded middle: $(P \ v-P)$

For example, we can take a proposition such as 'it is impossible for a man to have his cake and eat it' and symbolize it as follows: $-(P \ \& \ -P)$, which in fact is the law of non-contradiction.

Since the propositional calculus does not allow for breaking propositions down into their elements, it completely ignores the content of propositions. It can serve, therefore, only as a very crude formalization of natural language. For example, the connective '$\rightarrow$', which is translated into natural language as 'implies' or 'if-then', has a special meaning in the propositional calculus, known as *material implication*. Material implication does not express any relationship between the antecedent and consequent of a conditional proposition other than the purely logical one that the antecedent cannot be true and the conse-

28

Table 3.1

Antecedent	Consequent	If antecedent then consequent
true	true	true
true	false	false
false	true	true
false	false	true

quent false at the same time, as shown in the truth table (Table. 3.1). If, for example, we substitute the proposition 'the weather is fine' for the antecedent, and the proposition 'we go for a walk' for the consequent, then the conditional 'if the weather is fine we go for a walk' is false if the antecedent is true and the consequent false, and otherwise is true. It is obvious that the meaning of the premises is irrelevant to material implication because, as already pointed out, it is only a truth-functional connective. What matters is the truth or falsehood of the antecedent and consequent.

The logicians, though, have been aware of the dangers of translating '→'into 'if-then'. Both Strawson (1952) and Copi (1965) have pointed out that there are a number of different meanings of 'if-then' in ordinary language, and that these may express causal, logical, definitional or decision relationships between antecedent and consequent; while 'if-then' in the sense of material implication is specifically defined by the truth table, in natural language it is the content and communicative context of the premises that determines which of the possible meanings of 'if-then' obtains.

Mates (1965) has pointed out that the formalized language £ of formal logic is intended to be modelled on natural language, and the sentences of £ are intended to be 'counterparts' of sentences of the natural language (in a somewhat vague sense of 'counterpart'). However, he goes on to note that although we may read '&' as 'and' and 'v' as 'or' and '→' as 'if-then',

... serious confusion will result if one takes these readings to indicate some sort of synonymy . . . since such words as 'or', 'and', 'if . . . then' are not always (if ever) used truth-functionally in everyday language, their representation by the connectives of £ is always more or less questionable. (Mates, 1965, pp. 41 and 74)

Considering the obvious difficulties connected with the translation of propositional connectives into natural language, one might be surprised that until recently the psychology of deductive reasoning has been unaffected by these problems. In their attempt to study pure reasoning, psychologists have taken it for granted that whatever pure reasoning may be it can be isolated from the various non-reasoning impurities. This assumption has clearly been one of the effects of working within the Cartesian paradigm. The root of this assumption is to be found in the supposition that demonstrative knowledge can only be obtained from clear and distinct ideas—ideas which are not obscured or confused by the emotions (Descartes, *Principles*, p. 233).

The focus of the psychologists in the first instance was to discover whether the laws of logic are descriptive or normative of human reasoning (Henle, 1962). A trained logician is not only mentally able to separate the form of premises from their content, but this is how his job is defined. He must be able to substitute symbols for propositions and manipulate them according to the rules of deduction. For a person untrained in formal logic, correct manipulation with symbols cannot be taken for granted, just as the knowledge of mathematics cannot be taken for granted in an untrained person. The questions the psychologists put to themselves were *how much* logical knowledge an untrained reasoner possesses and *how* he uses it.

To explore these questions the following procedure has commonly been used: the subject, untutored in formal logic, has usually been presented with certain premises. He has then been required either to make his own inferences from these premises, or to select an inference he considers correct from a set of possible alternatives given to him. Presented with such a task, he has been assumed able to abstract to some extent from the 'irrelevant' aspects of the task, such as the language in which the premises are expressed, and such beliefs and attitudes that he may have towards the content of the premises, as well as from the communicative context of the premises. Moreover, it has been assumed that he is able, again to some extent, to use the rules of deduction, and the language connectives such as 'and', 'or', 'if-then', in a truth-functional manner. In fact, the extent to which the subject uses these connectives truth-functionally and the extent to which he is able to abstract from the non-reasoning aspects of the task is taken to define the level of his logicality. Wason and Johnson-Laird (1972) justified the use of the logical calculus on the following grounds:

The advantage of a formal calculus is that it brings order to a great variety of inferences, and that it allows the specific content of an inference to be ignored . . . The essential logical point about such inferences is that validity depends purely upon the position of the propositions within their framework of logical connectives . . . Once the form of the inference has been ascertained there are simple mechanical procedures which will reveal whether it is valid. (Wason and Johnson-Laird, 1972, pp. 40 and 41)

3.3 Syllogisms and conditional problems

So far we have been talking about 'logical tasks' and 'premises' rather generally.

What kinds of 'logical tasks' have actually been explored in the psychology of deductive reasoning? There have been a number of them, for example three-term serial problems, anagrams, propositional reasoning tasks, and syllogisms. In this section we shall only discuss reasoning with syllogisms and conditional problems, simply because these two kinds of task have been explored most extensively and there is an abundant literature based upon them.

Syllogisms virtually never occur or very rarely occur in daily life. At one time, however, they were thought to be the basis of philosophical argument, and they have played an important role in the history of logic. The theory of the syllogism was first developed by Aristotle, for whom the words 'reasoning' and 'syllogism' were synonyms (cf. Aristotle, *Topica*, 100ₐ, 25; *Analytica Priora*, 24ᵦ, 18). The Aristotelian or traditional syllogism consists of two premises and a conclusion, for example:

> All students are radicals.
> Some young people are students.
> Therefore, some young people are radicals.

The two premises have one term in common with each other (students), known as the *middle term* (M). One term in each premise is in common with the conclusion (radicals, young people), known as the *major* (S) and *minor* (P) terms respectively. The premise which contains the major term is called the major premise (All students are radicals) and the premise which contains the minor term is called the minor premise (Some young people are students). The terms are *quantified*, i.e. words such as 'all', 'some', 'no', are attached to them. According to the quantity (universal-particular) of the quantifier and quality attached to the terms (affirmative-negative) of the copula, the three propositions of the syllogism can each be of four types (giving $4 \times 4 \times 4 = 64$ different possibilities), and are symbolized by the capital letters A, I, E, O, where A and I come from 'AffIrmo', and E and O from 'nEgO':

A *universal affirmative*:   'All students are radicals'
I *particular affirmative*:   'Some students are radicals'
E *universal negative:*   'No students are radicals'
O *particular negative*:   'Some students are not radicals'

According to the position of the middle terms in the propositions, such as S–M, M–S, M–P, and P–M, there are four different figures of the syllogism:

Figure 1	Figure 2	Figure 3	Figure 4
M–P	P–M	M–P	P–M
S–M	S–M	M–S	M–S
S–P	S–P	S–P	S–P

Considering these four figures, the possibility of presenting the propositions in each figure in the forward and reverse orders, and the above types of propositions (A,I,E,O), we can construct 512 combinations of propositions (4 figures × 2 orders × 64 combinations of A,I,E,O). However, only from a minority of these combinations of propositions can valid conclusions be drawn.

The exposition of the syllogism in this form basically comes from Aristotle (except that Aristotle knew only the first three figures), who also gave general rules for syllogisms and the criteria for their correctness. The mediaeval scholastics elaborated the theory of the syllogism in various details, but there was virtually no real change in formal logic until the nineteenth century. In fact, it was its stagnation, immutability, and apparent completeness which led Kant to his claim that

... that logic has already, from the earliest times, proceeded upon this sure path is evidenced by the fact that since Aristotle it has not required to retrace a single step, unless, indeed, we care to count as improvements the removal of certain needless subtleties or the clearer exposition of its recognized teaching, features which concern the elegance rather than the certainty of the science. It is remarkable also that to the present day this logic has not been able to advance a single step, and is thus to all appearance a closed and completed body of doctrine. (Kant, *Critique of Pure Reason*, B viii)

Nowadays, syllogisms are honoured only in small print in the textbooks of logic. In the psychology of deductive reasoning, however, the study of syllogisms continues. It has developed into a whole tradition of research and the syllogism still appears as experimental material. The questions asked by psychologists today, though, are not exactly the same as they were seventy, or even thirty, years ago. The focus of the early studies was on the kinds of error the subject made and their possible explanation (cf. Section 3.4). Psychologists today are more concerned with how syllogisms are represented in the mind of the reasoner (e.g. Revlis, 1975) or what exactly makes some syllogisms more difficult to solve than others (Johnson-Laird, 1975).

Why do psychologists find syllogisms so interesting? The chief reason is that syllogisms give the impression that they are the kind of material by means of which deductive reasoning can be studied *pure*, separated from content, context, attitudes, and emotions—simply in isolation from everything that might interfere with pure thought. As we pointed out above, the system of syllogisms is complete, the combination of propositions by means of affirmation and negation, figures and moods, is easily defined, and it is easy to identify formal changes in syllogisms. In order, supposedly, to investigate pure reasoning, unadulterated by content or context, the subject has usually been presented with syllogistic formulae, either confined to symbols, or with content as unfamiliar as possible, or which are partly or even completely meaningless. For example, in the study by Sells and Koob (1937) syllogisms have been presented in the following form:

All Xs are Ys.
Some Ys are Zs.

The subject's task was either to draw his own conclusion from these premises or to select an appropriate answer from a set of alternatives:

All Zs are Ys.
Some Zs are Ys.
Some Zs are not Ys.
No Zs are Ys.

(cf., for example, Wilkins, 1928; Chapman and Chapman, 1959; Begg and Denny, 1969).

Unfamiliar content has been introduced, for example, in Wilkins' experiments (1928):

> All foraminifera are rhyzopoda.
> All foraminifera are protozoa.
> Therefore, some protozoa are rhyzopoda.

Sometimes, on the other hand, meaningful content is used in order to demonstrate that content either facilitates or distorts pure reasoning. Wilkins (1928) found that the ability to draw correct conclusions from syllogistic premises was considerably affected by the content. When the content was familiar and concrete, the subjects made fewer errors than when the content was abstract and unfamiliar. Bucci (1978) also found that children made fewer mistakes when presented with syllogisms with broadly rather than narrowly or abstractly based predicates. For example, the question

> All haunted houses are dark and quiet.
> This house is dark and quiet.
> Is it haunted?

attracted the answer 'not sure' more often than the question

> All birds have feathers.
> The animal I am thinking of has feathers.
> Is it a bird?

In the case of abstract contents, e.g. 'All the pink blocks are rectangles', there were even fewer 'not sure' answers. The children's answers demonstrated that broadly based predicates make it easier to think about counter-examples, such as about dark and quiet houses that are not haunted, than about animals with feathers that are not birds.

The other kind of problem studied in the psychology of deductive reasoning, connected particularly with the original studies of Wason and his students, is reasoning with conditionals. Conditional problems usually take the form of *hypothetical syllogisms*: the first premise is hypothetical (or conditional) and the other premise and the conclusion are categorical. Let us take our earlier example (p. 28):

> If the weather is fine, we go for a walk.
> The weather is fine.
> Therefore, we go for a walk.

The conditional premise has two propositions: the *antecedent* (the weather is fine) and the *consequent* (we go for a walk) being connected by 'if-then'. There are two valid moods of such a conditional problem: the one in which the categorical premise affirms the antecedent of the conditional premise, called *modus ponens*; and the other in which the categorical premise denies the consequent of the conditional premise, called *modus tollens*. Thus, the above syllogism is an example of modus ponens. On the other hand, the syllogism,

> If the weather is fine, (then) we go for a walk.
> We do not go for a walk.
> Therefore, the weather is not fine.

is an example of modus tollens. Arguments of any other kind lead to fallacies. For example, arguing in the following way:

> If the weather is fine, (then) we go for a walk.
> We go for a walk.
> Therefore, the weather is fine.

is known as the fallacy of *affirming the consequent*. Similarly, arguing in the following way:

> If the weather is fine, (then) we go for a walk.
> The weather is not fine.
> Therefore, we do not go for a walk.

represents the *fallacy of denying the antecedent*. The reader can check the validity and invalidity of all four arguments on the truth table on p. 28.

Readers interested in learning about the ways in which syllogisms and conditional problems have been explored are referred to reviews of deductive reasoning such as those of Wason and Johnson-Laird (1972), and Erikson and Jones (1978). Our own interest, once again, lies in the presuppositions of this extensive work. It is to the notion of error that we shall turn our attention for an answer. The notion of 'error' has been crucial to studies in deductive reasoning from their beginnings. To commit an error in conditional problems is defined as arriving at a conclusion that differs from the one determined by the logical calculus. To commit an error in syllogisms is defined as arriving at a conclusion that differs from the one determined by the rules of syllogistic inference.

Experiments in deductive reasoning have provided ample evidence that human beings often arrive at conclusions that do not agree with formal logic (see the above-mentioned reviews). The common occurrence of error has led over the years to different ways of explaining it and, finally, to the questioning of the theoretical presuppositions of reasoning studies. It is important, however, that none of the changes in the explanation of error have stepped outside the Cartesian framework. Formal logic has remained the *external standard* of reasoning.

3.4 Encoding and error

Clear and distinct ideas were *given* to the seventeenth century Cartesian reasoner intuitively, and more complex truths were arrived at through step-by-step deduction (cf. Section 2.6). Ideas representing the properties of external objects flowed into the mind from the outside and the mind could not refuse them (cf. Section 5.1). Thus, *the mind was passive as to what it encoded.*

Experimental psychology generally, and the psychology of deductive reasoning in particular, has traditionally taken passive encoding for granted. Typically, the experimenter has assumed that the subject encodes the task in the way he encodes it himself, or in the way he wishes the subject to encode it.

How do we know whether a subject has encoded the stimulus in the required way? Usually, it is considered sufficient for the subject to be given *instructions* designed to ensure that sets, biases, expectations, and irrelevant information are all eliminated, and that the task is encoded 'correctly', that is, in the way required by the experimenter. In tasks involving responses to perceptual stimuli, 'correct' encoding can be easily checked by asking the subject to perform the task on an example.

But while in the case of responses to perceptual stimuli, such as pushing buttons when a red light comes on, 'correct' encoding can perhaps be taken for granted, a difficulty arises when the subject is presented with symbolic material. For example, Smedslund (1969) has pointed out that the syllable 'RAR', which would be classified as meaningless in English, is meaningful in Scandinavian languages. It means 'strange' in Norwegian but 'nice' in Swedish. A subject's perception and memory of the syllable might, therefore, be affected by his associations, and an experiment based on the assumption that RAR is an objectively defined entity, i.e. the *same* stimulus for different subjects, would be ruined.

Even more problems arise when the experimenter wishes to explore human thinking, reasoning, imagination or problem-solving. While in perceptual experiments the unknown variable is usually the capacity of the information-processing system, or its reaction time (cf. Chapter 4), in problem-solving experiments the unknown variable is usually taken to be the subject's logicality, that is, his ability to infer information, to deduce, to apply rules or to find out rules. In such experiments, in order to meet the criteria on the basis of which the mind, as an information-processing system, functions, correctness of encoding simply has to be taken for granted because providing the subject with an example would ruin the experiment. The only possible check on the encoding is either the subject actually repeating the instructions or the experimenter asking 'Do you understand the instructions?' or 'Do you understand what you are supposed to do?' or 'Do you have any questions?' Smedslund (1970), however, argues against this approach. The relationship between logicality and understanding, or in our case between logicality and encoding, is circular and if we want to investigate one of these factors, that is, either logicality or understanding, then the other factor must be defined as constant. In traditional research on cognitive development, reasoning or thinking, it has usually been understanding (or encoding) which has been taken for granted, while the logicality of the subject has been tested. Such an assumption, Smedslund argues, is unjustified.

Understanding must be a variable, since it is a function of the relation between the meaning experienced by different individuals with different background. On the other hand, logic must be presupposed, since it is a characteristic of the activity of any integrated system and is a part of the very notion of a person. (Smedslund, 1970, p. 218)

In fact, the discovery that 'sometimes . . . people treat even the same situation in different ways' (Broadbent, 1973, p. 105) was something of a surprise to some experimental psychologists. Broadbent found that the same information was stored and organized differently by different subjects and that the same task led to different patterns of behaviour because of variations in encoding.

Some psychologists queried the commonly unquestioned assumption of correct encoding some time ago. Raaheim (1960, 1962) stated that, while some of his subjects failed to solve the problem because they could not find the method of solution, others failed to solve it simply because they did not encode it in the required way. Jensen (1960a, b) has criticized the customary interpretation of 'functional fixedness' and 'set' in the investigation of problemsolving. Both 'functional fixedness' and 'set' have been evaluated negatively and specifically interpreted as tendencies inhibiting certain behaviour. Luchins, for example, interpreted set as a negative factor which precluded the creative use of new problem-solving methods by the subject. But, as Jensen remarks,

Instead of asking the experimenter what kind of behavior is reinforced in the experiment on the *Einstellung* effect, we may ask in what way the situation is perceived and what type of problem is actually accepted by the subject. In this matter the subject may be expected to be, not indeed the only, but certainly a valuable source of information. (Jensen, 1960b, p. 168)

Henle (1962) pointed out in her celebrated paper 'On the relation between logic and thinking' that 'errors' in reasoning are often not errors in the deductive process itself but are due to changes the subject makes in the premises: the subject may fail to accept the logical task, he may restate the premises in such a way that the meaning the experimenter intended has changed, or he may omit or slip in another premise. She argued that before psychologists can explore logicality they must know what the subject has encoded.

Since Henle's influential paper, it is no longer taken for granted that a reasoning task is encoded by the subject in the way intended by the experimenter. In fact, the model of syllogistic reasoning developed by Revlis (1975) is based on the assumption that 'errors' in reasoning are due to miscoding. Johnson-Laird (1975) also focuses on the way the reasoning task is encoded and internally represented, rather than on whether or not a subject commits logical fallacies. However, we shall see in Chapter 5 that these changes in attention from 'error' to internal representation are only changes in focus. They are not connected with any major conceptual changes. The studies concerned with internal representation are still carried out within the Cartesian paradigm.

3.5 Compartmentalization and error

One of the most common explanations of errors in deductive reasoning, since the early studies in the nineteen-twenties, has been *the effect of interfering factors*. Interfering factors are of a non-reasoning nature, such as the 'atmosphere effect', the content of the premises, the emotions, attitudes, and beliefs of the reasoner, or the complexity of the language used in the premises.

Historically the first explanation proposed by Woodworth and Sells (1935) was in terms of the overall impression or 'atmosphere' of the premises. According to this theory, affirmative premises create an affirmative atmosphere while negative premises create a negative atmosphere. If, in a syllogism, both premises are of the same kind, i.e. of the same quantity or quality, for example both universal negative, such as 'No X is Y', or both particular affirmative, such as 'Some S is Y', the atmosphere of the premises taken together is the same as that of the premises taken separately and is carried over to the conclusion. If on the other hand the premises are of a different kind, i.e. of different quantity or quality, a particular quantifier overrides a universal, and a negative overrides an affirmative in the atmosphere carried over from the premises taken together to the conclusion. The erroneous conclusions of the subjects are, therefore, due to the subject's response to the superficial effect of atmosphere of a syllogism rather than to invalid logical reasoning.

Since the pioneering study by Woodworth and Sells the supposed atmosphere effect has been examined and re-examined by a number of investigators. Chapman and Chapman (1959) found that the atmosphere effect predictions were not substantiated. Rather, what appeared to be due to an 'atmosphere' in fact reflects our experience of reality in the following ways: first, both Wilkins (1928) and Sells (1936) found that subjects often interpreted statements such as 'All As are Bs' to mean also that 'All Bs are As'. And this, claimed Chapman and Chapman, is what we often find in reality, that a proposition and its converse are both true. For example, 'when the temperature is below zero, water freezes' and 'when water freezes, the temperature is below zero' are both true. Secondly, we often reach conclusions by probabilistic or analogical reasoning, arguing that things with similar properties are probably of the same kind and are therefore likely to have other properties in common, while things with different properties are not likely to be of the same kind. In syllogistic reasoning, such common properties are included in the middle term. To clarify this way of reasoning, Chapman and Chapman offered the following example:

> Yellow and powdery material has often been sulphur.
> Some of these test tubes have yellow powdery material.
> Therefore, some of these test tubes contain sulphur.

Although this syllogism is not valid, the conclusion has a certain degree of probability and a chemist who reached such a probabilistic inductive conclusion would test it by some other means.

It has also long been recognized that personality variables influence verbal reasoning. The older studies were mostly concerned with the belief that attitudes and personal convictions have a distorting effect on reasoning, and were therefore focused on the experimental demonstration of this effect. For example, Morgan and Morton (1944, p. 39) stated that 'A person is likely to accept a conclusion which expresses his convictions with little regard for the correctness or incorrectness of the inferences involved'. Experiments demonstrating the distorting effect of attitudes have usually been based on the syllogism (for example, Morgan and Morton, 1944; Lefford, 1946) or propositional calculus type of inferences (Thistlethwaite, 1950), with the content assumedly neutral in half the experiments and emotional in the other half. The inferences in the two groups of experiments were compared and it has usually been claimed that emotional content has a distorting effect on reasoning. The *Watson-Glaser Criticial Thinking Appraisal Test* (Watson and Glaser, 1951) is based on the same principle.

More recent studies have been more concerned with how the influence operates and what underlies it. Henle (1955) suggested various ways in which motivation might influence cognition, not necessarily negatively; for example, needs and attitudes might function by sensitizing us, i.e. by making us more sensitive to an item which would otherwise remain unnoticed; they might have an organizing effect; they might supply context; or arouse relevant memory traces, and expectations; or they might discourage the desire to understand the problem and cause us to overlook differences and distinctions; and so on.

McGuire (1960a, b) used syllogistic material to demonstrate the effect of *cognitive consistency* in reasoning tasks. Cognitive consistency theories are based on the assumption that people tend to maximize the internal consistency of their attitudes, beliefs, and values. For example, an involved member of the Labour party would not vote for the Conservatives under normal circumstances, a member of the Communist party would not go to church, a person who hates his neighbour would not invite him home to a party, and so on. McGuire was able to show that logical consistency between a subject's estimate of the probabilities of the premises and of the conclusion of a syllogism depends upon the relative desirability or undesirability of the events or states of affairs they describe. In other words, subjects' attitudes and wishful thinking affect their logical reasoning.

What do psychologists presuppose when they explain a reasoning error by means of interfering non-reasoning factors? Let us consider the titles of some of the papers concerned with this issue: Lefford (1946) entitled his paper 'The influence of emotional subject matter on logical reasoning'; Henle (1955) talks about 'Some effects of motivational processes on cognition', and Henle and Michael (1956) about 'The influence of attitudes on syllogistic reasoning'; Wason and Johnson-Laird (1972) entitle a chapter in their book 'Negation: the effect of context'. All of these titles lead the reader to believe, as the authors obviously do, that the mind consists of special compartments, one dealing with pure reasoning, one with emotions, one with beliefs, one with language, and so on. These compartments may 'affect' or 'influence' each other by interfering with each other's activities. In other words, Descartes' distinction between clear and distinct ideas on the one hand and passions of the soul on the other is emerging again.

The view that the mind is compartmentalized is reinforced by the findings that the brain has compartments; for example, emotions have their physiological basis in the hypothalamus while speech is dependent on the functioning of Broca's speech centre, and so on. Moreover, ordinary language reinforces the compartmentalists by labelling various mental states. Calling something by a name, such as 'emotion', 'attitude', or 'context' means acknowledging its independent existence.

3.6 The logical calculus as a yardstick

Studies in conditional reasoning started with the logical calculus being used as a yardstick (Wason and Johnson-Laird, 1972, p. 66) by means of which errors could be evaluated. The experiments demonstrated, however, that most of the subjects' inferences were not correct from the point of view of logical truth tables. Thus Matalon (1962) and similarly Peel (1967) found that children read 'if-then' predominantly as biconditional. Wason (1968) found that even highly intelligent undergraduates were unable to draw logically correct inferences when the negation of the consequent was given together with the conditional sentence. It was obvious that the subjects did not evaluate 'if-then' in the material implication manner.

In view of these findings, psychologists have finally started turning their attention to the kinds of rule people use in solving reasoning tasks. Thus, Wason (1966) suggested that instead of using two truth values (true and false), specified by truth tables, subjects might be using three truth values (true, false, and irrelevant). According to this hypothesis, subjects specified an irrelevant value for cases where the antecedent was false. Some experimental results (Wason, 1968; Johnson-Laird and Tagart, 1969) have supported this hypothesis. Taplin (1971, p. 224), on the other hand, reached the conclusion, on the basis of his studies, that 'no truth table exists for conditional sentences which is common to all individuals'. In addition, it has become more and more obvious that the meaning of premises is also important and determines the interpretation of conditionals (Wason and Johnson-Laird, 1972). Moreover, subjects' experience and familiarity with the experimental material has proved more influential in the reasoning process than the logical structure of the problem (Wason and Shapiro, 1971).

The position of psychologists with respect to propositional logic as a guide to reasoning has, therefore, been wavering for some time. As Wason and Johnson-Laird put it,

It is probably no longer sensible to ask whether the laws of logic are the laws of thought, because logic is no longer a monolithic body of doctrine . . . Much of the individual's thinking lies outside the realm of the calculus, indeed outside any established branch of formal logic, since it concerns questions of causality. (Watson and Johnson-Laird, 1972, p. 86)

Finally, it has 'become a truism that whatever else formal logic may be it is not a model of how people make inferences' (Johnson-Laird, 1975, p. 7).

What, then, is the alternative? Does it mean that the above considerations have led the psychologists actually to abandon their Cartesian presuppositions in the study of thought? In other words, does it mean that the assumption of compartmentalization of mental processes into pure reasoning and non-reasoning factors has been abolished? That references to formal logic have diminished? Not at all.

Having accepted that formal logic is not a model of how people make inferences, psychologists are now trying to find out the reasons for it. Thus, one of the main factors seem to be that subjects, presented with reasoning tasks, are concerned with issues other than the purely truth-functional relationships between the propositions. People seem to be involved more in *practical* reasoning rather than in *pure* reasoning (Wason and Johnson-Laird, 1972, pp. 67–85). In practical reasoning a subject is influenced by various factors such as temporal or causal relationships and these may prevent him from drawing correct, i.e. truth-functional, inferences. Subjects 'are always ready to leave the logical requirements of the task behind and try to establish some meaningful connection between events' (*ibid.*, p. 81). But practical deduction, involving temporal and causal considerations, the authors claim, depends to a great extent upon the content of the problem. It will occur if the reasoning material is concrete and involves issues of everyday life. On the other hand, if the material is abstruse or abstract, the subject will tend to think truth-functionally (cf. also Taplin and Staudenmayer, 1973).

Another reason why formal logic is not a model of reasoning is sought in language. Experiments have demonstrated that both syntactic and semantic manipulation of the reasoning material have effects on the kind of inferences subjects make (Evans, 1978). It seems to be supposed, however, that if content were excluded, or language suitably manipulated, the subject would be forced to apply pure reasoning after all. Thus we find Wason and Johnson-Laird saying: 'Hence the subjects were forced to try to think in a purely deductive way, and showed a striking lack of facility at so doing' (Wason and Johnson-Laird, 1972, p. 75). A lack of facility at doing something in which one is not trained would not, most probably, be surprising for any other activities. For example, one does not try to test the geometrical knowledge of a person who has not been appropriately trained. Or, one does not try to test a person untutored in Chinese in his knowledge of Chinese. So why is it interesting to test the logical ability of a person untutored in logic? It seems to me that the explanation lies in the fact that although human reasoning is now generally believed not to be modelled on the logical calculus, assumption of the possibility of pure reasoning has not been exorcized. It is the kind of material, its concreteness or abstractness, and the subject's familiarity with the material that determines whether or not he reasons 'purely' or 'impurely'.

Some psychologists have recently expressed their dissatisfaction with the state of the studies into reasoning. Thus, Evans (1978) has stressed the artificiality of experiments in reasoning, and argued that it is necessary to investigate reasoning with real-life problems. Erikson and Jones (1978, p. 83) are dissatisfied with the lack of theoretical integration in the psychology of reasoning, and consider that more effort should be made to explore the 'continuum from two-value logic through multi-value logic to continuous-value logic . . . with respect to different kinds of psychological judgment tasks'.

3.7 Conclusion

The purpose of this chapter has been to demonstrate that the studies of thought carried out in the Cartesian paradigm assess thought by means of an external standard. In the case of deductive reasoning, such a standard is formal logic. Deductive reasoning, of course, is not the only case of assessment of thought in terms of an external standard. Rommetveit (1978) introduced the notion of 'negative rationalism' to deal with the same issues in the work of Piaget and in psycholinguistics:

We may end up assessing deficiencies of language and reasoning in terms of deviance from alien and superimposed standards instead of assessing human communications and thought on premises adopted by the speaker and thinker himself. And the danger of such a negative rationalism is— despite Piaget's own truly great contributions to our insight into the unique and intrinsic nature of children's thought—particularly salient in a synthesis of Piagetian cognitive psychology and Chomskyan linguistics. (Rommetveit, 1978, p. 119)

The use of the notion of error in the studies mentioned in this chapter demonstrates that, in spite of their attempts to abolish the external standard of formal logic, psychologists have not succeeded in doing so and are moving in circles: on the one hand, it is claimed that formal logic is neither descriptive nor normative of human reasoning, but at the same time formal logic is still being used as a model with which the reasoner's actual performance is compared.

Kuhn (1962) pointed out that the first attempts to save a paradigm that is breaking down are carried out within the existing paradigm. New concepts are introduced and new theories put forward while the basic presuppositions of the paradigm are not changed. In the case of deductive reasoning, examples of such new concepts have been mentioned above, e.g. meaning, content, context. With respect to the nature of error, the theory of passive encoding has been replaced by the theory of internal representation (cf. Chapter 4). However, all of these changes are changes within the paradigm itself and do not concern the basic presuppositions of the Cartesian paradigm, defined by its conception of the knower, the known, and knowledge. The question still remains: can these difficulties be resolved unless the basic conceptual presuppositions of the Cartesian paradigm are changed?

CHAPTER 4

The Static and Predetermined Nature of Ideas, Concepts, and Internal Representations

The individualism introduced by the Cartesian paradigm had a profound effect upon Cartesian epistemology: the knowing subject on the one hand, and the object of his knowledge on the other, were no longer epistemologically equal. It was only the *knowing subject* that was epistemologically certain while the *object of knowledge* was thrown into shadow and doubt. Consequently, it became a problem for the Cartesian philosophers to explain how the knower's contact with the outside world was mediated and how it was possible to come to know it. For the philosophers of the Cartesian paradigm, *mediation* between the subject and object was possible through *ideas*. But new problems arose: if we cognize the outer and inner worlds mediately through ideas rather than immediately through the world itself, then how can the objects of that world produce ideas in the mind, and how can we, in any case, know that there are such objects or even that we have a body, senses, and a brain.

The notion of an 'idea' itself deserves a brief comment. As Kenny (1968) demonstrates, by an 'idea' Descartes meant all sorts of things ranging from an act of the mind to the content of such an act. For the purpose of this chapter, we shall use a definition according to which an idea is the form of a thought: *'Idea* is a word by which I understand the form of any thought, that form by the immediate awareness of which I am conscious of that said thought' (Descartes, *Arguments Demonstrating the Existence of God*, p. 52).

To questions such as 'how do ideas arise?' or 'how do ideas get into the mind?', the philosophers of the Cartesian paradigm replied similarly: the rationalists said that ideas were ultimately produced by the mind, and the empiricists indirectly implied the same answer. In both cases the position that ideas are products of the mind was a consequence of Cartesian dualism which claimed the absolute independence of body and mind.

4.1 The innate ideas of the rationalists

According to Descartes all ideas are innate. This fact may not be always clear

41

42

because Descartes discusses innateness in two different senses (cf. Copleston, 1964, pp. 82–4; Keeling, 1968, pp. 182–5) without making this sufficiently obvious.

In the first sense, *innateness is a capacity of the mind*. According to Cartesian dualism, body as unthinking extended substance and mind as unextended thinking substance had nothing in common (cf. p. 20), so there was no way in which stimulation of the senses could *produce* ideas in the mind. But 'the mind [was given] occasion to form these ideas, by means of an innate faculty' (Descartes, *Notes Against a Programme*, p. 443) when the senses were suitably stimulated by an external body. Therefore, when Descartes spoke of ideas as being innate, strictly speaking it was not the ideas that were innate, but the faculty of the mind producing them (*ibid.*, p. 442). Consequently, he did not consider that innate ideas existed fully-fledged in a baby's mind. Both Descartes and later Leibniz viewed innate ideas as dispositions of the mind to produce ideas when the senses were stimulated by the external world. Thus, Descartes says that similarly we can speak of a disposition to generosity being innate in some families, or of a person being born with a disposition to a disease like gout; not that such families or persons would act generously or suffer from gout at birth, but only that later in life, when faced with someone in need or as a result of heavy drinking, they would tend to be generous or develop gout (Descartes, *Notes Against a Programme*, p. 442). As Descartes puts it, following the sixteenth century philosopher Julius Scaliger, concealed in us are seeds of knowledge which are like the fire that lies hidden in a flint and is only revealed when a stone is struck upon it: 'philosophers extract them by way of reason, but poets strike them out by imagination, and then they shine more bright' (Descartes, Private thoughts, p. 4; also Leibniz, *New Essays*, p. 43).

When Descartes talks about innateness in the sense of a capacity of the mind, innateness refers to all ideas. But Descartes also uses the term 'innate ideas' when he classifies ideas according to their origin into three kinds: innate, adventitious, and factitious. He says (Descartes, *Meditations*, pp. 160–1, Letter to Mersenne, 16th June, 1641, p. 104) that adventitious ideas are those which come to us through the senses from external objects, such as the idea we have of the Sun; factitious ideas, on the other hand, are constructed by the mind from simpler ideas, for example, the astronomer's idea of the Sun is constructed from certain basic geometrical ideas; the third kind of ideas, innate ideas, are those which account for *universals* and make *universal knowledge* possible. All true knowledge starts with universal innate ideas, such as 'the idea of God, mind, body, triangle, and in general all those which represent true, immutable and eternal essences' (Descartes, Letter to Mersenne, 16th June, 1641, p. 104). And these ideas, which represent the 'immutable and eternal essences', are themselves immutable and eternal. They are 'primary germs of truth implanted by nature in human minds' (Descartes, *Rules*, p. 12). They are clear and distinct ideas known by intuition (cf. p. 22). We can say, therefore, that these ideas are innate in two senses: first, innate through the capacity of the mind to produce them; and, secondly, innate in the sense that they are produced by the mind independently of external stimulation, in contrast to adventitious and factitious ideas.

4.2 The Chomskyan revolution

Descartes' conception of innate ideas in both the above senses has persisted in philosophy and psychology right through to the present day. Chomsky, more than anyone else, has reawakened this Cartesian conception in recent years and, indeed, has made it a point of departure for a whole tradition of research in psychology and linguistics. Although his attachment to Descartes permeates all his work from *Syntactic Structures* (1957) up to his most recent accounts, Chomsky's (1966) *Cartesian Linguistics* is the most explicit acknowledgement of the influence of Descartes' notions of innate capacities and innate universals in the field of linguistics.

The main doctrine of *Cartesian Linguistics* is that the general principles which determine grammatical structure in particular languages are common to all human languages and are therefore linguistic universals. These principles, which, according to Chomsky, underlie the structure of the human mind, are of biological, rather than of logical necessity (Chomsky, 1977). The child at birth is endowed with an innate capacity for the acquisition of language, not of some particular language, but of human languages generally. Placed in an English-speaking community, he will learn English; in a Chinese-speaking community, he will, with equal facility, come to speak and understand Chinese (Chomsky, 1962). Having been equipped with this innate capacity, the child, in order to acquire a particular language, has to discover a specific grammar from a set of potential grammars which are determined by the above general principles (Chomsky, 1965). The grammar the child selects is the one appropriate to the linguistic experience available to him. On the basis of this experience, which in fact is very sparse and incomplete from the point of view of the complexity and richness of the adult language, it is possible to account for the fact that the child can learn language as quickly as he does, can construct sentences he has never learned before, and can derive the grammatical rules.

Influenced by Chomsky's ideas, linguists and psychologists have set themselves some challenging tasks: to discover the exact nature of the innate intellectual equipment necessary for the acquisition of language; to develop a theory of general linguistic description; and to find out whether innate principles are syntactic, semantic, cognitive, perceptual, motoric or a combination of a number of these. For example, McNeill (1971) approached the problem from the point of view of transformational grammar. He suggested that the grammatical universals are partly phonological and partly syntactic. In contrast to McNeill, Schlesinger (1971) thought that there was nothing specifically linguistic about the innate capacities, but rather that they were cognitive and that they determined the semantic intentions of the child. Postal (1966) and Bierwisch (1970) focused on innate semantic structures. Thus, Bierwisch claimed that 'semantic features cannot be different from language to language, but are rather part of the general human capacity for language, forming a universal inventory used in particular ways by individual languages' (Bierwisch, 1970, pp. 181–2). The Genevan school maintained that 'linguistic structures may well be yet another symptom of the very general, universal cognitive structures' (Sinclair-de-Zwart, 1973, p. 25).

For Chomsky (1980) it is a *modular mental structure* that is innate. Mental structures are innately endowed with high specificity. This high specificity, or modularity, is *predetermined* for human species in the same way that the specificity of any other biological organ, such as the heart, liver or eye, is predetermined. It is the highly specific innate biological endowment that makes members of certain species one like another:

> Were it not for this highly specific innate endowment, each individual would grow into some kind of an amoeboid creature, merely reflecting external contingencies, one individual quite unlike another . . . When we turn to the mind and its products, the situation is not qualitatively different from what we find in the case of the body. Here, too, we find structures of considerable intricacy, developing quite uniformly, far transcending the limited environmental factors that trigger and partially shape their growth. Language is a case in point, though not the only one. (Chomsky, 1980, pp. 2 and 3)

Several important points are included in this quotation. First, the nature of innate endowment is not qualitatively different for body and mind. In both cases it is the innate *biological* endowment Chomsky is talking about. It is quite clear, in this most recent statement from Chomsky, that the notion of the mind and that of the brain can be used interchangeably. Mental organs are organs of the brain in the same sense as an eye is an organ of the visual system (Chomsky, 1980, p. 3). Secondly, the role of environmental factors is limited to a triggering and partially shaping effect. Thus, what psychologists call language learning, concept learning, learning mathematics, and so on is an internally pre-determined course that is triggered and partly shaped by the environment (*ibid.*, p. 2). In this respect, Chomsky's position is very similar to that of Descartes. Just as for Descartes, so for Chomsky thinking exists in the human soul (in the brain for Chomsky), even in a mother's womb. And just as for Descartes the striking of the flint provides the 'occasion' on which 'seeds of thought' can manifest their 'hidden fire' (cf. p. 42), so for Chomsky the environment has a triggering and shaping effect.

There is yet another feature in Chomsky's theory of language: the creative aspect of the use of language. This feature was elaborated in *Cartesian Linguistics* (Chomsky, 1966). Creativity, or the ability of a child to produce and interpret sentences he has never heard before, is, according to Chomsky, a defining characteristic of language and a feature which distinguishes human language from animal communication. Once the child has mastered the grammatical rules he is able to create an infinite number of sentences in a given language quite independently of external or internal stimuli.

Bearing in mind the above discussion concerning the predetermined structure of 'mental organs', how can we interpret Chomsky's notion of creativity? It may be helpful to make a distinction between two different notions of creativity. The first notion, let us call it Creativity I, is a *self-contained* and *predetermined* creativity. It is the creativity of the rationalists, the creativity of the *Cartesian Linguistics*. Creativity in this sense is the process of generating new sentences from the internalized rules, and it has two essential features: first, it is rooted in certain static structures and predetermined principles and rules; secondly, it is self-contained in the sense that the role of the external factors is negligible (cf. 'the triggering and shaping effect'). The external factors, i.e. the factors of the environment, have the role of the stone which strikes the flint; they start the process off but they do not actually participate in the process. They shape the process by providing the child with information, but this shaping is, as Chomsky points out, 'narrowly constrained'.

The second notion of creativity, let us call it Creativity II, possesses neither of the two main features of Creativity I: it is neither predetermined nor self-contained. It is creativity in which the mind and the social environment are equal partners in starting the creative process. They are also equal partners during the whole process, in which they are synchronized and play a reciprocal role. Such a notion of creativity was given by romanticism and elaborated by Hegel, and is becoming established and taken for granted in many recent psychological studies into language and communication. We shall discuss its nature in Part II of this book.

In support of his ideas on creativity in *Cartesian Linguistics*, Chomsky discusses and quotes from Herder's *Essay on the Origin of Language*. According to Chomsky, Herder, one of the representatives of the German romantic movement, like Descartes, claimed that language is a product of the intellectually organized and specifically human mind; it is not to be found in animals, but is characteristic of man's freedom from control by external stimuli or internal physiological states. Moreover, Chomsky points out that 'a concern for the creative aspect of language use persists through the romantic period, in relation to the general problem of true creativity, in the full sense of this term' (Chomsky, 1966, p. 16). This comparison between the Cartesians and Herderians, however, is inappropriate and ill-conceived. We shall see in Part II that Herder's conception of language was in fact a strong reaction against seventeenth and eighteenth century rationalism in general, and therefore against the rationalism of Descartes. Herder, being a representative of the romantic movement, in waving the banner of Creativity II, was defending it against Creativity I.

4.3   The solution of Locke

Locke rejected Descartes' innate ideas and claimed instead that the mind at birth is like a blank sheet. The infant's mind is only gradually furnished with ideas as the infant spends more and more of his time awake rather than sleeping, and as more and more things affect him as he sees, hears, and touches them. All our knowledge is founded in experience, and is ultimately derived from it. Our experience is of two kinds: about external sensible objects and about the internal operations of the mind. These two kinds of experience are the two sources of knowledge from which we get our ideas.

Having repudiated innate ideas and substituted ideas obtained through experience, Locke claimed that certain ideas do, while others do not, resemble the qualities of the bodies that produce them in us. Those qualities of bodies that resemble ideas are primary qualities. Examples of these are solidity, extension, figure, and mobility. These qualities are inseparable from objects in the sense that no matter what the changes to which we may submit them, or the forces which may be applied to them, these qualities still remain. *Secondary qualities*, on the other hand, produce in us such ideas as taste, colour or sound, but nothing like our ideas exists in the bodies themselves. Secondary qualities are groups of primary qualities which, individually, are too finely divided to affect our senses. But if our senses were more acute, and, indeed, when our senses are assisted by the microscope, these secondary qualities would be and are resolved into their individual components, and we would and do perceive the ideas of the respective primary qualities instead (Locke, *Essay*, II, xxiii, 11).

But how do the primary qualities of objects produce ideas? Locke does not give a satisfactory answer to this question. In Book II of the *Essay* he suggests that evidently 'some singly imperceptible bodies' must come from objects to the senses and 'convey to the brain some *motion*, which produces these *ideas* which we have of them in us.' (*Essay*, II, viii, 12). But in Book I of the *Essay* he proposes not to trouble himself with examining or speculating

... by what motions of our spirits or alterations of our bodies we come to have any sensation by our organs, or any *ideas* in our understandings; and whether those *ideas* do in their formation, any or all of them, depend on matter or no. These are speculations which, however curious and entertaining, I shall decline, as lying out of my way in the design I am now upon (Locke, *Essay*, I, i, 2)

If we take Locke's non-committal position on this, together with the fact that he accepted the dualism of body and mind, then, strictly speaking, he must have accepted that it is the mind which produces ideas. Nevertheless the mind had no freedom whatsoever in this respect, and produced ideas when and only when the brain was activated by the stimulation of the senses by external objects. Consequently, it was just as if the mind was directly affected by such objects and ideas were directly conveyed to the mind.

However, Locke certainly did not accept that the mind could produce universals or universal laws (i.e. Descartes' second kind of innateness), and it is this sort of innateness he attacks in Book I of the *Essay*.

4.4   The ideas and concepts of the empiricists

According to Locke, *simple ideas of sensation* have their source in external objects. Examples of such simple ideas are the coldness and hardness of a piece of ice, the scent and whiteness of a lily, the taste of sugar, or the scent of a rose. External objects stimulate the appropriate senses, i.e. sight, taste, touch, and so on. The senses usually convey the stimulations to the mind simultaneously, and the mind has the ability to consider all of them together and to produce one *complex idea*:

... the complex idea which an Englishman signifies by the name *swan* is white colour, long neck, red beak, black legs, and whole feet, and all of these of a certain kind of noise, and perhaps, to a man who has long observed this kind of bird, some other properties: which all terminate in sensible simple ideas, all united in one common object. (Locke, *Essay*, II, xxiii, 14)

But the connections between our *ideas* are not of a necessary nature, they are only connections of co-existence; in other words, we perceive a swan as a swan because all the simple ideas, i.e. white colour, a special type of noise, long beak, and so on, are produced together. Because of this, however, our knowledge is purely contingent and any generalizations extending beyond our actual experience are prone to be erroneous. Locke's notion of a *complex idea* and the definitions of a *concept* (it was Kant who first used the term 'concept' to replace the expression 'idea') by some present-day psychologists are surprisingly similar:

Most natural concepts are defined by relevant attributes which affect several different sensory systems simultaneously. Members of the class of objects called 'banana', for example, are yellow (visual), elongated (visual or tactual), soft (tactual), and rather sweet (taste and smell). (Bourne, 1966, pp. 59–60)

Such definitions assume that concepts vary according to their constituent attributes, such as size, shape, colour, etc.; an appropriate collection of such attributes constitutes a concept. Those objects that display the collection of attributes constituting the concept in question have been called 'positive instances' of a concept, while those objects that do not display those attributes have been called 'negative instances' of the concept. Let us now consider how, according to this theory, a subject might acquire a concept.

Bruner, Goodnow, and Austin (1956) assumed that a subject has grasped a concept when he is able to select positive instances of a concept and eliminate negative instances. For example, the concept 'influential person' might be acquired in the following way. A stranger might come to a town where he has never been before and where he does not know anybody. An old resident might take him round and introduce him to different people in the town. After each encounter with a new person, the old resident might comment: 'this person is influential' or 'this person is not influential'. The task of the stranger is to discover which people in the town are instances of 'influential person' and which are not. Thus, being given positive and negative feedback as to who is and who is not influential, the stranger might discover that age, religion, apparent aggressiveness, economic status, and perhaps others make a person

48

influential, while their absence did not make him influential. Bruner, Good-now, and Austin, in order to simplify and exemplify the process of finding out what 'influential' means, selected four attributes, each with three discriminable values. These were *age* (under 35, 35–50, over 50), *economic status* (high, medium, low), *religion* (Catholic, Jew, Protestant), and *apparent aggressiveness* (high, medium, low). It was assumed that the concept was conjunctive, that is, that the four attributes with their particular values are combined together to form a concept. For example, the definition of 'influential person' could be: 'over 50, rich, Protestant, and moderately aggressive'.

Whole generations of psychologists such as Heidbreder, Smoke, Hull, Vygotsky, Bruner, Hovland, Bourne, and others have adopted the above approach to the laboratory investigation of concept formation and concept acquisition. A typical laboratory method for the study of concept formation based on this approach is the classical experiment by Bruner *et al.* (1956).

A subject is presented with a set of cards with single, double, or triple borders. Each card bears one, two, or three identical geometrical figures. The figures are 'plus' signs, squares or circles, and they are coloured red, green or black. 'Border', 'number', 'shape', and 'colour' are attributes, and each attribute can take three values. There are therefore $3^4 = 81$ different cards (cf. Figure 4.1). The experimenter tells the subject that he has chosen a certain combination of attributes and values to represent a concept, and that some of the cards on the table illustrate the concept (positive instances) and others do not (negative instances). The subject's task is to determine the concept. He should select a card for testing, one at a time, and will be told whether it is a positive or negative instance. To start him off the experimenter shows him a card that is a positive instance. The subject can offer as many hypotheses as he likes, but not more than one between tests. In this account, a concept is decomposed into attributes $A_1, A_2, \ldots, A_n$ which are items of equal weightings and can be easily quantified, for example in the case above, as high, medium, and low. Concepts are thus 'well defined' in terms of their attributes with equal weightings and are suitable for computer programming.

A model of concept formation for computer programming has been developed by Hunt (1962). This model consists of two stages. In the first stage a description of the stimuli is arrived at by the definition of attributes (e.g. in the case of people, age and religion) and values (e.g. under 35, 35–50, and over 50;

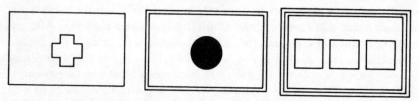

Figure 4.1. Card experiment. From Bruner, Goodnow and Austin (1958), *A Study of Thinking*. Reproduced by permission of the authors and John Wiley & Sons, Inc. Copyright © 1956 John Wiley & Sons, Inc

Catholic, Jew, Protestant). This, Hunt says, is really a problem in perception. The second stage is the discovery of an adequate concept by first designating a particular class of objects as positive instances of the concept and looking for features of the descriptions of these positive instances which they have in common. The procedures used in this stage are of an algorithmic nature (cf. Chapter 5) and are best represented by decision trees. The concept so obtained is finally tested against further positive instances to ensure that it is correct.

4.5 The meanings of words

The theories of the meanings of words in linguistics and psychology that have emerged in the nineteen-sixties and seventies are clear examples of rationalism and empiricism combining their efforts together. Thus, on the one hand, they assume that the meanings of words can be decomposed into their elementary components in the same way that concepts can be broken down into attributes and values. This is the empiricists' assumption. On the other hand, these theories presuppose the existence of *semantic universals*. This is the rationalists' assumption.

Just as the attributes of concepts are of a binary nature and are either present in a concept or not, so the elementary components of the meanings of words are either present in a word or they are absent.

To acquire the meaning of a word is to discover what combinations of elements are present together. The meanings of words, according to this assumption, can be expressed as follows (Bierwisch, 1970, p. 169):

(a) *boy:*   ANIMATE and HUMAN and MALE and NOT ADULT
(b) *girl:*   ANIMATE and HUMAN and FEMALE and NOT ADULT
(c) *man:*   ANIMATE and HUMAN and MALE and ADULT
(d) *woman:*ANIMATE and HUMAN and FEMALE and ADULT

Just as the presence and absence of attributes and their values express relationships among concepts, so the presence and absence of atomic semantic components such as ANIMATE, HUMAN, MALE, ADULT, and so on, express semantic relationships between words. For example, as we can see above, the difference between the meanings of the words 'boy' and 'girl' concerns the elements MALE and FEMALE, while the difference between 'woman' and 'girl' concerns the elements ADULT and NOT ADULT. Rules of combination ensure that only certain combinations of semantic components count as meaningful words.

So how does a human being acquire the meanings of words? Just as concepts are acquired by identifying attributes and their values, so meanings are acquired by identifying their elementary discrete components. Let us consider how both the behaviourists and cognitivists arrive at this answer.

Skinner has no difficulty in explaining how a child learns the meanings of words when he is responding to visible stimuli:

A child learns to distinguish among different colours, tones, odours, tastes, temperatures, and so on only when they enter into contingencies of reinforcement. If red candies have a reinforcing flavour and green candies do not, the child takes and eats red candies. Some important contingencies are verbal. Parents teach a child to name colours by reinforcing correct responses. If the child says 'Blue' and the object before him is blue, the parent says 'Good!' or 'Right!' If the object is red, the parent says 'Wrong!' (Skinner, 1973, p. 105)

Such straightforward reinforcement by attaching labels to objects, however, is not possible when the child is learning to respond to stimuli inside his body, such as hunger or pain. Such sensations are private, and the teacher-parent cannot make fine distinctions among stimuli when only their visible signs are accessible to him. Thus, it is when the child eats ravenously or gives some other signs of hunger that the parent says 'hungry'. Moreover, because the teacher-parent himself once had to be taught the meanings of words referring to private sensations, the language which refers to such sensations is necessarily inaccurate and imprecise and very often when we describe our emotions we use metaphors or analogies.

Skinner's belief that our sensations are incommunicable suggests the existence of a *private language*. According to Wittgenstein (1953) a private language is a language which 'refers to what can only be known to the person speaking: to his immediate private sensations. So another person cannot understand the language' (Wittgenstein, 1953, §243). Thus it could be argued that although the child's language learning may proceed in a public context, in the presence of his parents, it is still basically private and individualistic because all that is required for successful learning is the reinforcement: 'Right' or 'Wrong'. In that case the role of the parent-teacher could quite easily be taken by a push-button machine producing a sound, electric shock or sweet, with a reward for a correct and punishment for an incorrect response. The role of the parent-teacher in such a scheme is reduced to the one of reinforcement, which can be achieved by a mechanism. All the child learns is to label objects correctly, whether the objects are external or internal, with the latter being more difficult and therefore the labelling less precise. Other people, of course, according to this scheme, do not have access to the child's inner experiences, they can only infer his internal changes from his external observable behaviour.

Let us turn now to the cognitivists' approach to the acquisition of meanings. There are, of course, substantial differences between them and the behaviourists. However, there are also some important similarities between them because both behaviourists and cognitivists are descendants of Cartesianism. The cognitivist theories of meaning are individualistic and presuppose identification of invariants just as do the behaviouristic theories. Thus, according to Clark's (1973) *semantic feature hypothesis* the meanings of words can be broken down into elementary components which she calls features. When the child learns the meanings of words, he originally acquires only a limited range of features rather than the whole combination of features which are present in adult meanings. Only gradually does he learn more features which he adds to his existing range. This early stage of his semantic acquisition is characterized by an overextension of meanings. For example, when learning the meaning of the word *dog* he may originally acquire the semantic feature four-legged and so apply it not only to dogs, but also to pigs, cows, horses, and so on. However, when he adds on another feature, such as *relatively small*, he narrows down his overextended meaning to smaller animals only. When he adds on the feature *barking*, he finally narrows down the meaning of *dog* to dogs only. The child's early referential errors, therefore, are due to the fact that he delimits categories differently from the adult (Clark, 1973). The question which Clark posed for herself, as to what exactly a feature is and whether children use the same features as adults, could not be answered on the basis of the existing theoretical and empirical evidence. She maintained, though, that 'in an ideal world where we knew what the universal semantic primitives were, we could assume these would be used by both child and adult' (Clark, 1973, p. 74). This assumption, again, is typical of the Cartesian paradigm. Leibniz's claim that 'there must be simple substances because there are compounds' (cf. p. 16) has been taken for granted by the psychologists who assume the existence of semantic elements or conceptual attributes as *ready-made substances*. Thus, 'maleness' or 'redness' are substances that have a universal and eternal existence and do not submit themselves to any changes or development. The consequences of this view are numerous.

First, the essential feature of the above theories of concept and meaning acquisition is that it is the purely referential aspect of concepts and meanings that is considered. A person is assumed to form hypotheses about concepts or the meanings of words on the basis of the components of the concepts or word meanings in question. In forming such hypotheses, the person is supposed to refer to objects in terms of their perceptible features, combine these features together, and test his hypotheses against them. It is thus not only considered possible but it is *taken for granted* that the formation of concepts and meanings is to be studied as a purely *referential process*.

Secondly, since the elements are ready-made substances, mixing and combining them together produces new concepts and new meanings of words.

Thirdly, the idea of ready-made perceptible substances led the psychologists to a concern with the study of those objects, concepts, and meanings, in which the perceptible elements are distinctly manifested. For example, studies of concept acquisition have been concerned with objects that can be easily mentally analysed in terms of simple properties such as geometrical figure, size, and colour. Or the acquisition of meanings has been studied with the names of animals (cf. above) or of simple physical objects such as a chair, cup or ball. It can be argued, of course, that in child development these are the objects with which a child becomes acquainted first and, therefore, the concepts and meanings of words he acquires first. But even if it were true that the first words and first concepts are acquired by mental analysis of perceptual properties of objects, the question still remains as to how *other* meanings of words and concepts are acquired, for example, how concepts such as 'can', 'uncle', 'friend' are acquired. No satisfactory answer has been given by those working in the

Cartesian paradigm. Their assumption seems to be that *all objects* can be conceived in terms of elements; that *all concepts* are decomposable into attributes; that *all meanings* are decomposable into semantic elements. Therefore, it is sufficient to demonstrate this fact on 'simple' objects, 'simple' concepts, and 'simple' meanings.

Finally, the decomposability of objects, concepts, and meanings into their simple components has led to the assumption that the acquisition of knowledge is a *yes–no affair*. But this is the subject matter of Chapter 5.

4.6   Kant's *a priori* modes of knowledge

Just as for all philosophers of the Cartesian paradigm, so for Kant our contact with the outside world was not direct but mediated. But Kant accepted neither the innate ideas of the rationalists nor the conception that our ideas are derived from experience, defended by the empiricists. Instead, Kant maintained that 'all our knowledge begins with experience, [though] it does not follow that it all arises out of experience' (Kant, *Critique of Pure Reason*, B 1). For our empirical knowledge may contain material that is supplied by the mind in the act of knowing. Such knowledge is called *a priori*, in contrast to *a posteriori* knowledge, which is derived from our sensible impressions.

What is Kant's *a priori* knowledge? Kant is opposed to the Cartesian conception that we have innate dispositions, and certain specific knowledge such as of innate ideas of God, the soul, etc., which means that we are born with the ability to form ideas with empirical content. In his polemics against Eberhard (Allison, 1973), Kant insists that there is no divinely implanted or innate knowledge. Representations of space and time, for example, are *a priori*, being amongst the conditions of any kind of experience, but are, nevertheless, acquired, and therefore not innate. They must, however, be grounded in something that *is* innate. It is the constitution of the mind that makes such representations as space and time possible. The mind has an innate receptivity to receive representations according to its subjective constitution: 'Only this first formal ground, e.g. the possibility of a representation of space, is *innate*, not the spatial representation itself' (Allison, 1973, p. 136).

There are two basic features which distinguish *a priori* knowledge from empirical, i.e. *a posteriori*, knowledge: it is necessary, and it has universal validity. For knowledge to be necessary means that any possible alternative or exception is excluded because such an alternative or exception would not be intelligible, though Kant does not make it quite clear whether it would not be intelligible on logical or psychological grounds. Universal validity or 'strict universality' refers to the fact that *a priori* judgements are absolutely valid, i.e. valid for all possible beings in all possible conditions. These two criteria, necessity and universality, are applicable to *a priori* knowledge only because it is *not* derived from experience. In contrast, as Kant says, *empirical* universality, applicable in the case of *a posteriori* knowledge, is only an arbitrary extension of what we believe is the case on the basis of our experience. Thus, we may say that all bodies are heavy because, according to our experience, all bodies with which we have so far been in contact have had weight. And Kant in fact sets it for himself as a general programme to find out how *a priori* knowledge is possible and how exactly we apply this *a priori* knowledge to specific instances of our experience. *A priori* knowledge is possible, not because our ideas resemble objects as Descartes and Locke believed, but because *objects as we know them* must conform to our own concepts (Kant, *Critique of Pure Reason*, B xvi–xviii), and thus it is through *a priori* principles that *the mind gives laws to nature* (*ibid.*, A 127). This is perhaps the most fundamental thesis of Kant's first *Critique* and he himself compares it with the Copernican revolution in physics.

However, there is no agreement among the commentators on Kant as to how exactly his *a priori* principles and the mind's law-giving nature should be interpreted. For our discussion, I shall use what I believe is Hegel's interpretation of Kant. This interpretation has also been accepted by some present commentators on Kant and also by recent cognitive psychology. According to this interpretation, to call an element *a priori* means that such an element is

attributable entirely *to the nature of our cognitive constitution* [my italics] and not at all to the nature of those things, as they are in themselves, which affect that constitution to yield experience. (Strawson, 1966, p. 68)

This interpretation was also accepted by Copleston (1964) who, in order to clarify Kant's position on *a priori* principles, uses the analogy of a man born with 'red vision'. Copleston invites the reader to imagine a person whose visual and cognitive systems are so constructed that everything this person perceives in the world seems to him to be red. However, in order to give a correct account of Kant we would have to add that *the category of colour itself* was attributable to the structure of the cognitive system, just as Kant held that such categories as space, time, and causality were attributable to the structure of the mind. Under these conditions, if a person perceives everything red, then two hypotheses are possible: first, everything in the world really is red but this is only contingently true: secondly, although things may have other colours they necessarily appear red because of the structure of that person's visual system. Let us suppose, first, that the man believes that everything really is red but that during the course of time he finds certain facts which cannot be explained by this supposition. Consequently, he turns to the alternative hypothesis, that he necessarily sees things red because of the structure of his visual system. And this, in fact, is Kant's position: the man will not be able to see what objects are really like; what he perceives is determined by his visual and cognitive system. However, his *reason* tells him that behind these perceptions or *appearances* there is a *real* world.

According to this interpretation we only have knowledge of *appearances* (empirical objects, empirical selves) while we are utterly ignorant of *things-in-themselves* (objects-in-themselves, selves-in-themselves). Objects- and selves-in-themselves *affect* our senses and understanding and on the basis of

54

their effects we then construct empirical objects and empirical selves. This interpretation of Kant ascribes to Kant's theory the claims of a *psychological* rather than a *conceptual* nature. This interpretation has had a significant influence on cognitive psychology.

4.7 Kant and internal representations

The belief that we only have contact with ideas or appearances rather than with the 'real' world (world-in-itself) has also become, implicitly or explicitly, part of the assumptions of cognitive psychology. As the distinguished cognitive psychologist Neisser put it:

There certainly is a real world of trees and people and cars and even books, and it has a great deal to do with our experience of these objects. However, we have no direct, immediate access to the world, nor to any of its properties . . . Whatever we know about reality has been *mediated*, not only by the organs of sense but by complex systems which interpret and re-interpret sensory information. (Neisser, 1967, p. 3)

A page of print, Neisser continues, is just an array of blobs of ink in a certain arrangement on the page; this objective stimulus, with which we have no direct contact, is 'distal stimulus'. The sensory input, transmitted to us by light rays or in some other cases by sound waves, is a 'proximal stimulus'. The patterns of light or sound fall on the retina or on sensory cells in the ear and transmit the stimuli to the brain. Only now does the constructive process start, leading to a representation of the object. Brunswik (1952) and Heider (1958) refer to this model of perception as the *lens model* (Figure 4.2). The foci of the lens are the distal stimulus, which in Kantian terms would refer to the real world, i.e. the world-in-itself, and the final percept, which would correspond to Kant's appearance. The diverging lines represent the mediation of information from the distal stimulus into sensory inputs (proximal stimulus). The constructive

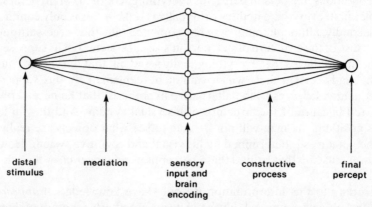

distal   mediation   sensory   constructive   final
stimulus   input and   process   percept
                                   brain
                                   encoding

Figure 4.2   The lens model. Adapted from Brunswik (1952), *The Conceptual Framework of Psychology*, in Neurath, O. *et al.* (gen. eds), *International Encyclopedia of Unified Science*, Vol. 1, No. 10. Reproduced by permission of The University of Chicago Press. Copyright by the University of Chicago

process, in Kantian terms the process by which the mind gives laws to nature, is represented by the converging lines. We may thus note that psychologists, just like those of Kant's commentators who accepted a 'double-affection' interpretation, have taken Kant's words literally:

I am not, therefore, in a position to *perceive* external things, but can only infer their existence from my inner perception, taking the inner perception as the effect of which something external is the proximate cause. (Kant, *Critique of Pure Reason*, A 369)

With the development of experimental cognitive psychology, however, the Kantian position in psychology with respect to the world-in-itself and *a priori* cognitive structures has undergone significant transformations. The 'real' world, the world-in-itself, has lost its attraction. Brunswik and Heider at least pay lip service to the world-in-itself in their concern as to the relationship between the distal stimulus and the final percept. For most cognitive psychologists, however, because we know the world-in-itself only through the information entering our senses, we may just as well take *this* information as the point of departure for our enquiries and ignore the world-in-itself completely. In this respect, Kant's transcendental idealist position has been replaced by a kind of realism to which he strongly objected: appearances or representations of the world-in-itself have been replaced by a position according to which appearances in fact are things-in-themselves.

Kant's *a priori* knowledge was empty of any empirical content; it was only a condition for empirical knowledge. Moreover, it was universal and necessary, and attributable to the nature of cognitive constitution. In the work of the present experimental psychologists, the structures and the postulated different kinds of 'red vision' systems have been given different names, depending upon the psychologist's particular specializations and psychological biases, as well as upon his biases concerning imports from logic, mathematics, computing science or even from philosophy. Thus, we have mental maps (Tolman, 1948), internal representations, (Gregg, 1967; Bobrow and Collins, 1975; Newell and Simon, 1972; Michon, 1972; and others), mental representations (Chase and Clark, 1972), mental operations (Trabasso, 1972), tacit knowledge (Polanyi, 1966; Franks, 1974), and internal linguistic structures (Chomsky, 1968), while sometimes these labels are used with little discrimination. Inner structures, or representations of the outer world, are sometimes supposed to be empty of empirical content and sometimes to have empirical content and depend on experience. An example of a theory that treats inner structures as empty of empirical content is the model of the internal representation of the syllogism developed by Johnson-Laird (1975). This model is based on the representation of the subjects and predicates of the syllogism in two separate classes:

The model assumes that human reasoners represent a class by imagining an arbitrary number of its members. For example, a class of artists is represented by a set of elements that are tagged in some way as artists. The nature of the elements and their tags is immaterial—they may be vivid visual images or ghostlike verbal tags. The crucial point is simply that they are discrete elements. A statement such as 'All the artists are beekeepers' relates two separate classes and it is represented in the following way:

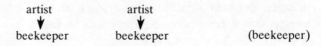

where representatives of one class are mapped onto representatives of the other class, and the parenthetical item indicates that there may be beekeepers who are not artists. (Johnson-Laird, 1975, p. 42)

Such representations can be generalized. All universal affirmative statements (cf. p. 30), e.g. *All S are P*, can be represented as follows:

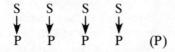

A particular affirmative statement, e.g. *Some S are P*, can be represented as follows:

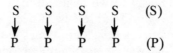

(P) and (S) represent those subjects and predicates that are not P and not S respectively. Negative universal and particular statements involve negative links and for details the reader is referred to Johnson-Laird (1975, p. 42ff). The main problem for the reasoner is to make correct mappings of subjects and predicates of the syllogistic premises. Some combinations of A, I, E, O, figures, and orders of propositions may make the task a rather difficult one. The reasoner's task is to abstract the linguistic form of the premises from the content (and context) and to apply logical rules of inferences. The model assumes that the human reasoner and the PLANNER of the theorem-proving machine process information using the same general principles.

Revlis's model of syllogistic reasoning characterizes a reasoner as a processor of information. Information is given to the reasoner in the form of premises and is formally represented in his mind. If the information is syntactically too complex for the reasoner, then the internal representation of the premises may be erroneous. Errors in reasoning, according to this model, are due to 'a flawed representation of the propositions' to which 'formally correct operations' are applied (Revlis, 1975, p. 97).

These two models of internal representation are based on the representation of the deductive reasoning tasks of the kind discussed in Chapter 3. They assume a certain organization of cognitive structures that determines the way a problem is encoded and processed.

Schank and Abelson (1977) have argued, however, that 'tight logical systems' which can be mechanistically applied to artificial laboratory tasks are unsuitable for dealing with the problems of real life. 'The real world is messy and often illogical' and therefore a different kind of approach is necessary, which should take the person's experience into consideration: it is not only the logical structure that is important in comprehension but also the content. To be quite fair, the importance of content in comprehension and reasoning has been *admitted* by other researchers (Wason and Johnson-Laird, 1972; Johnson-Laird, 1975). However, Schank and Abelson have *not only admitted* the importance of content but they have also *made it part of their basic assumptions*. In fact their theory of knowledge structure and conceptual dependency provides a representation of meanings of texts, as against the meanings of individual sentences. And, as they say,

If our theory is apt, it will provide a model of the human observer of the human scene; it will also explain how to construct a computer observer of the human scene, and lead to the eventual building of a computer participant in the human world. (Schank and Abelson, 1977, p. 4)

The understanding of events and situations in the social world, and of texts describing them, depends, according to Schank and Abelson, on the possession of *scripts*, and the existence of scripts depends on the fact that many of our social activities are stereotyped, and therefore predictable. A script represents what is common to the sequences of physical and mental events that constitute social activities of the same kind. It is because we have scripts that a few words can tell us a great deal. Scripts make for enormous economy in written or verbal texts because a minimum of information is sufficient to activate the appropriate script in the reader or listener and enable him to give specific values to the variables in the script. Thus, for example, people have scripts for taking a taxi, behaving at a party, dining in a restaurant, participating at a business meeting, and so on. Scripts are thus internal representations by means of which the person controls and predicts his physical and social world.

Knowledge of a script is knowledge of a 'structure [which] is an inter-connected whole' (Schank and Abelson, 1977, p. 41), each step of which presupposes the previous step. The acquisition of scripts depends upon the repeated experience of the type of social activity in question, which in turn depends upon learning of the conceptual or quasi-causal relationships between the different stages of the activity, so that a complete representation of a text as intended by the speaker or writer requires both the knowledge structure of the script and the conceptual dependency of the states and events described in the text.

The essential characteristic of script-based understanding is that 'a person must have been in that situation before' (*ibid.*, p. 67). People can act upon the situation sensibly only if they understand it, that is, if they

match what they see and hear to pre-stored groupings of actions that they have already experienced. New information is understood in terms of old information. By this view,

58

man is seen as a processor that only understands what it has previously understood. Our script-based program, SAM [Script Applier Mechanism], works this way. (Schank and Abelson, 1977, p. 67)

How do people cope with entirely new situations in which they have not found themselves before, though? They do not have scripts for new situations. They do, however, have the ability to make plans, and this ability enables them to cope with entirely new and unexpected situations. It was pointed out earlier that everyone has at his disposal a vast conceptual equipment that enables him to cope with innumerable kinds of situations by connecting them to other stages of familiar social activities. In order to cope with or understand a situation that is not part of a stereotyped social activity, a person has to make use of this conceptual equipment to make *plans* which hypothesize series of actions by which his goal might be achieved.

Plans describe the set of choices that a person has when he sets out to accomplish a goal. In listening to discourse people use plans to make sense of seemingly disconnected sentences. By finding a plan, an understander can make guesses about the intentions of an action in an unfolding story and use these guesses to make sense of the story. (Schank and Abelson, 1977, p. 70)

Thus, the understanding of events is sometimes based on scripts, sometimes on plans and sometimes on a mixture of both. It is important, though, that a person must have at least some ability to anticipate actions and in order to anticipate actions he must have some idea as to how actions are connected. What then comes first: plans or scripts? Schank and Abelson (1977, p. 72) say that scripts come from plans. In this context they evidently mean *new* scripts, but all scripts are surely new at some time. If this is the case, then it must mean that a person must have the ability to predict actions before he actually is acquainted with them. Does he possess such knowledge innately or *a priori*? The authors do not say so. They point out, however, that a child four months old showed knowledge of certain scripts (*ibid.*, p. 225). Did he have any general knowledge necessary for planning beforehand? If so, where did such generalized knowledge come from?

There are no satisfactory answers to these questions. On the one hand, 'scripts are constantly elaborated on with each successive experience' (*ibid.*, p. 224) and, at the same time, script-based understanding 'is a process by which people match what they see and hear to pre-stored groupings of actions that they have already experienced', and explain new information in terms of old information (*ibid.*, p. 67). What is the role of experience, then? Can scripts in fact be elaborated in any creative way or are they only new combinations of already existing information? According to Schank and Abelson's conception, prediction is a construction out of mirror images of past experience. And this is exactly what all thinkers of the Cartesian paradigm would say (cf. p. 18). It is a reflection of the past. It is not reflexion, that is the past seen through the present experience, not the activity with its capacity for development that we shall find in the Hegelian framework.

We can thus conclude that although 'scripts' and 'plans' and perhaps some other terms introduce 'context' and 'experience' into the understanding of language and events, the conceptual framework has not changed. We may say that the theory of 'scripts' and 'plans' is an example of the attempts to save the collapsing Cartesian paradigm. The conceptual framework with which the theory has been developed, however, does not step outside Cartesianism. Although 'content' and 'context' and 'past experience' have become parts of the assumptions of this theory, the conceptualization itself is Cartesian: scripts and plans exist only because a person has been in that particular situation before and is simply matching the pre-stored representations to his new experience. People can cope with new situations because they can understand them in terms of their previous experience, because they can re-organize the pieces of information they already have in their internal representations. No actual development is taking place: the apparent development of plans and scripts is really only a regrouping of static and predetermined elements of information. And, of course, this is where the authors see an overlap between man and computer. Computers too can use scripts and make plans using pre-stored and already built-in elements (cf. Chapter 5).

Predetermined and static elements have been taken for granted in the innate ideas of the rationalists, the experience-based ideas of the empiricists, and the internal representations of the cognitivists. For the rationalists and cognitivists, innate ideas and mental structures are predetermined and stable. For the empiricists, ideas represent objects in the world, and consequently these objects themselves are predetermined and stable. There is no real development either in mental structures or in objects. Therefore, we can say that modern psychology, based on the assumptions of the Cartesian paradigm, has not, in fact, accepted the idea of evolution as developed by the Darwinians and Hegelians in the nineteenth century. Or at least it only pays lip service to evolution, for evolution certainly has not been built into its conceptual assumptions.

It is the supposed stable and predetermined nature of inner structures decomposable into elementary units that has become suitable material for the postulation of hierarchical trees and design of computer programs, as we shall see in Chapter 6.

CHAPTER 5

The Passivity of the Knower in the Acquisition of Knowledge

5.1 The views of the Cartesian philosophers

We pointed out earlier that seventeenth century philosophy waved the banner of individualism, and of the freedom and intellectual ability of human beings. At the same time, it was deeply preoccupied with a painstaking effort to find rock-bottom certainty. And certainty was identified with truth.

For Descartes, as well as for his followers, the search after truth proceeded through meditation and the contemplation of the contents of the mind. We must be *passive* towards the objects of knowledge in order to obtain knowledge of them.

According to Descartes, the senses receive impressions from external stimuli by virtue of passivity in the same way that a piece of wax receives an impression from a seal (Descartes, *Rules*, p. 36). But it is not only perception that is passive. Understanding, too, 'is the passivity of the mind' (Descartes, Letter to Regius, May, 1641, p. 102), in the sense that our clear and distinct ideas are passively contemplated in the process of understanding.

But Descartes did not claim that the mind is only passive in the process of knowing. The mind has two main modes of thought. Only one mode is passive: it consists of perception (perception encompassing sense-perception, imagining, and the conceiving of ideas) and the operation of the understanding. The other mode of thought is active, and consists of volition, or the operation of the will. Willing encompasses desiring, having aversions, affirming, denying, and doubting (Descartes, *Principles*, p. 232).

While mere perception and understanding cannot lead us into any misapprehension because they are passive, the will, the active faculty of the mind, sometimes makes us fall into error. The ideas which the mind perceives clearly and distinctly are always true, and as long as the will restricts itself to what the mind clearly and distinctly perceives there can be no error. Very often, however, we make assertions that extend beyond our clear and distinct ideas, or make judgements about propositions, affirm or deny them, rather than seek first what is clear and distinct in them. So we abuse our freedom by making judgements about things we do not know exactly, or which go beyond what we know exactly, and it is the active component of the mind, the will, that then deceives us. The passivity of the understanding and the activity of the will are easily confused with one another. In fact,

because we cannot will anything without understanding what we will, and we scarcely ever understand something without at the same time willing something, we do not easily distinguish in this matter passivity from activity. (Descartes' Letter to Regius, May, 1641, pp. 102–3)

But as it is through meditation and contemplation that we acquire knowledge, the passivity of understanding 'should always precede the determination of the will' (Descartes, *Meditations*, p. 176).

Just as for Descartes so for Locke the mind has two main faculties, an 'active power' and a 'passive power'. *Willing* or *volition* is the activity of the mind; it is the mind's ability to choose the course of its own action and 'to put itself into action by its own power' (Locke, *Essay*, II, xxi, 72). On the other hand, the faculty of acquiring knowledge, that is of *perception* or *understanding*, is the passive power of the mind. Passivity of the mind in Locke's theory is connected with *simple ideas* which are of two kinds, of sensation and of reflection. Simple ideas are passively accepted by the mind and the mind cannot refuse them:

These *simple ideas*, when offered to the mind, *the understanding can* no more refuse to have, nor alter when they are imprinted, nor blot them out and make new ones itself, than a mirror can refuse, alter, or obliterate the images or *ideas* which the objects set before it do therein produce. As the bodies that surround us do diversely affect our organs, the mind is forced to receive the impressions; and cannot avoid the perception of those *ideas* that are annexed to them. (Locke, *Essay*, II, i, 25)

While in perception the mind is mostly passive (Locke, *Essay*, II, ix, 1) because it cannot avoid perceiving, in memory, on the other hand, 'the mind is often-times more than barely passive' because memory depends on the will (Locke, *Essay*, II, x, 7). The mind is also active in thinking 'when it with some degree of voluntary attention, considers anything' (Locke, *Essay*, II, ix, 1), and in retention, important for fixing ideas in the memory and for reviving them later (Locke, *Essay*, II, x, 1). Thus, some modes of thinking are controlled by intentions and the will.

Gibson (1917), when analysing Locke's theory of knowledge, pointed out that Locke's insistence on the passivity of the understanding was extremely important for him. Locke conceived of the passivity of the understanding as the only possible guarantee that nothing arbitrary appeared in the ultimate data of our cognition. Anything wilful, any activity on the part of the mind, could modify the ultimate cognitive data and obstruct the possibility of achieving the truth. This position, quite common in the seventeenth century, applied to both Descartes and Locke. But while Descartes' theory of knowledge is based on clear and distinct ideas, and for him the ultimate cognitive data, universals and universal principles, are innate, Locke says that all knowledge comes from experience. Experience, to his mind, provides a guarantee of the correspondence between cognitive data and real objects.

While for Locke the understanding is completely passive in accepting simple ideas of sensation and reflection, usually in the form of combinations of these simple ideas, the will is actively involved in comparing and abstracting from ideas, and in compounding new complex ideas from existing simple ideas. Thus, for example, the ideas of golden, solidity, and a particular shape can be actively, voluntarily composed into the complex idea of a golden mountain. Similarly, the mind can compose complex ideas of 'beauty, gratitude, a man, an army, the universe' from the constituent simple ideas (Locke, *Essay*, II, xii, 2).

Hume, too, believed that perceptions are accepted by the mind passively, in fact they 'strike upon the mind'. Hume distinguishes two kinds of perceptions, *impressions* and *ideas*, which, however, are not essentially different from one another. Impressions, comprising sensations, passions, and emotions, enter the mind with considerable force and violence (Hume, *Treatise*, p. 1). When these impressions cease they leave behind faint copies which he calls ideas. Ideas, therefore, are simply faint images of impressions. Our perceptions of external objects are nothing but successions of certain impressions such as colours, shapes, and forms. These impressions we perceive as unique objects because their coherence and comparative constancy lead the imagination to attribute to them an identity which, properly speaking, they do not have (Hume, *Treatise*, pp. 194–5). We can thus conclude that Cartesian man acquires knowledge through the passivity of perception and understanding rather than by any form of activity. He is *a thinker* rather than *a doer*. Objects in the world must not be distorted by any active faculties of the mind if true and certain knowledge is to be obtained.

The idea that we must be passive in the acquisition of knowledge has been taken up by a number of modern philosophers and scientists who claim that knowledge can be acquired only by observation, and is limited to what is observable and actually observed. The extreme position in this respect was held by the physicist and philosopher, Ernst Mach, in his doctrine of the economy of thought. For Mach,

The ideal of science is the most complete, precise and economical description of facts. Facts are constituted by elements (sensations) in certain relations and description is in terms of resemblance and differences between these elements . . . Scientific explanation is just the complete precise and economical description of phenomena in terms of the relations between their elements. (Alexander, 1963, pp. 16 and 21)

Mach's programme for the re-establishment of science on absolutely secure foundations was developed by the logical atomists and logical positivists (for details, see Urmson, 1956), for whom a problem, that of the connection between *language* and *observation*, quickly arose.

5.2 The picture theory

Descartes and Locke were well aware that although the material for knowledge lay in ideas (cf. Chapter 4), *knowledge itself could only deal with propositions*. For Locke *mental* propositions consisted of ideas put together or separated by the mind. *Verbal* propositions consisted of words as signs of ideas put together or separated by the device of affirmation or negation (Locke, *Essay*, IV, v, 5–6). Verbal propositions were true if the ideas were put together or separated in the same way as the things they represented.

There is a general assumption, underlying Locke's account, that in a perfect language there would be a one-to-one relationship between words and things. This is even more true of Hume, for whom any word that did not correspond to a sense impression was to be rejected as meaningless (Hume, *Enquiry Concerning the Human Understanding*, p. 22). Thus we have the basis for the 'picture' theory of language proposed by Wittgenstein (1922) in his *Tractatus*. Although subsequently repudiated by Wittgenstein himself, the 'picture' theory has considerably influenced the studies of language in philosophy, linguistics, and psychology.

According to Wittgenstein, language does not picture *things* but *facts* because the world we know does not consist of things but facts. This distinction is important. If I see an apple *as* red or sweet, I see that *it is* red or sweet. In other words, the apple presents itself to us as a fact, and it is a *proposition* we use to state a fact. Each proposition has one of the two truth values: true and false. Complex propositions can only express facts if they are truth-functions of elementary propositions, that is if they are formed by combining elementary propositions by logically defined connectives. The truth value of the resulting complex proposition is explicitly determined by the truth values of the constituent propositions. Wittgenstein also suggested that truth-functional language was the logical basis of ordinary language and that every complex proposition of ordinary language could be decomposed into atomic propositions. Since, moreover, propositions are made true by the facts they purport to state, it followed that the world was constituted of independent, atomic facts, and that molecular facts were simply collections of atomic facts. It is in this sense that the relationship of language to the world is that of propositions to facts. The term 'picture', used by Wittgenstein in his theory that propositions are pictures of facts, is misleading. The term 'analogue' would probably express better what Wittgenstein meant. His point is that propositions have the *same logical structure* as the facts which they express:

A gramophone record, the musical idea, the written notes, and the sound-waves, all stand to one another in the same internal relation of depicting that holds between language and the world. They are all constructed according to a common logical pattern. (Wittgenstein, 1922, 4.014)

Wittgenstein continues by saying that there is a *rule* which enables one to *reconstruct* the symphony repeatedly from the gramophone record and back again. This rule is *the law of projection*. It is the rule by means of which the language on the gramophone record can be translated into the language of the musical score. There is thus an underlying assumption in Wittgenstein's picture theory that all sentences of ordinary language can be expressed by means of the propositions that constitute them. This assumption has been explicitly elaborated by Chomsky in his analysis of deep and surface sentence structure (Chomsky, 1965) and has inspired a great many studies in psycholinguistics in recent years.

To illustrate the point, we have chosen to discuss the experiments by Clark and Chase (1972) and Chase and Clark (1972) concerned with comparing sentences with pictures. The aim of their research was to identify the mental operations and their order used in comparing atomic sentences and atomic pictures. We have to warn the reader about the confusing terminology, though: in the Wittgenstein theory, propositions are pictures of facts; in the Clark and Chase experiments, however, pictures (and we mean *literally* pictures, such as ‡ stand for facts. It is important, however, that, just as in the picture theory, propositions have the same structure as the facts they express, so it is the assumption of Clark and Chase that sentences and pictures are represented in the same 'mental format' which basically can be expressed in the manner of Chomskyan propositional analysis. Thus, sentences are interpreted by the mind in terms of their deep structure propositions, and pictures (facts) when they are encoded are also interpreted as propositions. For example, the sentence *A is above B* is supposed to be represented as $((A)_{NP}(above\ B)_{VP})_{S}$ where NP is noun phrase, VP is verb phrase, S is sentence, and the parentheses indicate the tree structure of the sentence. The negative sentence *A is not above B* is supposed to be represented as $((((A)_{NP}(above\ B)_{VP})_{S})_{NP}(false)_{VP})_{S}$ as shown graphically in Figure 5.1. In other words, each sentence is decomposed into its underlying propositions and these are stored in the long-term memory

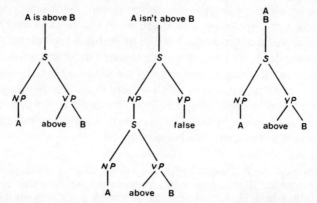

Figure 5.1   Deep structure representations for a positive sentence, a negative sentence, and a picture. From Chase and Clark (1972), in Gregg (ed.), *Cognition in Learning and Memory*. Reproduced by permission of John Wiley & Sons, Inc. Copyright © 1972 John Wiley & Sons, Inc

of the knower. Encoding of pictures is similar but we have to distinguish between cases where the sentence is encoded *before* the picture and *after* the picture. When the sentence is encoded before the picture and contains the preposition 'above', the picture ^A_B is encoded in exactly the same way as *A is above B* (see Figure 5.1). If the sentence contains the preposition 'below' and is encoded before the picture, the picture too is interpreted as *B below A*. However, where no sentence precedes, the picture is supposed to be interpreted as *A above B* because evidence has shown, as the authors say, that people normally scan things from top to bottom, and therefore verticality is usually encoded from top to bottom, in our case *A above B*.

The actual experiment of Clark and Chase consisted of presenting sixteen different relationships between sentences and pictures. Each sentence was paired with one of two possible pictures, a star above a plus *, or a plus above a star *. The subjects had to indicate as quickly as possible whether the sentence was true or false by pushing a 'true' or 'false' button.

The authors conceive the task of composing the sentences and pictures as consisting of four discrete stages employing different types of mental operations. At each stage the subject constructs a tentative response as to whether the sentence is true or false of the picture. At stage 1, the subject encodes the sentence and represents it in terms of its underlying propositions. For example, the sentence *Plus is above star* is represented as ((plus)NP(above star)VP)s. At stage 2, while holding in short-term memory the propositional form of the sentence, the subject encodes the picture in the same mental format as the proposition. Stage 3 consists of several operations in which the subject compares the representations produced at stages 1 and 2. These operations compare each subpart of the two representations as to their identity, producing at each substage a tentative answer 'yes' or 'no'. Stage 4 is the executive stage in which the subject pushes the appropriate button 'true' or 'false'. All mental operations are of an algorithmic nature (cf. Section 5.8). In addition to the type and order of mental operations, reaction time was measured. The greater the number of mental operations that are involved, the longer the process of comparison takes because the time needed by each mental operation accumulates in an additive manner. Thus, the authors were able to predict the reaction time on the basis of the number of operations presumed to be involved in the task.

Just as Wittgenstein argued that the language of the gramophone record can be translated into the language of the musical score, so Clark and Chase argue that there is a 'common "interpretive" system that must be handled by one set of principles no matter whether the source of a particular interpretation is linguistic or perceptual' (Clark and Chase, 1972, p. 515). And like the logical atomists, Clark and Chase assume that knowledge is constructed from simple atoms of knowledge, from atomic propositions matched with atomic facts, in their particular case, with atomic pictures. Although they raise the problem of how to extend this type of propositional analysis to more complex pictures and sentences, they assume that basically the same method of encoding and comparing would be involved. Just as atomic sentences and pictures are interpreted in terms of their underlying propositions, so the complex sentences and pictures are expected to be reduced in internal representations to their simplest forms before being verified, though 'the details of such a proposal . . . clearly wait on future research' (Clark and Chase, 1972, p. 513). Such optimism can only be based on the assumption which we have already encountered in Locke and the logical atomists, that all big truths are decomposable into little atomic truths. Clark and Chase assume that their kind of analysis is also applicable to other cognitive tasks such as deductive reasoning, iconic and pattern recognition by computers, sentence verification, question answering, imagery, and so on. It is their conviction that the processes by which people compare sentences with pictures 'are far more general than they might appear, for they suggest a particular way of looking at *meaning* as it is applied to sentences, to pictures and even to visual imagery' (Chase and Clark, 1972, p. 205). We have shown that this particular way of looking at meaning is the picture theory postulated by Wittgenstein in his *Tractatus*.

What do we learn from this study? We learn that the data from Clark and Chase's experiment support the theoretical model the authors set out to test. However, the model itself is based on the assumptions that:

(a) Sentences are internally represented as propositions.
(b) Pictures are represented as propositions.
(c) Complex propositions and complex pictures are decomposable into atomic propositions.
(d) The greater the number of operations, the longer it takes to perform the task.
(e) Mental operations are of a yes–no nature.

This means that the design of the experiment presupposes the very hypothesis it is supposed to test: both the pictures and the sentences are as simple as they possibly can be. Since no context is provided for these simple pictures and sentences there are no choices left for the subject as to how to encode them. Complexity of the task is increased by making the sentence false or negative.

The study is an example of how the presuppositions in which the scientist is imprisoned determine the way he perceives and constructs his research study: he holds certain presuppositions, constructs the experiment on the basis of these presuppositions, tests these presuppositions, and finds they are correct. The existing paradigm thus perpetuates itself by producing a vicious circle: a particular seeing of the world determines the way one constructs this world. It is symptomatic in the case of Clark and Chase's experiments that the testing of more complex pictures and sentences is left to the future. More complex pictures and more complex sentences, of course, might not fit into their framework based on static and predetermined elements.

5.3 One-way information-processing systems

There is a close parallel between the philosophical views concerning the passivity of the mind and the presuppositions of information-processing approaches to cognitive processes. The assumption of the seventeenth century philosophers that external and internal stimuli impinge upon our senses and that these accept information for further processing has also been adopted by modern psychologists concerned with the study of cognitive processes. The statements of the empirical philosophers, such as 'impressions strike upon the mind' or 'ideas enter the mind through the senses', have been altered into the more modern one, 'information enters the cognitive system through sensory processes', but the gist of these statements remains the same.

The passivity that was a feature of seventeenth century philosophy was largely due to the influence of the mechanical science of the day. The emphasis on mechanical causality in the physical sciences, with its focus on the effect of forces on objects, has also had paradigmatic consequences for psychology. Just as a photocell accepts light and causes a bell to ring, or a mixture of fuel and air is ignited by an electric spark and causes an engine to run, or photons impinge on the retina and cause the sensation of light, so the mind is affected by an external object and produces ideas. In this mechanical model of the mind, all that is necessary for an event to occur is that information should enter the system and that the parts of the system should be in good mechanical order.

In the information-processing theory, the human mind is conceived as an information-processing system. The system accepts stimuli from the environment through the sensory *receptors* and translates them into signals which are understood by the *processor*. In addition, the function of the processor is to hold the input and output signals in a short-term memory while the main *memory* section stores the information for longer periods. Instructions as to the responses of the system to the stimuli are then transmitted to the *effectors* (Newell and Simon, 1972, pp. 19–20).

This rather simplified account of information-processing systems makes the following fact fairly obvious: that the relationship between the 'environment', or 'stimuli', or 'information', on the one hand, and the individual, on the other, is that of *one-way flow*, from 'outside' to 'inside'. The pervasiveness of this assumption is well illustrated by the fact that one-way flow has been pre-supposed not only by individual cognitive psychology but also until recently by social cognitive psychology.

Thus the main body of research in social cognitive psychology has most commonly been preoccupied with such problems as a person's behaviour under the influence of other people; the extent to which he conforms to and is affected by group pressure; with changes in attitudes, beliefs, and values under the influence of external agents; how he resists the power of others; and so on. In fact, one of the most commonly used definitions of social psychology has made the processes of influence the focus of attention (cf. Tedeschi, 1972). The word 'influence' has been taken literally as meaning '*in*flowing', '*in*fluxing', '*in*fusing', and social influence is thus studied as a one-way process with the direction IN rather than OUT or IN AND OUT. The individual, like a piece of wax, accepts the impressions made on him by something stronger and harder, in this case by society. The individual's reactions to such various types of pressure can be measured, evaluated, and predicted. The predictions are usually made on the basis of the individual's internal conditions, such as the level of cognitive complexity, personality characteristics, postulated level of cognitive dissonance, apparent feelings, and motives.

The amount of literature bearing on information-processing in cognitive psychology is tremendous and a full account would go far beyond the scope of this book. All we can do is to support our assertion concerning the one-way character of the information-processing model of the mind using examples.

5.4 The filter model

Since an information-processing system is a complex mechanism, the most obvious questions about such a system are those related to the capacity of the system and its parts, the time needed to process information, the possibility of increasing the capacity of the parts and the system as a whole, the conditions under which the information can be processed, and so on. Such questions have, in fact, concerned the psychologists who have adopted the information-theory approach. For example, Broadbent has carried out a number of experiments on listening to more than one stimulus, on problems of selective listening, and on effects on performance achieved by varying the physical characteristics of the input. These experiments involved changing the frequencies of sounds, manipulating the auditory location of the message, increasing or decreasing the amount of simultaneous stimulation, and so on.

On the basis of Cherry's (1953) information theory of communication and MacKay's (1956) principle of a 'generalizing filter' in intelligent automata, Broadbent (1958) proposed his *filter theory* of attention and selective listening. According to this theory, the human operator is viewed as an information-processing system which can cope with only a limited amount of information. An information flow-diagram for such a system is shown in Figure 5.2. Information enters the system through several parallel input channels such as the channel of hearing, vision, and others. The incoming information enters into and is held in a short-term memory store with no definite limit on its capacity before it reaches the selective filter. This selective filter or 'bottleneck' lets only a certain amount of information flow into the limited capacity channel, the brain, because the limited capacity channel has a smaller capacity than the senses and input channels. Messages which are not selected for further processing are held in the short-term memory compartment for a few seconds and are then degraded and new information allowed in. We can see in the flow-diagram that a signal can return to the short-term memory compartment for a rehearsal and signals can also enter a long-term memory store. The end of the system is connected with the output motor-response mechanism.

Several similar bottleneck theories have been suggested in order to account for certain inadequacies in the Broadbent (1958) model (for details see, for example, Moray, 1969a, b; Kahnemann, 1973), differing basically as to where

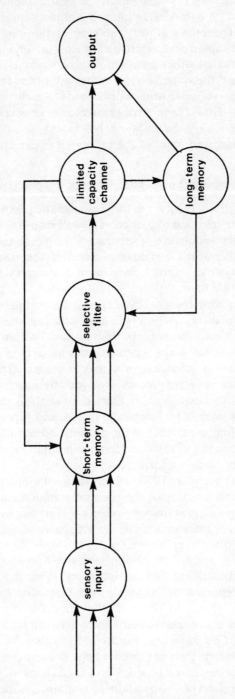

Figure 5.2 A filter model flow diagram. Adapted from Broadbent (1958), *Perception and Communication*. Reproduced by permission of Pergamon Press Ltd

in the system the bottleneck is to be placed. For example, while in Broadbent's model the bottleneck is placed before the central limited channel, in Deutsch and Deutsch's (1963) model it is located at or just before the stage of selecting a response. In Treisman's (1960) variation of the model, information is not simply *either* accepted *or* rejected in a yes–no manner, but the rejected message is merely attenuated rather than completely abandoned. In all variations of the model, however, the system *accepts* information, and information flows in (or *enters in*) to the system. In other words, as in Descartes' or Locke's conception, the knower is *passive*. His mind does not change or develop. It is preserved as a static storehouse while the empty shelves in its various compartments become stored with more and more of the processed information.

5.5 Neisser's position: perception changes the perceiver

Neisser (1967, 1976) objects to the theory of the passive filter model. According to him, the selection of particular stimuli is an active rather than a passive process and the postulation of separate filter mechanisms of attention is not required. In other words, certain stimuli are not picked up, not because they are filtered out by some internal mechanism, but simply because the perceiver chooses to ignore them.

In his earlier book Neisser (1967) maintains that perception consists of two stages. At the first stage, which is an automatic pre-attentive process, a person picks out an object in its entirety from its environment and separates it from other objects. At this stage a person is aware only of global features of the object. For example, a block of print may be separated from the rest of a page. This passive, pre-attentive process is followed by an active constructive process of analysis-by-synthesis. What is selected for analysis and synthesis is dependent upon the contextual information, biases, and expectancies of the system, upon the previous experience of the person, and upon the pre-attentive stage. Thus, only the messages relevant from the point of view of the system's biases are selected for further information processing.

However, Kahneman (1973) claims that, although Neisser objects to the filter theory, the selection of the relevant stimuli for analysis-by-synthesis is not, in fact, any different from the selection of stimuli by a filter. Moreover, he argues that the predictions made on the basis of the analysis-by-synthesis model do not differ from the predictions made on the basis of the filter theory (Kahneman, 1973, pp. 126–7). So is Neisser's position in fact any different from that of Broadbent and his followers? Yes, it is. However, since the experiments reported by Neisser in his *Cognitive Psychology* (1967) are basically very similar to those of the filter theorists, it was difficult for Kahneman to see any essential difference between the two sides. Moreover, it was not until *Cognition and Reality* (1976) that Neisser really stated his assumptions clearly. Only in this later book does he claim that cognition is the activity of knowing, that it proceeds in a social context, and that psychologists must make the effort of understanding cognition as it occurs in a natural human environment as a purposeful activity. The operations of the mind are not simply operations in the head of the perceiver but are *transactions with the world*. The activity of cognition does not consist only of *in*forming the perceiver but also, and perhaps more importantly, of *trans*forming him (Neisser, 1976, p. 11). Neisser's claim that 'no two perceptual acts can be identical' (*ibid*., p. 57) reminds one, perhaps too closely, of Heracleitus's doctrine that a man cannot enter the same river twice. But what Neisser means is not just to point to the ever-changing perceptual flux. Rather, since the perceiver is active, every act of his perception is the act of reconstruction and development of his already existing cognitive system. The world is infinitely rich with information and in the process of interaction with this world the perceiver constantly transforms himself. The information-processing approach, in contrast to this position, pays no attention to the *kind* of information reaching the perceiver. It is concerned only with the processing of information and with the internal cognitive structure of the processor. No transactions between the perceiver and his world are considered. It implies that no real biological or social development takes place. The only changes are of a quantitative nature. Consider the effect on experimetal design:

Contemporary studies of cognitive processes usually use stimulous material that is abstract, discontinuous, and only marginally real. It is almost as if ecological *in*validity were a deliberate feature of the experimental design. Subjects are shown isolated letters, words, occasionally line drawings or pictures, but almost never objects. These stimuli are not brought into view in any normal way. Usually they materialize in a previously blank field, and they often disappear again so soon that the viewer has no chance to look at them properly. They are drawn as if suspended magically in space, with no background, no depth, and no visible means of support. (Neisser, 1976, p. 34)

Such presentations of stimuli, lasting only a fragment of a second during which the subject is not allowed to attend to the object properly, or to touch or hear it, and in which he is isolated from the rest of the world by the artificial enclosure of the laboratory, are made to serve as the evidence on which our understanding of what human perception is all about is based.

In thinking about this kind of study, it is helpful to bear in mind the assumptions of the logical atomists discussed earlier in this chapter. There is a close parallel between such *atomic* presentations of stimuli by experimental psychologists and the postulation of atomic facts by Wittgenstein. Therefore, Kahneman cannot be right in saying that predictions made on the basis of Neisser's model do not differ from those made on the basis of the filter theory. He cannot be right simply because Neisser's theory applies to kinds of data that have never been produced by the filter model theorists.

The question that remains to be answered is whether Neisser's position is so different from the information-processing approach that it makes a complete break from the Cartesian paradigm. Neisser's position is certainly not that of a one-way flow of information, but is it a two-way flow? Strictly speaking, it is not. As often happens at the edge of a paradigm crisis, Neisser's position is not consistent. Although, according to him, perception is a transaction between the perceiver and the world, it is only the perceiver who is being transformed, and *not* the world. As he puts it, perception

differs from performances like sculpting and tennis playing in that the perceiver's effects on the world around him are negligible; he does not change objects by looking at them or events by listening to them. (Neisser, 1976, p. 52)

But if looking at physical objects does not change them, touching, another kind of perception, certainly does change them. And looking can be conceived as an extension of touching, and to a certain degree looking can function in the same way as physically touching, eyes being 'extended hands'. An infant, as Neisser himself is well aware, coordinates the exploratory activities of touching, seeing, and listening in order perceptually to grasp an object or a person. But an adult, as Schuetz points out in his review of Sartre, does not need hands physically to restrict the freedom of the other person and keep him under his control:

If another looks at me, a basic change occurs in my way of being. I become 'self-conscious' in both meanings of this word, namely, aware of myself as being an object for another, placed in a situation not defined by me, and ashamed or proud of this fact. I am no longer myself but by reference to the Other. He, by merely looking at me, becomes the limit of my freedom. Formerly, the world was open to my possibilities; now it is he, the Other, who defines me and my situation within the world from his point of view, thus transforming my relations to objects into factors of *his* possibilities. The world and my existence within it is no longer 'world for me': it has become 'world for the Other'. (Schuetz, 1948, p. 188)

Coordination of looking and non-looking, and synchrony in mutual gaze between two people, is certainly of tremendous significance for both participants, for their relationship and their cognitive-social development. We are thus not dealing with the problem as to whether a *single physical object* is changed by touching or looking. The problem is *conceptual*, for 'perceiving is a kind of doing' (Neisser, 1976, p. 52), and any kind of doing affects the world and consequently *must* change it, as we shall see in Part II.

5.6 The limits of capacity in one-way systems

One of the main assumptions of one-way systems generally and the filter model in particular is that there is a physical limit to the system's capacity. The system can accept only a certain amount of information. As Neisser (1976) points out, such an assumption is common not only to experimental psychology but also to other disciplines such as neurophysiology or computing science. The nervous system can accept only a certain quantity of information and the brain is thus protected from overloading. This suggests the importance of exploring the system's ability to cope with multiple messages, to measure reaction time under various conditions such as stress and tiredness, and to investigate the physical characteristics of stimuli. Such issues seem to arise whether the system in question is a machine or a human mind. In many kinds of performance, all that is required from the information-processing system is precision, reliability, and effectiveness. Driving a car, piloting a plane, calculating, playing chess, attending to several stimuli simultaneously, are all tasks in which the success of performing depends upon the effective processing of information.

However, Neisser argues against the view that a human cognitive system has a fixed capacity regulated by filters. Although human abilities are limited in some way, these limitations should not be conceived of in simple quantitative terms as is the case with machines. 'The very concept of "capacity" seems better suited to a passive vessel into which things are put than to an active and developing structure' (Neisser, 1976, p. 98). It is a misconception of the man–machine approaches that the mind can be thought of as a storehouse with a danger of becoming overloaded. Neisser points out that there are no long-term memory limits to acquiring new languages, exploring new places, and meeting new people. There is no evidence that would justify the postulation of a central filtering system protecting one from general overloading. Thus, the difficulty of performing several tasks simultaneously may not be due to a central limiting system but to the simple fact that a particular individual has not had sufficient practice in simultaneous performances. Or, the tasks may require the body to carry out incompatible movements such as playing the piano and painting at the same time. In other words, other explanations concerning apparent limits in information processing should be sought.

5.7 Minds and computers

A good example of the postulation of the passive nature of the knower are theories of cognitive processes based on the assumption that cognition can be understood and explained in terms of computer programs. Indeed, in the optimistic nineteen-fifties it was forecast that it would one day be possible for all mental phenomena to be explained in terms of computer programs.

Turing, one of the pioneers of modern computing, claimed that 'the problem is mainly one of programming', that too little was known about the complex functioning of the adult human mind, which was a very complicated machine. Why not, therefore, try to develop a program of the child's mind first. As Turing put it

Presumably the child brain is something like a notebook as one buys it from the stationer's. Rather little mechanism, and lots of blank sheets. (Mechanisms and writing are from our point of view almost synonymous.) Our hope is that there is so little mechanism in the child brain that something like it can be easily programmed. The amount of work in the education we can assume, as a first approximation, to be much the same as for the human child. We have thus divided our problem into two parts. The child programme and the education process. These two remain very closely connected. We cannot expect to find a good child machine at the first attempt. One must experiment with teaching one such machine and see how well it learns. One can then try another and see if it is better or worse. There is an obvious connection between this process and evolution, by the identifications

Structure of the child machine = hereditary material
Changes of the child machine = mutations
Natural selection = judgement of the experimenter.

(Turing, 1963, pp. 31–2)

Since this influential paper by Turing, the idea that the human mind can be explained as a complex computer program has become generally accepted among information-processing theorists. As Pylyshyn (1980) says, 'the view that cognition can be understood as computation is ubiquitous in modern cognitive theorizing, even among those who do not use computer programs to express models of cognitive processes'. There are two fundamental reasons, according to Pylyshyn, why cognition and computation can be viewed as essentially of the same kind: first, both are physically realized, cognition by the brain and computation by the computer; secondly, both are governed by representations and rules.

If a system is a *physical device*, then its performance or behaviour is presumably governed by physical laws: such a device is a one-way system capable of accepting, encoding, processing, and storing information. The interaction with the environment is next to zero, limited probably to the effect of physical forces on the device, such as oxidation, the pressure of the air or gravitation. If the performance of a system is governed by representations and rules, then it means that the system has built into it some structure that determines the way the system interprets information and processes it according to built-in rules. And we are back again to the Kantian idea of 'red vision' (cf. p. 53): once the information enters the system, it is the internal representation and pre-programmed rules that determine the output.

The belief in the similarity of minds and computers, however, goes far beyond the belief that the behaviour of both is governed by rules and representations and that both are physical systems. It is the presupposed nature of the rules that makes this similarity particularly significant. We mentioned earlier that for Descartes one of the ways of the acquisition of knowledge was deduction from clear and distinct ideas. To deduce, for Descartes, meant to infer from true and known principles by the step-by-step succession of elementary thoughts. Each step had to be firmly based on the previous step so that no wilful and, therefore, erroneous thoughts could interfere with the process of the acquisition of knowledge. Only deductive systems were certain, immutable, and independent of time and space. The rules of present-day cognitivists and computer scientists are based on the same principles as Descartes' deduction. They are *algorithmic*, that is, each step is dependent on the successful completion of the previous step. And algorithms, just like Cartesian deduction, carry a further important implication: algorithmic processes exist independently of any *embodiment*, whether mind or computer, and therefore are immutable and timeless. We shall consider the algorithmic nature of the rules and their separation from embodiment in the remainder of this chapter.

5.8 The algorithmic nature of cognitive processes

The term 'algorithm' comes from the name of the ninth century Uzbek mathematician Al-Khowarizmi who discovered simple rules for performing the basic arithmetic operations, addition, subtraction, multiplication, and division. An algorithm is a 'list of instructions specifying a sequence of operations which will give the answer to any problem of a given type' (Trakhtenbrot, 1957). The important aspect of algorithmic operations is that it is possible to proceed to the next operation only if the previous one has been successfully completed.

Let us consider the following example. Human problem-solving and thinking have often been conceived as processes in which the subject is trying to find out a *method* of solution, i.e. an algorithm for a problem of a given type. Since Duncker's (1945) pioneering work, problem-solving behaviour has been defined as the activity of filling the gap between the initial data known to the subject and the final goal of which he is also aware. Bearing in mind this definition, how does a subject proceed in his attempt to find the solution of the problem of how to win the game NIM? NIM is a game for two and is played as follows: there is a pile of chips from which both players take alternately either one or several chips according to rules fixed in advance; the player left with the last chip is the loser. Thus, the subject knows what is given and knows the goal, and his task is to find out how to achieve the goal. In other words he has to find a method of playing which would be effective every time he plays the game, i.e. an algorithm which would specify operations leading to his winning.

The number N of chips at the beginning is not random but is given by the formula $m(k+1)+1$, where m is a positive integer and k is the maximum number of chips that may be taken by either player in a single round. If, in each round, the second player makes the number of chips taken up to $x=k+1$, he will always win, even if the first player also knows the winning strategy. Suppose, for example, that $k=2$ (i.e. $x=3$) and the total number of chips is 13 (i.e. $m=4$). Then if the first player takes 2 chips the second should take 1, and if the first takes 1 the second should take 2, so that 3 chips are taken in each round. After 4 rounds 12 chips have been taken, and the first player is forced to take the last chip. Thus, the subject discovers the algorithm of winning if he realizes that the number of chips to be taken in each round is x.

The essential characteristic of the algorithmic approach to information-processing is that the whole process is broken into elementary steps and each step is dependent on the successful performance of the previous step. Newell, Shaw, and Simon devised computer programs to simulate problem-solving processes. Their *Logic Theorist* (Newell and Simon, 1956; Newell, Shaw, and Simon 1957, 1958) was the first attempt on the basis of a computer program to discover proofs for theorems in elementary symbolic logic. Their later devised *General Problem Solver* (Newell, Shaw, and Simon, 1960) uses program methods that consist of the sequential solution of subgoals of the original goal. The solution of the subgoal at each step is algorithmically dependent on the solution of the subgoal at the previous step, so that the problem-solving activity must proceed in a determined sequence of decisions. Sequences of decisions thus result in a narrowing and final closing of the gap between the initial data and the goal. The problem-solving activity is completed when a human being or computer achieves the final closing of the gap.

Since Newell, Shaw, and Simon's pioneering work in artificial intelligence, the view that 'mental activity can be viewed literally as the execution of algorithms' (Pylyshyn, 1980) has pervaded most of the work in cognitive information processing. This assumption is to be found, for example, in the studies into deductive reasoning discussed in Chapters 3 and 4. In order to *explain* human deductive reasoning, Johnson-Laird (1975) has developed a model of propositional reasoning. The model has an executive component that controls various attempts to make inferences from premises; it has a component that actually carries out inferences; there is a component for making hypothetical assumptions on which inferences are based; and, finally, there is a component for detecting contradictions. All of these four components are of an algorithmic nature, and each elementary subproblem of the reasoning task can be answered in a yes–no fashion. If the answer to the elementary subproblem is 'yes' then the program can proceed to the next step. If the answer is 'no' the program has to proceed through a route that will finally get it onto the correct track. Each of the four components can be represented in a scheme like the one given for the executive component of the complete model (see Figure 5.3). Johnson-Laird (1975, p. 36) points out that the model is, of course, a simplification of what the human reasoner actually does, and its correspondence with actual human performance is to be tested empirically. But he maintains that various kinds of modification will gradually make it more and more similar to actual human reasoning.

The view that knowledge is acquired in a yes–no fashion is not only an assumption of information processing theorists but also of Piaget. In his analysis of Piaget's theory of conceptual development, Hamlyn (1971) points out that although Piaget reacts strongly both against 'geneticism without structure' (empiricism) and 'structuralism without genesis' (rationalism), his own approach suffers from the very misconceptions that he himself criticizes. Thus, Piaget assumes, like the empiricists, that knowledge consists of fixed and constant units of understanding. When a child fails to accomplish the task concerning the constancy of volume, the Piagetians assume that it is the concept of constancy that is missing from the child's cognitive repertoire. At the same time it is taken for granted that the child's concept of water does not differ from that of an adult. According to the Piagetian conception the child has acquired certain elements of knowledge but is unable to solve the task given to him by the experimenter because he still has not acquired other ready-made bits of knowledge. Hamlyn maintains, however, that we have no grounds for supposing that

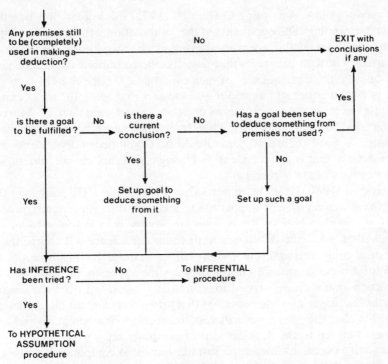

Figure 5.3 The executive component of the complete reasoning model.
From Johnson-Laird (1975), in Falmagne (ed.), *Reasoning: Representation
and Process in Children and Adults*. Reproduced by permission of the author
and Lawrence Erlbaum Associates, Inc

there are bits of understanding—the understanding of what water is, the understanding
of what volume is, and the understanding of what mass is—so that we can compare and
contrast the relations that hold between them in a linear way. The child's understanding
of what water is will be quite different on the occasions when he does not know or
appreciate that water poured from one vessel into another of a different kind remains the
same water, when he appreciates this but does not appreciate the constancy of volume,
and when he appreciates all of these things ... knowledge is not and cannot be an
all-or-none affair, and ... it is not formed out of fixed and constant units of understanding, so that we can without qualification speak of identical or similar structures, as
Piaget does. (Hamlyn, 1971, pp. 9 and 10)

All these examples demonstrate the pervasiveness of the basic assumption of
the Cartesian paradigm that knowledge is acquired through a succession of elementary steps in which every following step is firmly based on the previous step.

5.9 The separation of cognition from its embodiment

It is sometimes argued that computational systems cannot provide
explanations of human cognition on the grounds that computers could not have
feelings or intentions, could not experience pain, or actually cry out with pain

and produce tears. According to Dennett (1978) this argument is based on a misunderstanding. The opponents of the computational theory fail to appreciate that artificial intelligence is not concerned with the *physical modelling of the behaviour* but with programs that describe the conditions of such behaviour and describe the consequences of such conditions. Descriptions of such a kind are, in fact, theories of behaviour and the fact that some theories cannot be rewritten as programs simply means that they are not good theories. Moreover, the fact that human beings and animals feel pain has nothing to do with theories of pain. A good theory of pain should be developed independently of its embodiment, that is, independently of living organisms and computers, which may or may not *experience* pain.

Pylyshyn (1980) strongly supports Dennett's position. He points out that it was the discovery that it is possible to study 'formal algorithmic processes without regard to how such processes are *physically* instantiated in an actual device' that led to the development of computer science. Of course the idea that there could be a coherent notion of *process* considered in abstraction from a *physical* process was not entirely new. After all, mathematical and logical deduction systems have existed for centuries. It was, however, the discovery that the languages of some processes that *prima facie* are not mathematical or logical in character were, nevertheless, amenable to mathematical and logical analysis that led to the development of computer science.

Cognitive processes, therefore, just like any other computational processes, can apparently be studied and explained *without regard to their physical embodiment*. A set of well formed problems, a set of symbols and the rules of their manipulation, seem to be sufficient to model a cognitive process:

A crucial aspect of the assumption that there exists a fixed formal vocabulary for addressing a significant set of psychological questions is the view that such questions can be answered without appealing to the material embodiment of the algorithm, and without positing additional special analytical functions or relations which themselves are not to be explained in terms of algorithms. In fact, as I shall argue presently, one can take the position that this proprietary vocabulary or level of description *defines* the notion of cognitive phenomenon in the appropriate technical sense required for explanatory theories. (Pylyshyn, 1980, p. 116)

This last point is most important: cognitive processes here are *by definition* processes that can be modelled by means of algorithms, so those who argue that feelings or consciousness cannot be accounted for in terms of algorithms must have unclear ideas concerning the very notion of cognition. Although cognition presumably has its own compartment in the brain (or mind), it can be accounted for independently of it. It can be treated also without reference to emotions, motives and feelings. Such non-cognitive processes, according to this theory, presumably must be embodied and cannot be treated in terms of algorithms. And yet it is supposed that they can 'interfere' with the pure cognitive processes and thus be responsible for errors made by a subject (cf. Chapter 3). But, of course, we also remember that the interference of wilful activities with the passivity of perception and understanding in the acquisition of knowledge had already worried the Cartesian philosophers of the seventeenth century.

Finally, it is important to point out that the assumptions of the passivity of the knower have been applied by experimental psychologists usually when dealing with relatively simple phenomena: in the comparison of simple sentences and diagrams, the acceptance of information based on single words and single sentences, the solving of well defined problems, and so on. More complex tasks, such as the solving of ill-defined problems involving creativity, the comparison of texts and complex pictures, and the processing of information under conditions of ecological validity (Neisser, 1976) still await future research. Does this mean that psychologists have not yet tried to apply the passive approach of information processing to such phenomena or does it mean that this approach is not suited to such phenomena? Bearing in mind the curiosity of human beings (and perhaps of computers too?), it seems highly unlikely that no psychologist has attempted such a challenging task. In fact such attempts have been made. For example, Schank and Abelson's (1977) script analysis certainly is an attempt to deal with complex phenomena involving the content and context of information rather than just its formal characteristics. However, we pointed out earlier (cf. pp. 58–59) that scripts and plans do not, in fact, explain the acquisition of *new* information. They explain the acquisition of new information only in terms of the regrouping of the already built-in elements of information. So perhaps the passive one-way approach is not suitable for dealing with complex phenomena?

Let us return to Kuhn (1962). Perhaps one might suppose that for simple cases the information-processing approach is quite appropriate, just as Newtonian physics was quite suitable and appropriate for dealing with low speeds. Could we not conceive that the present Cartesian framework in psychology is 'correct' when dealing with 'low speeds' and with 'short distances'? But would it not mean, then, that for more complex human behaviour we need a different framework, just as physics, unable to cope with complex phenomena, needed the Einsteinian framework? However, if this is so, then our understanding of the above 'simple' phenomena also needs a complete overhaul. We said earlier (cf. p. 6) that Newton's equations may be identical *in form* with Einstein's when dealing with simple phenomena, but that *they do not have the same meaning*. This may also be so in our case. Our analogy between the human mind and computer programs, showing a close similarity between the functioning of the two *in form*, does not seem to extend to its *meaning* even when dealing with simple phenomena. It may be superficially similar but its essence is different.

CHAPTER 6

Mechanisms, Causes, and Effects

6.1 The world as a rational system

The Renaissance and the subsequent rise of modern science retained many of the presuppositions on which Christianity was based and which were an inherent part of mediaeval thought. The Renaissance, for example, inherited the presupposition according to which the world was conceived as a rational system guided by universal laws and where nothing was accidental and irrational.

Mead (1936) pointed out that the conception of the world as an absolutely rational system was peculiar to Christian theology and was unknown in Greek philosophy.

The conception of the world as a rational order came through the theology of the church. The doctrine was built around the gospel of Jesus and the conception of St. Paul when he undertook to formulate the Jewish theory in such a form that it would be made universal. (Mead, 1936, p. 1)

The historian of mediaeval science, Duhem (Randall, 1962, Vol. I, pp. 267–82), maintained that Galilean science was not simply a creation of the sixteenth and seventeenth centuries but that all the main principles and the essential propositions of mechanics were laid down by physicists of the Middle Ages at the Universities of Oxford and Paris in the fourteenth century. According to Duhem, it was a delusion of the sixteenth and seventeenth centuries that they were substituting modern science for the peripatetic physics of the Middle Ages. Duhem claimed that while the sixteenth century physicists were celebrated as revolutionists and creators of Renaissance science they were, in fact, only continuing the tradition of the Middle Ages and quite often they were mere plagiarists. Whatever might be the objections to Duhem's interpretation, it remains true that the Christian presupposition of the absolute intelligibility of the world permeated the thought of those who are considered to be the founders of the new physics such as Copernicus, Galileo, Descartes, and Newton.

Let us take Galileo, for example. For Galileo the universe could be understood only through the language of mathematics, with triangles, circles, and other geometrical figures as its objects (Galilei, *The Assayer*). Since the world is rational it is governed by rules and therefore it is also explicable. And it is mathematics that is the rational tool given to man in order to conquer the rational world. People should not give up contemplating things just because they are remote from them, such as, for example, the sunspots. Even if it may seem impossible to determine the true nature of things, we do learn at least some of their properties and through this partial knowledge we can proceed to further knowledge (Galilei, Letters on Sunspots, pp. 123–4). This world that is rational is created by God, 'the source of all light and verity'. God works through Nature in the most perfect fashion and the physical laws should be established through sense-experience and demonstrations rather than through the authority of scriptural passages. Both the Bible and Nature proceed from the same source, from the divine Word, and God is not 'any less excellently revealed in Nature's actions than in the sacred statements of the Bible' (Galilei, Letter to the Grand Duchess Christina, p. 183).

The rational universal order and the laws of mechanics became also the essential assumptions of Cartesian philosophy. God retained ultimate authority over this world, but otherwise all things and all living organisms were subject to mechanical laws. The Aristotelian world, in which inanimate objects, animate organisms, and unmoved movers all had their place in a hierarchical order, and were described in terms of their specific properties, vanished. It was replaced by a world in which everything was reducible to matter and motion, and was quantitatively analysable by mathematics. 'Give me matter and motion and I will make a world' Descartes was supposed to have said.

Both for Galileo and for Descartes material substance was conceivable only in terms of the laws of mathematics and mechanics. It was because of our senses that we perceived objects as having colours, tastes or smells and that we gave names to such qualities. But

if the living creature were removed, all these qualities would be wiped away and annihilated. But since we have imposed upon them special names, distinct from those of the other and real qualities . . . we wish to believe that they really exist as actually different from those . . . To excite in us tastes, odors, and sounds I believe that nothing is required in external bodies except shapes, numbers, and slow or rapid movements. (Galilei, *The Assayer*, pp. 274 and 276)

This conception of matter is best illustrated by Descartes' example as to what happens to wax when it is melted: the colour changes, the smell and taste disappear, the shape is lost. It becomes liquid and undergoes all sorts of other alterations. Nothing eventually remains of those properties of the wax which depend solely upon the senses:

. . . all these things which fall under taste, smell, sight, touch, and hearing, are found to be changed . . . certainly nothing remains excepting a certain extended thing which is flexible and movable. (Descartes, *Meditations*, p. 154)

Descartes maintained that there are no occult qualities in plants and stones, no 'wonders of sympathies and antipathies'. There is simply nothing in the whole of Nature which could not be traced back solely to corporeal causes devoid of mind and thought (Descartes, *Principles*, IV, 187).[4]

For Newton, Nature consisted of fixed and discrete particles of matter. These fixed, impenetrable, and solid particles do not undergo any real qualitative changes. The changes concerning these particles are only external to them and affect only the relations between them. Such relations can be expressed mathematically. They are 'to be placed only in the various Separations and new Associations and Motions of these permanent Particles' (Newton, *Optics*, p. 400).

According to Hume, too, the world was a great machine. He expressed this view in many places in his work, but perhaps the most explicit is in the *Dialogues Concerning Natural Religion*. In the *Dialogues*, Cleanthes contemplates the world and its parts. The world is

nothing but one great machine, subdivided into an infinite number of lesser machines, which again admit of subdivisions to a degree beyond what human senses and faculties can trace and explain. All these various machines, and even their most minute parts, are adjusted to each other with an accuracy which ravishes into admiration all men who have ever contemplated them. (Hume, *Dialogues*, p. 22)

Hume, of course, was not the only philosopher who adopted the mechanistic picture of the world. The mechanistic conception of the world was quite common even among the general public in the sixteenth and seventeenth centuries. For example, Nature was often compared to the big clock of Strasbourg Minster whose complexity and ingenious structure reminded the public of the ingenious structure of living organisms. And for Descartes all living bodies including those of human beings were mechanisms decomposable into their components, all of them in constant motion (Descartes, *Treatise on Man*, pp. 112–13).

6.2 Hierarchical structures in cognitive psychology

There are two points in the above quotation from Hume that have become reflected in recent philosophy and psychology: the hierarchical subdivision of a machine into a number of lesser machines, and these in turn into their 'most minute parts'.

To take the second of these first, Hume's 'most minute parts' were transformed into *logical atoms* in the earlier years of this century. Logical atomism, which had its foundation in the logic of Russell and Whitehead, was developed to provide an account of the whole of mathematics in terms of a minimum of axioms and logical concepts. This logic conceived of mathematical language as consisting of absolutely simple or 'atomic' propositions. These propositions can be bound together by logical connectives with a minimum of meaning, thus producing complex or 'molecular' propositions.

The subdivisions of the world into hierarchically organized lesser and lesser machines is also mirrored in present psychology. As Winograd puts it

One of the most powerful ideas of modern science is that many complex systems can be viewed as nearly decomposable systems, and that the components can be studied separately without constant attention to the interactions. If this were not true, the complexity of real-world systems would be far too great for meaningful understanding, and it is possible (as Simon argues) that it would be too great for them to have resulted from a process of evolution. (Winograd, 1975, p. 191)

It is thus implied that just as the carburettor or ignition coil or cooling system of an internal combustion system can be decomposed into smaller and smaller parts and studied without constant reference to the engine as a whole, so perhaps an eye, a circulatory system or a liver can be decomposed into smaller parts and studied independently of the organism as a whole. The decomposing of a brain into various 'mental organs' has already been discussed in Chapter 4.

The hypothesis that knowledge is stored in the mind in hierarchical layers has become ubiquitous among scientists working in the field of artificial intelligence and in cognitive psychology. Forehand (1974, p. 164) maintains that 'the very recognition of knowledge as a hierarchical structure casts light on the problem of specifying the extended outcome of a learning experience'. And, as he says, the postulation of hierarchical structures and decision trees enables psychologists to represent detailed pieces of knowledge and their relationships to an extent that was not possible previously.

Let us consider some examples of studies based on the assumption of hierarchical cognitive structures.

A classic case of the hierarchical structure approach is the already mentioned *General Problem Solver* (GPS) computer program of Newell, Shaw, and Simon (1960) and Newell and Simon (1963). The program consists of the sequential solutions of subgoals of the original goal. For example, the problem in symbolic logic of finding a method for the transformation of object A into object B is solved by means of setting up subgoals associated with particular methods. As can be seen in Figure 6.1 objects are first compared so that the difference between them becomes clear. Then the subgoal is set up to reduce this difference. The result of this procedure is a new object A' which is closer to object B than the original A. In order to reduce the difference between the objects the GPS uses a set of *operators* that can be applied to the objects. An operation is a transformational expression of which the left part has a certain property and the right part is an expression which can be substituted for the left part. For example in A & B = B & A, the only difference is the order of the symbols A and B. If operators are applied to objects, they produce objects with new properties, usually ones that are closer to the final goal objects (see 'Goal: Apply operator Q to object A' in Figure 6.1). Although the GPS is a computer program, it has its counterpart in human problem-solving. In fact, the authors claim, it was their attempt to simulate human problem-solving that led them to develop the computer program. It was on the basis of the experimental subjects' *thinking aloud* that the computer program was constructed.

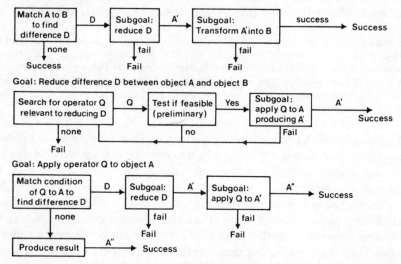

Figure 6.1   Sequential solution of subgoals by GPS. From Newell, Shaw, and Simon (1960), in *Information Processing: Proceedings of the International Conference on Information Processing*, 1960. Reproduced by permission of Unesco. Copyright © Unesco, 1960

A model of the hierarchical structure of semantic memory was proposed by Collins and Quillian (1969, 1972). Although the authors originally developed this model as a computer program, they also considered it as a model of human semantic memory applicable to sentence comprehension (Figure 6.2). According to this model the words an individual knows are stored in his memory as node-points which are connected by 'pointers' to other related words, the whole corpus of stored words forming a network. 'Canary' and 'yellow bird that sings' might be stored together at the same node (thus providing a definition). 'Canary' is linked to 'bird' as a category or superset name. Property names like 'can fly', 'has wings', and 'has feathers' are for economy linked directly only to 'bird' instead of to the names of each kind of bird, being true of birds in general. The sentence 'canary can fly' can be inferred from 'canary is a bird' and 'bird can fly'. The sentence 'canary eats' can be comprehended by tracing the path: 'a canary is a bird', 'a bird is an animal', 'an animal eats'. In general, to comprehend sentences in natural language means to be able to find paths through the semantic network. The structure of the network, that is, of the interrelationships between words, is built up in the process of learning. Learning involves the building of new structures on the basis of the already existing semantic network.

The applicability of the model to human semantic memory was tested by means of reaction times (Collins and Quillian, 1972). The subject was presented with a number of sentences, some true and some false, for example: 'An oak has acorns', 'A pine is barley'. The subject had to press the button if he considered the sentence true and a different button if the sentence was false. The reaction time was measured in each case. The assumptions concerning the retrieval time are worth mentioning because, once again, they remind one of

Figure 6.2   A model of semantic memory. From Collins and Quillian (1969), *Journal of Verbal Learning and Verbal Behavior*, **8**. Reproduced by permission of Academic Press, Inc. (New York) and the authors. Copyright © Academic Press, Inc. (New York)

the Humean mechanistic position. The most important of these assumptions are the following. First, it is assumed that it does take time to get through each step; for example, some time is needed to get from a node to a superset, or to get from a node to a property. Secondly, the time needed through several nodes is additive; for example, it takes longer to press the button if the subject is required to retrieve 'a canary eats' than to retrieve 'a canary is yellow'. In the former case the path to be followed is 'a canary is a bird', 'a bird is an animal', 'an animal eats', therefore 'a canary eats', while in the latter case the property 'is yellow' is assumed to be stored together with 'canary'. Thus the latter path is much shorter than the former. These assumptions, of course, are functions of the presupposed mechanistic and hierarchical structure of the semantic network. Just as it takes a car longer to get through several road junctions than to get through one, so it takes longer to get through several nodes in the mind than to get through one node.

Unfortunately, the experimental results concerning reaction time were not as simple as predicted by the mechanistic model. The authors found that the experimental conditions as well as the meanings of the words unpleasantly interfered with the model and made the results rather untidy. However, the authors 'have not given up hope of finding a technique that will get at the question of how people utilize stored information in comprehension' (Collins and Quillian, 1972, p. 136).

Another example of a hierarchical mechanistic model is the one developed by Abelson and Kanouse (1966). This model is applied to concepts. According to Abelson and Kanouse, concepts can be viewed as organized in hierarchical structures in one's mind (Figure 6.3). Starting with any specific concept, such as that of 'choral music', one can move down the hierarchy to levels of increasing specificity, first to subclasses of choral music, such as masses, oratorios, and

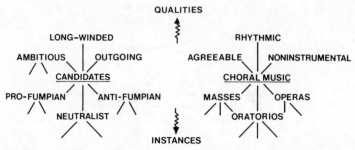

Figure 6.3 Hierarchical structure of concepts. From Abelson and Kanouse (1966), in Feldman (ed.), *Cognitive Consistency*. Reproduced by permission of Academic Press, Inc. (New York) and the authors. Copyright © 1966 Academic Press, Inc

operas, and then to sub-subclasses of choral music, e.g. German, Italian, and French operas, and so on. In Abelson's terminology, these are *instances* of choral music, and instances of instances, and so on. The minute elements of instances thus represent *atoms*, to use the terminology of the logical atomists. Similarly, one can move up the hierarchy to levels of increasing generality. Choral music now appears as a subclass of the classes of agreeable sounds, rhythmic sounds, and non-instrumental sounds. In a like manner one can move another stage up the hierarchy by analysing the qualities of these different kinds of sound, and so on. Eventually, one arrives at what Abelson calls the 'global concept' of sound.

A corresponding analysis may be carried out in the case of the concept of a candidate (for an election). The subclasses are in terms of the different political parties, pro-Fumpian, anti-Fumpian, and Neutralist candidates, while the qualities of candidates are found to be that they are ambitious, long-winded, and outgoing, so that the higher-level classes are those of ambitious individuals, long-winded individuals, and outgoing individuals.

We can now form a wide variety of statements from these two hierarchies, by taking one of the concepts of individuals as *subject*, and one of the concepts of sounds as *object*, and binding them with a *verb*.

Taking now the basic levels of the concepts of 'candidates' and 'choral music', we can form the statement 'Candidates like choral music'. We can also form statements the subject or object of which is at a lower level, such as 'Neutralist candidates like choral music'. And finally, we can form statements at a higher level, such as 'Ambitious individuals like non-instrumental sounds'. Such lower-level and higher-level statements can be used as *evidence* supporting the basic-level statement or, in the negated forms, as undermining it. If the movement from evidence to hypothesis is one of increasing generalization, the evidence is said to be inductive: if of decreasing generalization, it is said to be deductive. Thus in the above examples, 'Neutralist candidates like choral music' is inductive evidence, and 'Candidates like agreeable sounds' is deductive evidence for the statement 'Candidates like choral music'. It should, however, be noted that the terms 'inductive' and 'deductive' as used here are misnomers, since they refer only to the direction of the movement from

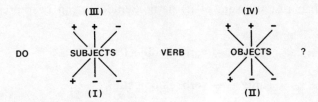

Form I. Inductive, subject-specific
Form II. Inductive, object-specific
Form III. Deductive, subject-specific
Form IV. Deductive, object-specific

Figure 6.4 Four inference forms. From Abelson and Kanouse
(1966), in Feldman (ed.), *Cognitive Consistency*. Reproduced
by permission of Academic Press, inc. (New York) and the
authors. Copyright © 1966 Academic Press, Inc

evidence to basic statement. From this point of view terms like 'lower' and
'higher' or 'subordinate' and 'superordinate' would be less misleading.

In his experiments Abelson either kept the object constant and varied the
subject at the same conceptual level (subject-specific evidence); or he kept the
subject constant and varied the object (object-specific evidence). He thus has
four kinds of evidence, subject-specific or object-specific 'inductive' evidence,
and subject-specific or object-specific 'deductive' evidence (Figure 6.4). Here
are some examples of the items Abelson used.

Subject-specific 'inductive' evidence:
Altogether there are three kinds of candidates: pro-Fumpian, Neutralist, and anti-
Fumpian.
Pro-Fumpian candidates produce choral music.
Neutralist candidates do not produce choral music.
Anti-Fumpian candidates do not produce choral music.
Do candidates produce choral music?

Object-specific 'deductive' evidence:
All choral music is agreeable, rhythmic, non-instrumental sound.
Candidates produce agreeable sounds.
Candidates do not produce rhythmic sounds.
Candidates produce non-instrumental sounds.
Do candidates produce choral music?
(Abelson and Kanouse, 1966)

A subject participating in the experiment was required to give a 'yes' or 'no'
answer to the question. Two pieces of negative evidence to one of positive
evidence were found to be sufficient to yield considerable agreement with the
statement in the 'inductive' case, but in the 'deductive' case two pieces of
positive evidence were necessary if significant agreement was to be
obtained.

We have gone to much pain in describing Abelson's study so that its assumptions are highlighted; a sentence, in this conception, can be broken up
mechanically into independent elements, since a whole is assumed to be

no more than just the sum of its parts. Sentences can be represented as follows:

sentence$_1$:   subject$_1$ — verb$_1$ — object$_1$

sentence$_2$:   subject$_2$ — verb$_2$ — object$_2$

sentence$_n$:   subject$_n$ — verb$_n$ — object$_n$

In so far as these words are treated only as marks on paper, with their meaning ignored, we could take the sheet of paper on which they are written, cut out the subjects, verbs, and objects, and mix the subjects together in one hat, the verbs in a second, and the objects in a third. Then we could take the three hats and ask a blindfolded person to choose one item from each hat and so construct, completely at random, new sentences from the old ones, obtaining, for example:

sentence$_1$:   subject$_2$ — verb$_7$ — object$_3$
sentence$_2$:   subject$_1$ — verb$_n$ — object$_2$

sentence$_n$:   subject$_4$ — verb$_3$ — object$_n$

The number of sentences which can be constructed in this way is n^3, though Abelson and Kanouse only used a 'balanced subset' of these sentences.

It is only fair to point out that Abelson and his students have been concerned to demonstrate in items such as those above that the *verb* is more important than the *subject* and *object* for a person when drawing conclusions from such inductive or deductive evidence. It remains true, though, that the underlying assumptions of such studies are the same as those of Hume and the logical atomists: atomic units, in this particular case words, have an independent and static existence of their own.

While Collins and Quillian's and Abelson and Kanouse's models were concerned with the hierarchical structures of individual items such as *categories*, *properties*, and *concepts*, more recent models have attempted a description of the hierarchical structures of much bigger units of knowledge.

Minsky (1975) claimed that the problem with most cognitive theories was that they were too 'local' and 'minute'. Mental activities occur in much larger and structured units which he called *frames*. A frame is a hierarchical structure of a particular knowledge domain, for example, *a room*. It can be thought of as consisting of nodes and relationships as in Collins and Quillian's model. At the 'top level' of the frame are representations of things that are supposedly always true about a particular object or situation. Thus, rooms have supposedly invariant features such as a ceiling, walls, floor, and so on. These are the features one 'expects' to find before entering a room. The 'lower levels' of a frame have *terminals*, i.e. slots that have to be filled by particular observations.

For example, a particular room may have walls with windows, walls decorated with flowers, and so on. The levels of a frame are thus hierarchically arranged with top levels representing fixed features of objects or situations and lower levels representing their variable features. Minsky's original model has been elaborated by a number of psychologists and applied to recognition (Kuipers, 1975) and natural language (Winograd, 1975), or to the representation of stories (Schank and Abelson, 1977). Although these various models differ in detail as to how knowledge is actually represented, their main assumptions of a Humean mechanistic and hierarchically organized structure of lesser and lesser machines are common to all of them.

6.3 Invariants and homogeneous time

Since the belief in the rationality of the world became one of the presuppos-itions of Newtonian science, this science has made it its aim to discover the nature of rationality in things and events. This search for rationality has taken the form of a search for *invariants*. Although there does not seem to be a logical connection between the search for rationality and the search for invariants, there certainly is a psychological relationship between the two. Events that regularly repeat themselves or are regular and repeatable give one a feeling of security, predictability, and therefore of intelligibility. A human being, whether a layman or a scientist, appears to have a psychological threshold beyond which change and flux cannot be tolerated; and in order to make some sense of things and events one must feel that there is something regular and permanent about them. Therefore, the search for invariants is essential to the naive layman's epistemology and seems to exist even in very young babies (Bower, 1967, 1971, 1974).

The search for invariants in science results in the search for *laws*. Thus, although things are variable and change in time and space, the laws according to which they change are themselves immutable. For example, iron and oxygen change into iron oxide and such a change is subject to the immutable laws of conservation of matter and energy.

According to Meyerson it was the discovery of the immutable laws of nature that made it possible for science to reduce the changes and differences in things and events to *identities* that can be expressed by mathematical equations. For example, the principle that 'nothing is created' and 'nothing is lost' forms the basis of chemical experiments, and chemical equations express the identity between the antecedents and consequents in chemical reactions (Meyerson, 1908, p. 226).

Meyerson also makes the important point that chemical equations, by identi-fying the antecedent represented by the left side of the equation, and conse-quent represented by the right side, tend to *eliminate time*. It is not that reactions do not *take* time, but that the reactions that occur do not depend on the time when they occur. Time has no influence on a reaction because the reaction can be repeated *at any time* if certain chemical and physical conditions obtain. In other words, such reactions are *timeless*.

Timelessness has become a general assumption for the experimental natural sciences. It has been taken for granted not only in physical and chemical experiments but also in psychology. If the same 'psychological' conditions obtain then the experiments are supposed to be repeatable. They also, therefore, are timeless in this sense.

As an example of the assumptions of invariance and timelessness in experimental psychology, let us take the studies by Abelson and his co-workers on the effect of the verb, discussed above. The antecedents of the study, defined in terms of *independent variables*, are different verbs. The consequents, defined in terms of *dependent variables*, are the subjects' responses, 'yes' or 'no'. No other assumptions have been made by the experimenters and the experiment is supposed to produce the same results when repeated over and over again. There is, of course, nothing special about Abelson's experiments with respect to timelessness. In the majority of psychological experiments, just as in physics, time is commonly eliminated. Repeatability of scientific experiments is the criterion of the correctness of the established facts.

Another form of the tendency to eliminate time in natural science is the *spatializing* of time. The spatializing of time in the natural sciences is based upon one important assumption: that time is a *homogeneous medium* 'which in itself and from its own nature *flows equally* without relation to anything external' (Newton, *Mathematical Principles*, I, Def. VIII, Sch. I). According to this picture, time is like a river. Since we observe the passage of time, we are not being carried along with the river: we are onlookers while the river flows uniformly past us. Changes are occurring all around us, including changes in our bodies and minds, and the rate at which these changes occur is measured by the number or degree of such changes which occur while a standard length of the river passes by. It is this notion of time in the physical sciences and philosophy of the seventeenth century that, according to Bergson, has a *spatial* rather than a *temporal* character.

Bergson's point comes out very clearly in his example of the clock:

When I follow with my eyes on the dial of a clock the movement of the hand which corresponds to the oscillations of the pendulum, I do not measure duration, as seems to be thought; I merely count simultaneities, which is very different. Outside of me, in space, there is never more than a single position of the hand and the pendulum, for nothing is left of the past positions. (Bergson, 1889, pp. 107–8)

In other words, when I see the hands of the clock, I see them as they are *now*, and there is no difference in this respect between a clock which is going, and a clock that has stopped. A single position of the hand of the clock does not have any duration, it is an instant. If the clock is going, these positions of the hand are sharply distinguished from one another; they are a succession of instances and they do not coincide. If a pen were connected with the hand, we would actually be able to see the distance the hand passed in the same way that a shooting star leaves a trail behind it (Bergson, 1922). The movement of a shooting star is spread out in space in our present perception, and we can measure its length.

Thus we measure the passage of time by means of movement, and since movement, as we have just seen, can be represented as a trail or a line which occupies a certain space, we can say that time is measured by means of space. Moreover, one can select a point on a line, and one can conceive of a line as made up of points. Likewise in spatialized time the present can be thought of as an instant—indeed, a *point*—in time, and time as made up of instants. But instants do not have duration, any more than points have size. And finally, we can also measure the speed of the movement by comparing the length of the line or trail with the distance covered by the hands of the clock. Measuring reaction time in psychology has precisely the purpose of measuring the speed of movement. In the experiments discussed earlier it was the speed of the 'movement' of mental operations that was measured, the number of mental operations and their assumed complexity.

There appears to be a general tendency to eliminate time whenever a search for invariants takes place, not only in science but also in everyday life. Thus it is a child's age, that is the distance from his birth to the present, that determines whether he is ready to start school, or when his primary and secondary education has been completed, or whether he should be considered responsible for his actions and so on. Even the *developmental theory* of Piaget can be said to be of that kind. The study of child development is based on principles of operations that are *universally* valid, i.e. universally invariant. The child's mind unfolds according to a predetermined biological programme that moves through a certain time sequence, i.e. through a series of points in time. The cognitive progress of a child can be evaluated by means of a specified point on a time line, regardless of the child's educational experience:

Whether we study children in Geneva, Paris, New York or Moscow, in the mountains of Iran or the heart of Africa, or on an island in the Pacific, we observe everywhere certain ways of conducting social exchanges between children, or between children and adults, which act through their functioning alone, regardless of the context of information handed down through education. (Piaget, 1970, p. 35)

In sum, there seem to be two ways in which time has been eliminated from psychology. First, it is ignored completely and excluded from experiment, as in Abelson's studies. Or, it is treated as a dependent or independent variable. An example of time treated as a dependent variable is reaction time. In Piaget's studies, in which time is taken as the distance from birth to the present rather than based on a person's experience, time is an independent variable. All of these cases in psychology use the Cartesian conception of physical time which is defined as a succession of instants that can be measured. Physical experiments, of course, presuppose that no change occurs in objects due to 'experience'; experiential time has no place in physics. Nor was experiential time considered by the Cartesian philosophers with respect to psychology. For Locke, as for Leibniz and Hume, time was a succession of ideas and any concept of time that was concerned with experience and, therefore, with true development, would be incompatible with the Cartesian paradigm. Consequently, experiential time has no place in the psychology of the Cartesian paradigm.

6.4 Causes and effects

Another form that the search for invariants in science has taken is the search for causes and effects. The modern version of causal explanation is usually associated with Hume and, as Harré and Secord (1972) claim, the Humean conception of causality has had a tremendous impact on experimental psychology.

Although Hume believed in the existence of an external world, he claimed that 'we have no perfect idea of anything but of a perception' (Hume, *Treatise*, p. 234). While we keep talking of houses and trees, these are only perceptions, not objects themselves. The reason why we can really only be talking about perceptions and not about objects themselves is that we simply can never discover what such objects are. Perceptions are distinct and separable existences. They are substances, that is things that exist independently of one another. These distinct and separate perceptions can only be connected by a habit of mind. Some of them come to the mind in a certain succession and order, and the mind learns through repeated experience to associate them together. 'We then call the one object, *Cause*; the other, *Effect*' (Hume, *Enquiry Concerning the Human Understanding*, p. 75). (Hume usually talks about 'objects' rather than about 'perceptions' when he refers to what ordinary people think.) We experience the change in the one object as causing the change in the other but in fact there is no real connection between the objects. They are conjoined, but the connection is imagined. Hume's favourite example of conjoined events apparently connected is the one of a billiard ball lying on a table and struck by another ball moving towards it. To the mind such an event appears as a cause–effect connection, although nothing is perceived except the movements of the two balls. Moreover, similar balls in similar situations produce the same effect. Thus, Hume maintains, contiguity in time and place and a constant conjunction between objects results in a cause-effect appearance (Hume, *Treatise*, p. 173). It is only such frequent repetition of experiences that could induce the mind to expect the one event to be followed by the other. Even the connection between heat and flame is only imagined by the mind. It is only their invariable conjunction that makes them appear to be connected as of necessity.

This does not mean, however, that Hume rejected the existence of *real* causal relationships among things. Real causes do exist at the level of things in themselves but as such are permanently hidden from us. Hume calls the real causes the *unknown causes*:

We are placed in this world, as in a great theatre, where true springs and causes of every event are entirely concealed from us... We hang in perpetual suspense between life and death, health and sickness, plenty and want; which are distributed amongst the human species by secret and unknown causes, whose operation is oft unexpected, and always unaccountable. The *unknown causes*, then, become the constant object of our hope and fear. (Hume, *The Natural History of Religion*, p. 316)

It thus follows that if we were able to perceive real things rather than perceptions only, we would also have access to real causes rather than just to correlations.

So what kind of causes are explored in psychological experiments? Harré and Secord (1972) argue that it is the correlational relationships between events that experimental psychology is concerned with. Thus, the psychologist postulates his independent variables and measures their effect on the dependent variables. Although such experiments purport to be studying causal relationships in the sense of factor A exerting an influence upon factor B, all that they actually do is to explore the degree of correlation. For example, in Abelson's experiments the different verbs (independent variables) seem to be causing differences in the subjects' responses (dependent variables). However, all that such experiments show is that different verbs correlate more or less with the subjects' 'yes' or 'no' responses. All we have are statistical relationships between the variables. We cannot predict which subjects will give a 'yes' and which will give a 'no' answer. Harré and Secord argue that if they generally did study the causal rather than just statistical relationships between phenomena, psychologists would have to take into consideration *internal personal parameters* such as intentions, reasons, and actions, rather than just the external manipulation of variables.

6.5 Purposeful action

It has been apparent to some psychologists and philosophers that the mechanistic model of man that excludes what Harré and Secord call internal personal parameters, is untenable. Instead, psychology must take actions, intentions, purposes, and other internal personal parameters into account.

There is a great deal of philosophical literature bearing upon the analysis of the concepts of action, intention, and reason. The majority of such analyses are concerned with describing the states of affairs that must be fulfilled for an action to occur. For example, Alston (1974) gives three conditions that must be fulfilled for an action to take place. These are bodily movement, success, and purpose. In other words, the concept of action can be applied if X underwent some bodily movement, the bodily movement occurred because X wanted to bring about a particular state of affairs, i.e. had some purpose in his mind, and the bodily movement was successfully completed. Alston (1974, pp. 88–9 and 97) is concerned whether psychological theories have the necessary conceptual equipment and whether they 'do, or can . . . use intentional action concepts to represent their dependent behavioural variables'. He then came to the conclusion that the physicalistic and stimulus–response types of theory do not have the conceptual resources for representing intentional action. The reasons for this claim are to be seen in the fact that behaviouristic theories are concerned only with observable behaviour which can be objectively analysed and measured. The study of inner states or mental phenomena is excluded. The cognitive–purposive theory of Tolman (1932), on the other hand, Alston saw as having such resources, and therefore as having more promise for the study of intentional action.

Let us examine briefly Tolman's cognitive–purposive theory. In contrast to 'strict' and 'near' behaviourism, Tolman calls his version of behaviourism 'purposive'. Thus, behaviour is not molecular, as the former two versions of behaviourism claim, but is molar, i.e. 'Gestalted' (Tolman, 1932, p. 418). The responses of animals and human beings are purposeful, they are always directed towards specific goals. Animals learn that one pattern of stimuli is related to another pattern. In other words, they learn 'what leads to what'. They build up cognitive maps of the ways things and events relate to each other. In order to explain behaviour, one has not only to postulate independent variables and measure dependent variables but also to assume intervening variables. Intervening variables are the actual determinants of behaviour and are of three kinds: purposive and cognitive determinants, capacities, and behaviour-adjustments. These determinants can be inferred from behaviour by backward analysis and, as Tolman says,

they are to behaviour as electrons, waves, or whatever it may be, are to the happenings in inorganic matter. There is nothing private or 'mentalistic' about them. They are pragmatically conceived, objective variables the concepts of which can be altered and changed as proves most useful. They are not the dictates of any incontrovertible moments of immediacy. (Tolman, 1932, p. 414)

Tolman's intervening variables are therefore logical constructs that serve to achieve economy of description and explanation of phenomena. Tolman's reference to electrons and waves clearly demonstrates that the status of intervening variables is purely fictional and of the same kind as the status attributed to electrons by Russell: 'The persistent particles of mathematical physics I regard as logical constructions, symbolic fictions enabling us to express compendiously very complicated assemblages of facts' (Russell, 1917, p. 96).

We can see that behaviour generally and action in particular, both in philosophy and psychology, are explained by means of a chain of variables. First, there are independent variables of a physiological or hereditary nature, or environmental stimuli, or variables arising from past learning of the organism. Then some intervening variables, desires, wants for some state of affairs, intentions and purposes, are constructed and presupposed to determine the dependent variables, the bodily movements. A conception of this kind, once again, is typical of the Cartesian paradigm and has its place in physics. The state of physical objects does not change unless preceded by some external force or stimulus. Thus, changes from non-motion to motion, or changes in motion, in the Newtonian system were due to mechanical forces. Such forces can arise through attraction between bodies or through impact of one body upon another. The independent variables, or the determinants of motion and change, are forces of impact, or of attraction. Commencement of motion, or change in motion, are characterized as dependent variables. Complex events that cannot readily be incorporated into the scheme of independent and dependent variables are accounted for by postulating logical constructs called intervening variables.

Is there any alternative to the Cartesian presupposition that actions should be explained in terms of dependent variables? We shall see in Part II that in the Hegelian framework action is an essential characteristic of a living organism, and as such has to be treated as a *primitive* concept and is not decomposable into elements forming causal changes. An action does not have any determinants because it is the action itself that determines all the other characteristics of the living organism.

6.6 Purposeful explanation in information-processing

The language of artificial intelligence and information-processing abounds with words such as 'purpose', 'reason', 'intention', and so on. Boden (1978) maintains that the logic of purposive or teleological explanations[5] is essential to account for information-processing goal-directed systems; causal or mechanistic explanation is not powerful enough and cannot be a substitute for purposeful explanation. On the other hand Nagel (1961) argues very cogently that purposive explanation *can* be translated into causal explanation and vice versa without loss of explanatory power. Although from our point of view it does not particularly matter whether causal *language* is sufficiently rich for these purposes, it *is* significant that both Boden and Nagel should deny that there is any radical difference between living organisms, including man, and non-living physical goal-directed systems. Both kinds of system have a certain structure or internal organization and have the ability of representing and misrepresenting the external world (Boden, 1978, p. 2). According to Boden, the logical and conceptual analysis of purpose demonstrates that it is not necessary to postulate a special psychic cause in order to explain purposes and intentions. Rather, according to her reductionist position, purposive phenomena are 'totally dependent on causal (neurophysiological) mechanisms'. The internal organization of information-processing systems explains the 'special logical (intensional) features characterizing purposive accounts of behaviour'; and the mind should be thought of as a set of mutually interlinked representational models. Therefore, a complete account of how goal-directed behaviour arises can be given in causal, mechanistic terms alone:

Purposive psychologies may properly be regarded as basically mechanistic, no matter how 'molar' or 'humanistic' their theoretical terms may be. To regard all purposive creatures as basically physical mechanisms is not to deny the reality of mind, nor to assert the inhumanity of man. (Boden, 1978, p. 341)

Purposeful explanation in the Cartesian paradigm is based on several assumptions. First, it is the internal and formal organization of the system that underlies its purposefulness. The *essential nature* of the system, that is whether the system is an artefact, a living organism, or anything else, is disregarded. The criterion of the *essential nature* of the internal organization is whether the performance it affects can be simulated as a program. In fact, those holding this position often criticize those who ignore the distinction between the program on the one hand and its embodiment on the other. For example, Boden accuses Taylor (1964) of blurring this distinction and emphasizing the different natures of purposive organisms and mechanistic systems. We mentioned earlier (cf. pp. 77–78) the same kind of criticism by Dennett.

Secondly, purposes follow solely from the internal organization of the systems. The assumption of a static and predetermined nature of the knower has already been discussed in a different context in Chapter 4. It is a pre-Darwinian and pre-Hegelian conception in which purposefulness means the unwinding of a built-in algorithm rather than the result of an interaction between the system and its world.

Thirdly, purposive behaviour is fully predictable, whether by psychological or physical laws. This again is implied by the algorithmic nature of purposeful processes.

And, finally, it is assumed that the difference between causal and purposeful explanation is that the order of events is reversed. While in a causal explanation the cause is either past or present, in purposeful or teleological explanation the logical antecedent of the effect is in the future. For example, in order to clarify the difference between explanation by causes and explanation by purposes, Braithwaite (1953) maintains:

In a causal explanation the explicandum is explained in terms of a cause which either precedes or is simultaneous with it: in a teleological explanation the explicandum is explained as being causally related either to a particular goal in the future or to a biological end which is as much future as present or past. It is the reference in teleological explanations to states of affairs in the future, and often in the comparatively distant future, which has been a philosophical problem ever since Aristotle introduced the notion of 'final cause'. (Braithwaite, 1953, p. 324)

Such a conception seems to have two kinds of consequence. The first is an attempt to reduce teleological to non-teleological explanation (e.g. Rosenblueth *et al.*, 1943; Nagel, 1961). It tries to show that the notion of purpose is superfluous in evolutionary theory, to show that biological phenomena can be fully explained in terms of genetics, adaptation, natural selection, and so on. Secondly, in trying to demonstrate that there is no basic difference between natural living organisms and man-made machines, these philosophers and scientists are changing the meaning which the word 'purpose' has customarily been taken to possess. According to Taylor (1964), a teleological explanation is based on 'the assumption that the system concerned 'naturally' or inherently tends towards a certain result, condition or end . . . [whereas] the claim that a system is purposive is a claim about the laws holding at the most basic level of explanation' (Taylor, 1964, pp. 17 and 18). Taylor's point is that the behaviour of a system may be superficially teleological or goal-directed, but that this behaviour may be governed by more basic laws of a non-purposive character. In this case one cannot properly say that the system *naturally* or *inherently* tends towards a goal. The system is basically *non-purposive*. If, on the other hand, the purposive account *is* the basic level—if it cannot be reduced to a non-purposive account—then the system is *essentially* purposive. For example, if a mechanical dog were constructed and programmed to behave like a real dog, the laws describing its external behaviour would be teleological like those of its real counterpart. Such laws would characterize the behaviour as goal-directed. However, underlying this goal-directedness are laws that are different in kind, laws that are causal and not purposive. Thus, the distinction between purposeful living organisms and 'purposeful' machines cannot be made on the basis of what is superficially observed. As Taylor says, explanation by purposes is incompatible with the view that a natural tendency towards a certain condition can be accounted for in terms of laws which themselves are other than purposive in character.

But can one talk about purpose in Nature? For Kant a tree reproduces itself in two senses. What it reproduces is of the same *genus*: 'In the genus, now as *effect*, now as *cause* [my italics], continually generated from itself and likewise generating itself, it preserves itself generically' (Kant, *Critique of Judgement*, Part II, p. 18). But the tree reproduces itself also an an *individual*. The growth of the tree is different in kind from a mechanical *quantitative* addition to a machine. The tree assimilates and then organizes matter which is foreign to its body and 'bestows upon it a specifically distinctive *quality* which the mechanism of nature outside it cannot supply and it develops itself by means of a material which, in its composite character, is its own product' (*ibid.*, p. 18).

The problem for Kant, however, was how to account for the agency present in Nature. There seemed to be two possibilities: either to presuppose that matter has a property called life, or to presuppose that life is associated with a principle foreign to matter, a soul. But in any case 'the organization of nature has nothing analogous to any causality known to us' (Kant, *Critique of Judgement*, Part II, p. 23). As our reason is incapable of comprehending the origin of purposiveness in Nature, all it can do is to postulate it as a *regulative a priori* principle rather than as a constitutive one, that is only treat it *as if* it existed; in this case, purposiveness in Nature is treated *as if* it existed, but only for heuristic purposes. Such a presupposition guides us in scientific enquiry, but does not form any part of scientific knowledge. Teleology, therefore, has no essential place in natural science but is relegated to theology (*ibid.*, p. 34). Natural science can only be concerned with mechanical aspects of nature which are observable and measurable; what follows, then, is that although we must presuppose purposiveness in organisms, we cannot explain it scientifically.

We have emphasized earlier in this book that Kant was a philosopher of crisis. His treatment of teleology is an example of his inability to shake off his commitment to the Newtonian conception of Nature and of explanation in terms of mechanistic causes and effects.

6.7 Mechanisms and organisms

Hegel pointed out that it was Kant who reawakened Aristotle's organic conception of nature, claiming that 'life has there been made an end to itself' (Hegel, *History of Philosophy*, II, p. 160). Kant maintained that living organisms are only intelligible as self-organized beings and as such are totally different from aggregates such as earth, stones, and minerals. Aggregates and mechanisms can be made intelligible in terms of causes and effects but living organisms only in terms of purposes. Kant demonstrates the basic differences between these two kinds of thing by the example of a *watch*. Although one might say that a watch has its purpose, the purpose is not contained in the nature of the watch, but lies outside it, in an agent called a watchmaker. It is true that one part of a watch affects the movement of another part, but this movement is not due to any agency on the part of the watch. Moreover, one watch does not *produce* other watches. It is unable to consume any external material, organize it and produce instruments similar to itself; nor is it able to repair or replace its own parts. But all of these things and activities we take for granted and expect in living organisms:

An organized being is, therefore, not a mere machine. For a machine has solely *motive power*, whereas an organized being possesses inherent *formative* power, and such, moreover, as it can impart to material devoid of it—material which it organizes. This, therefore, is a self-propagating formative power, which cannot be explained by the capacity of movement alone, that is to say, by mechanism. (Kant, *Critique of Judgement*, Part II, p. 22)

Thus, there are two essential characteristics of organisms which are not to be found in machines: first, the parts of an organism can *only* function in relationship to the whole to which they belong, and, secondly, organisms have the ability to reproduce themselves. A part of a watch can be used either as it is or to serve some 'purpose' in another instrument, or it can be melted down and re-made into something else. A part of an organism can fulfil a function only in relationship to the whole to which it belongs. Thus the leaves of a tree live only when part of a tree but at the same time they maintain the tree too: repeated defoliation would kill the tree, for the growth of the tree is dependent on the action of the leaves.

Kant's 'formative power' as characterizing natural organisms has become the main line of attack against those who have tried to bring the doll to life. Foster's (1935) account is particularly illuminating. Discussing the failure in Greek thought properly to distinguish the relationships between parent and offspring on the one hand and artificer and artefact on the other, he points to the following differences between the two: First, the parent shares his *nature* with his offspring but the artificer conceives the object of his production by his reason. Since the manner of production of the offspring and the artefact is different, their natures too are different. The offspring is *like* the parent, whereas the artefact bears no resemblance to the artificer. The artificer can, of course, make a statue of himself, but the resemblance is only one of shape. Secondly, the offspring *grows* as its potentiality to become an adult is gradually realized, the agency of growth is *internal*, and *food* is converted into its own substance (cf. Kant, above). The artefact, on the other hand, gradually takes shape or becomes more complex as the artificer gradually realizes his *concept* in his material. The agency by which this is achieved is *external* and the material is not converted into the same substance as that of the artificer. Living organisms have an intrinsic spring or principle of activity. An artefact, on the other hand, needs a source of energy to make it work; this source is extrinsic, even if it is inside it, as in an internal combustion engine. As Foster puts it, the nature of the parent is embodied in the offspring 'as spontaneous active power' but the artefact remains dependent on the artificer for 'that spring or activity which the living creature can supply from within itself' (Foster, 1935, p. 447). Finally, artefacts are *influenced* by their environment, living organisms *interact* with it:

. . . living creatures exposed to a gale of wind do not remain merely passive to its force. On the contrary, each reacts against it according to its own kind, and the nature of each is exhibited in the active endeavour to subdue the element [i.e. wind] to the end of its own better preservation, whether by flight, or by such a disposition of the body as will minimize the surface exposed, or by turning to account the force of the wind itself, as soaring birds do to enable them to ascend . . . But artefacts possess no 'nature' in this sense of the word at all. Pieces of crockery do not react to pressure of wind each according to its kind, and no understanding of what constitutes the difference between a teapot and a jug will enable us to predict the different movement which will be imparted to each by the impact of an external force. (Foster, 1935, pp. 458–9)

The concept of *internal* and *external force* is also essential to Heider's (1958) theory of *personal* and *impersonal* causality. Personal causality is characterized by intentionality, equifinality, and local causality. Impersonal causality, on the other hand, possesses none of these characteristics. Thus, personal causality refers only to acts that are intended and wanted. For example, if a person breaks something, Heider talks about personal causality only if such an act was intended: if it was the weight of a person's body that caused something to break, it was impersonal causality that was involved, and the person's body functioned exactly like any other physical object. Equifinality refers to invariance of the goal and the variability of the means. For example, in the game of cricket, the goal of each side is to get more runs than their opponents but the means of reaching this goal are varied. In cases of impersonal causality there is no such thing as a goal. Finally, personal causality is local, by which Heider means that it is internal to the organism. On the other hand, a marble rolling about in a bowl is in motion because an external force is affecting it. The marble will follow a very complicated path before it eventually comes to rest at the bottom, but the forces leading it towards the endpoint are not located in any specific part of the marble.

We can thus see that although different philosophers and psychologists have discussed the distinction between mechanisms and organisms in various contexts, the conclusions they have reached rest on similar arguments: organisms are characterized by intrinsic causality or purposefulness and they manifest it in their interaction with their environment. Living organisms cannot stop interacting. Interaction is so essential for their existence that, if it stops, the organism is dead and cannot be resuscitated. It takes things from its environment, changes them into things characteristic of its own body, changes itself through growth of its parts, and also changes the environment through its own activity. Experience, which in fact is the totality of interactions between the organism and its environment, must, therefore, be part of explanation by purposes.

The fact that computers can simulate some human activities is an interesting technological development and one would not deny its practical usefulness or that it has led to some important contributions to theoretical progress in psychology. But any comparison between man and machine concerns only small aspects of their activities. The basic laws of their functioning are totally different because in living organisms they are based on the interaction between the organisms and their environment, which is not the case with machines. Nevertheless, some might still argue that it is an empirical question whether one day human beings will construct interacting, self-reproducing, and self-unfolding machines.

PART II

The Hegelian Framework for the Study of Thought and Language

Everything that from eternity has happened in heaven and earth, the life of God and all the deeds of time simply are the struggles for Mind to know itself, to make itself objective to itself, to find itself, be for itself, and finally unite itself to itself; it is alienated and divided, but only as to be able thus to find itself and return to itself. (Hegel, *History of Philosophy*, I)

CHAPTER 7

The Individual in the Hegelian Framework

7.1 Introduction

The emphasis on the self, introduced by the Renaissance and humanism, and nurtured by the rationalism of the seventeenth and eighteenth centuries, had its second blossoming in expressivism. The term 'expressivism' was coined by Berlin (1965) and has been adopted by Taylor (1975) to characterize the broadly based philosophical and artistic movement that reacted violently against the prevailing rationalism. This movement was mainly represented by romanticism, which penetrated the arts, literature, music, and philosophy in Central Europe after the failure of the French Revolution. But expressivism encompassed much more than romanticism. It became the *Zeitgeist* of the end of the eighteenth century and first half of the nineteenth century: its spirit guided the growth of nationalism, and it penetrated science where it led to the substitution of evolutionism for mechanistic rationalism.

The peak of expressivism, in my opinion, is Hegel's *Phenomenology of Spirit* (1807), a social psychology of the cognizing mind in its development. It was in this book that all the fundamental ideas of artistic expressivism were transformed and formulated into the propositions of scientific expressivism. Although Hegel's ideas owed a great deal to romanticism, it was the systematic manner, internal consistency, and logicality with which they were refined and elaborated that led Taylor to make the claim that because of 'a certain rigour and consequence in his thought' Hegel cannot be called a romantic (Taylor, 1975, pp. 42–3).

Like the Renaissance, expressivism reacted strongly against the contemporary political systems and social establishments of Europe, and against the prevailing ideas in philosophy and science. In particular, it was a revolt against the reactionary regimes established throughout Europe after the failure of the French attempt to give shape to a new social contract based on equality of the people and freedom for everybody.

The expressivist movement was strongest in Germany, one of the most economically backward countries in Europe at that time, with no political consolidation. The territory of Germany was divided into about 300 little states and free cities governed by feudal and Church oligarchies. These governing bodies met with virtually no political resistance. The feudal system itself was despotic and corrupt, and pursued expansionist politics. The backward economic situation did not allow Germany to participate in the industrial growth that was enjoyed by countries such as France and Britain. But as sometimes happens in history, it was this desperately backward political and social system that gave rise to a stormy reaction and created the need for a revolution in people's minds. As early as in the eighteenth century the poet Klopstock introduced into German literature themes of national pride and heroism, and personal freedom. Klopstock is often called the forerunner of the movement of the angry young men, *Sturm and Drang*, which shocked feudal German society during the period 1770–78. *Sturm and Drang* was a movement of artists, in particular of those concerned with literature. In contrast to the rationalists' beliefs in the infinite power of reason, *Sturm and Drang* celebrated *human genius*: human creativity, imagination and feeling, subjectivity, and individual experience were the main themes and motives in their work. It was a revolt of youth against tradition and the established values of society; it claimed that there were no prescribed ways of thinking or moral behaviour, no definitions of what was good and what was bad. Instead, according to *Sturm and Drang*, each human being had his own measures of right conduct.

We can thus see that the precedents and beginnings of the expressivist focus on the individual were very similar to those of the Renaissance: a human being is born with immense potentialities and freedom of will, he is filled with an inner energy that is revealed in various human activities, and all his potentialities and powers are destined to be developed to their maximum capacity in the enjoyment of a full life.

7.2 Expression is the realization of the individual

Although the ideas of expressivism concerning the nature of subjectivity started off as being very similar to those of the Renaissance, the similarity did not last.

We may recollect that it was in his search for certainty that Descartes finally turned to his own thoughts and consciousness: 'I think, therefore I am' became the starting point both for the Cartesian conception of the self and for Cartesian epistemology. The Renaissance mind, originally a unity of a multitude of human powers and capacities, was eventually reduced to ratiocination alone. In addition, as the individual found his only certainty in his own thought and relied solely upon his own reason, he became totally alienated both from nature and from other human beings. Satisfied with his own thought and the ideas he himself produced, the individual remained wholly *egocentric*.

In contrast to the Cartesian concentration on *reason*, the expressivists strived for the full *expression* of a human being. One of the main representatives of

Sturm and Drang, Herder, whose work on thought and language will be discussed later, wrote in his poem *St John's Dream*:

> I am not here to think! but to be! to feel!
> To live! to rejoice!
> (Herder, *Sämtliche Werke*, XXIX, p. 366)

As Taylor (1975) maintains, to see the life of a human being as an expression means to see him both as self-realization and as full self-awareness and understanding of that self-realization:

It is not only the fulfilment of life but also the clarification of meaning. In the course of living adequately I not only fulfil my humanity but clarify what my humanity is about. As such a clarification my life-form is not just the fulfilment of purpose but the embodiment of meaning, the expression of an idea ... Human life is both fact and meaningful expression. (Taylor, 1975, p. 17)

The act of expression is not something *added* to other human characteristics: rather, everything we do, every aspect of human activity, is a form of expression, i.e. a form of self-realization and self-unfolding. Leibniz's conception of the self-unfolding monad (cf. pp. 16–17) had a significant influence upon German expressivism. Just as monads are unrepeatable, so for expressivism every human being is unrepeatable. He has his own history and his own individual potentialities, and unfolds himself in accordance with these. But the expressivists went far beyond Leibniz. The monad's activity and its development was part of a universal system of individuals in pre-established harmony with one another; the monad unfolded itself with absolute necessity according to a plan predetermined by God. The expressivists, in contrast to Leibniz, and in agreement with Kant, postulated an individual who himself determined his own actions. According to Kant, it was *human rationality* that determined the human freedom to act: since a human being was rational, he had a duty and obligation to act in such a way that his actions were in harmony with those of everyone else:

So act as to treat humanity, whether in thine own person or in that of any other, in every case as an end withal, never as a means only. (Kant, *Critique of Practical Reason*, p. 47)

Free action, according to Kant, was *the action of reason* and excluded any action based partly or totally on irrational motives, desires or emotions. But it was at this point that expressivists departed from Kant. Rationality, the crucial notion of the Cartesian paradigm, does not determine human freedom to act. There is no universal moral code applicable to all mankind as Kant proposed, in the sense that there are universal laws of nature. Instead, each individual is unique. Each person develops and unfolds according to his own code and has his own measure (Herder, *Sämtliche Werke*, XIII, p. 292).

The expressivists' conception of individual freedom had important consequences for their conception of society and cultural progress: for them, cultural progress could not be achieved through moral and intellectual improvement. Instead, human history and human life must be understood in terms of the inner energy of people: human history is determined by the self-realization and self-unfolding of individuals.

7.3 Expression and consciousness

A fundamental feature of expressivism is evolutionism. An evolutionist approach started to emerge in various aspects of political, social, and scientific life in the middle of the eighteenth century, first as a reaction against the static framework of formalism in the Enlightenment, and then as a general idea.

The work of Leibniz and Kant had made it apparent that the dynamic characteristics of individuals, such as their self-unfolding nature and freedom to act, could not be conceived of in terms of mechanistic rationalism. Instead, the expressivists sought to make these characteristics intelligible in terms of *historical* categories. Moreover, for the expressivists, it was not only the individual's life that self-unfolded, but whole societies and cultures proceeded through various stages of self-unfolding. Herder's claim that history is much more than battles won and lost, and the achievements and failures of kings (Herder, *Sämtliche Werke*, XVI, 587), was not entirely new. But it was the strength and richness of his work, demonstrating the relativity of contemporary values, and arguing that the people as a whole were active participants in creating history, that made Herder's work so new and topical. Like Kant, Herder insisted that humanity was never only a means to something else; everything in history is both a means and an end at the same time (Herder, *Sämtliche Werke*, V, 527). This claim, however, could have no meaning for an a-historical mechanistic rationalism which evaluated historical events in black and white terms as they appeared in the light of contemporary values. Mead, for example, has pointed out that while ancient Greece was evaluated by the Enlightenment as the height of harmony and beauty, mediaeval culture was evaluated only negatively. Thus the Goths and Vandals were barbaric tribes that invaded Europe during the third to fifth centuries of our era. The *Oxford English Dictionary* gives one definition of 'Goth' as 'an uncivilized person, especially one who destroys works of art', and it was in exactly this sense that the Enlightenment intended the term when they used it in their disparagement of mediaeval architecture. It was only with romanticism that mediaeval culture was re-evaluated, and that the term 'Gothic' as applied to architecture took on the meaning that it has for us today (Mead, 1936, pp. 57–8).

The expressivists were profoundly aware of the relativity of the values and norms of individual cultures, historical epochs, and societies. Each stage in history is necessary for the next one; it is wrong to scorn at the towns, enclosed guilds, and habits of the Middle Ages, as Hume, Voltaire, Robertson, and others did (Herder, *Sämtliche Werke*, V, 524–5). It is wrong to despise events in the past and judge them only by temporary criteria, by present standards and morals. Although history is a progressive unfolding, it does not mean that it always appears as a progressive continuum to those who evaluate it. Mediaeval feudalism and suppression of individual freedom appeared to Hegel to be unquestionably inferior to the practices of ancient Greece. It had, nevertheless, its positive features: it was a necessary stage through which Western Europe had to go in order to progress.

A proper appreciation of history does not consist of praising what agrees with our present values and condemning what does not. One cannot understand the history of a nation or grasp its meaning without deeply immersing oneself in it and reconstructing that meaning for oneself (Herder, *Sämtliche Werke*, IV, 202–3). This, of course, is a very difficult task: it is an enormously complex and ambitious operation to empathize even with an individual human being, to understand his actions and feel his emotions.

If this is so, what happens when one tries to master an entire ocean of peoples, times, cultures, countries, with one glance, one sentiment, by means of one single word! Words, pale shadow-play! An entire living picture of ways of life, of habits, wants, characteristics of land and sky, must be added, or provided in advance; one must start by feeling sympathy with a nation if one is to feel a single one of its inclinations or acts, or all of them together. (Herder, *Sämtliche Werke*, V, 502)[6]

What is so very important for us in this book is that it was this particular aspect of expressivist historicism, this genuine attempt to feel oneself into everything ('fühle dich in alles hinein') (Herder, *Sämtliche Werke*, V, 503), *to empathize with other human beings, with other nations, and with their past*, that led to the expressivist notion of *self-consciousness*.

One of the characteristics of the expressivists generally, and of the romanticists in particular, was that they sought refuge in the past. But they did not attempt, simply, to turn the clock back (Mead, 1936, pp. 57–8). For them, a return to the past was possible only through a re-appreciation and re-interpretation of that past. And such a re-interpretation was based on empathy, as Herder himself constantly emphasized. In order to empathize one has to think oneself into the place of the other, or take the role, or the attitude of the other. If one is able to do that, one is also able *to see oneself through the eyes of the other*. In other words, one becomes *self-conscious*: to re-appreciate the past means to project one's own self into the world of the time, to see the past through one's own experience, and so to identify the past with one's own self. In this sense it means that *the self becomes its own object*. As Mead puts it

The word 'itself', you will recognize, belongs to the reflexive mode. It is that grammatical form which we use under conditions in which the individual is both subject and object. He addresses himself. He sees himself as others see him. The very usage of the word implies an individual who is occupying the position of both subject and object. In a mode which is not reflexive, the object is distinguished from the subject. The subject, the self, sees a tree. The latter is something that is different from himself. In the use of the term 'itself', on the contrary, the subject and object are found in the same entity. This very term 'itself' is one which is characteristic of a romantic phase of consciousness.' (Mead, 1936, p. 74)

But Mead also points out the peculiar characteristics of this romantic self-consciousness: while turning attention upon one's self could lead to subject-ivism, to a self-centred attitude and selfishness—and we noted that this was exactly what happened to the Renaissance self—the peculiarity of romanticism was the projecting of the self into the world, seeing the world through one's own experience and externalizing one's self into the world. 'The self-centered attitude may be one which is anything but romantic' (Mead, 1936, p. 75).

While the Cartesian consciousness was inseparable from thought, the romantic consciousness was inseparable from the expression of the person as a whole. While Cartesian reflection referred to consciousness of one's thought, the romantic reflexion referred to consciousness of one's expression, of one's actions. But in the latter case a human being is reflexive only because he is able to empathize, to take the attitude of the other. Reflexion is the process of reconstruction. It is not *reading* one's old diary as was the case with Lockean reflection, but *writing* one's story in the light of one's past experience in the social context. According to Mead, the existence of reflexivity is a proof of the social nature of human beings. Of course, *thought*, which is one aspect of expression, plays a fundamental role in reflexion. We reflect upon things when 'the ordinary stream of action is interrupted' because a problem has arisen (Mead, 1934, p. 90). Automatic activities and the taken-for-grantedness of normal situations do not require reflexion. It is only when activity cannot continue its ordinary flow that reflexive thought is mobilized. Reflexive thought arises as an individual tests the possibilities for resolving the problem or the ways of adjusting to a conflict situation. The inhibition of normal action initiates the invention of a set of hypothetical ways of continuing an action which has been interrupted (Mead, 1938, p. 79). However, in any problem-solving activity a human being is using his *social skills*, that is, his freedom to break the stream of his biological habits, to achieve his goal.

Neither thought, nor consciousness, nor reflexion is given to a human being in a ready-made form. Possession of these activities is the result of the labour of past generations. A human being must make of himself what he is to become in the process of history. This *becoming* of a human being is not a passive movement similar to the movement of natural bodies such as the Sun and Moon. In fact, in order to achieve humanity, a human being must liberate himself and shake Nature off from himself. The product of this process is his free mind (Hegel, *History of Philosophy*, I, p. 94). Thus, the development of the individual as a human being was impossible without the development of society at the same time. Human beings have developed as they gradually conquered Nature by their social activities, and these activities have taken particular forms in history. And history is the history of the journey of the mind towards self-consciousness.

7.4 The world-for-consciousness and the world-in-itself

We demonstrated earlier in the book (p. 20) that by proclaiming 'I think, therefore I am' Descartes separated the world-of-consciousness from the world-in-itself, or, in other words, the knowing subject from the object of his knowledge. The self's certainty comes only from the inside, from his own thoughts, while nothing certain can be said about the outside world.

Hegel (*Phenomenology*, pp. 46–7) pointed out that by making consciousness and the rest of the world two independent existences, traditional epistemology, including both rationalistic and empiricistic epistemology, set a problem for itself. The problem was the following: before philosophy can begin it must come to some sort of decision as to what can and what cannot be regarded as knowledge and how to delineate its boundaries. Descartes, as we have seen, separated the Cogito from the external world, i.e. the 'inner' from the 'outer' and, as a consequence, the questions were: Is the cognizing subject certain that what he cognizes is the truth? How can he be sure that the world he cognizes, i.e. the world-of-consciousness, is the same world that exists independently of him, i.e. the world-in-itself? Hegel pointed out that traditional epistemology, i.e. the epistemology of the Cartesian paradigm, offered two possible solutions to this problem. One possibility was to assume that knowledge could be viewed as a *passive medium* 'through which the light of truth reaches us'. Although Hegel does not mention names, his analysis could be interpreted as directed towards Descartes and Locke. We may remember that for Descartes the mind was passive in understanding, and clear and distinct ideas were passively contemplated by the thinking subject in the acquisition of knowledge. In Locke's theory of knowledge, simple ideas 'when offered to the mind, the *understanding can* no more refuse to have . . . than a mirror can refuse' the images of objects. The other alternative of traditional epistemology was, according to Hegel, the view that knowledge is an instrument by means of which we take hold of reality. In this case, knowledge is an activity of the mind. Hegel probably refers here to Locke's complex ideas that are actively constructed by the mind from simple ideas, and to Kant's constructive synthesizing activity of the mind (cf. pp. 62 and 127).

Hegel is critical of both of these solutions. Concerning the 'passive medium' solution, he pointed out that the mind does not receive the truth *as it is* but only *as it appears* through the medium. And concerning the 'instrument' solution, here again knowledge of 'absolute reality' is not attained. Using an instrument on a thing means that the thing is not left as it is but is altered by the instrument; it is made different from what it was by itself. Thus, Hegel claims, in both of these cases the final outcome is just the opposite of what was originally intended. The problem of traditional epistemology is insoluble: if we try to remove the medium, no information reaches us any longer; if on the other hand we try to discount the effect of the instrument and remove from the altered object what the instrument has done to it, then we apprehend nothing. Thus, Hegel argues, the problem of traditional epistemology, of how to bridge the gap between independent consciousness and independent reality, has not been solved. In both cases, what is directly available to consciousness is *only* the world-of-consciousness, and since the only contact that consciousness has with the world is through a veil that cannot be removed, i.e. either through the active application of an instrument, or by passive exposure through a medium, traditional epistemology necessarily led to scepticism.

For Hegel, however, the problem of traditional epistemology is a pseudo-problem which arises from the presupposition that consciousness and the world-in-itself are two independent entities.

What, then, is Hegel's alternative?

It is important, first, to point out the difference between Descartes' and Hegel's notions of consciousness. We remember that for Descartes consciousness is inseparable from thought. Thought is given to human beings while in their mothers' wombs, at least in its dispositional form; the dispositions manifest themselves whenever the senses are stimulated in particular ways by the external world.

For Hegel, consciousness is defined much more broadly (Chapter 8). It starts with sensory awareness and by its development reaches higher forms in perception, understanding, self-consciousness, and reason. This does not mean, though, that Hegel held some sort of psychobiological theory of the development of consciousness. We have to bear in mind that Hegel developed his theory before Darwin, and although evolutionism and historicism were the *Zeitgeist* of the nineteenth century, Hegel was not concerned with biological development. His philosophy, like that of other philosophers before him, starts with what he considered to be the most elementary form of cognizing, i.e. sensory awareness, and it was through *experience*, he believed, that consciousness attained its higher forms. Hegel's notion of 'experience', however, owes nothing either to empiricism or to behaviourism. For he saw experience as a *form of expression* as other expressivists did. Let us examine the nature of Hegel's notion of experience in some detail.

As already pointed out, traditional epistemology separated the thing-in-itself and the thing as it appears to consciousness. Since, however, in the process of knowing, consciousness only has access to objects either actively by applying an instrument or passively by exposure via a medium, all it has access to in either case is reality as it appears to consciousness, rather than reality as it is in itself. Consequently, there is no *external standard* available to consciousness with which it could compare what it believes it knows. Yet although quite aware of it, the science based on traditional epistemology postulated external standards as if they were actually available. Discussing the method of scientific inquiry, Hegel says:

For an examination consists in applying an accepted standard, and in determining whether something is right or wrong on the basis of the resulting agreement or disagreement of the thing examined; thus the standard as such (and Science likewise if it were the criterion) is accepted as the *essence* or as the *in-itself*. (Hegel, *Phenomenology*, p. 52)

For example, in Chapter 3 we saw that systems of logic have been taken as external standards for deductive reasoning; and in Chapter 5 we were concerned with the postulation, by the logical atomists, of elementary facts as standards by which the truth values of propositions could be determined, and with the effect this viewpoint has had on the theories and methods of cognitive psychology.

The postulation of external standards, Hegel argues, is wrong. Since consciousness has access only to the world *as it exists for consciousness*, the standards can only be *internal*, lying within consciousness itself: 'Consciousness provides its own criterion from within itself, so that the investigation becomes a comparison of consciousness with itself' (Hegel, *Phenomenology*, p. 53).

But how should we understand this claim? Is Hegel saying that no *objective* scientific knowledge is possible and that all our knowledge is *subjective*? Not at all. We have, on the one hand, consciousness of the object, and, on the other hand, consciousness of our knowledge of that object. The methods of enquiry, whether scientific or non-scientific, about objects, rests upon this distinction. What consciousness does in the process of knowing is to compare its experience of an object with its knowledge of the object. In other words, the process of knowing is a constant comparison of what we think the object is with how we actually experience the object, what we can do to it, and what the object does to us. The process of comparison shows whether the two aspects are in agreement. If they are in agreement, we can believe that consciousness has achieved true knowledge. If they are not, then consciousness must change its knowledge so that it conforms to the object. But as consciousness changes its knowledge of the object, the object itself changes because it is only an object for consciousness, not an object for itself. The testing criterion thus always lies within consciousness itself: if 'knowledge does not correspond to its object, the object itself does not stand the test; in other words, the criterion for testing is altered when that for which it was to have been the criterion fails to pass the test; and the testing is not only a testing of what we know, but also a testing of the criterion of what knowing is' (Hegel, *Phenomenology*, pp. 54–55). Perhaps we should add that the correspondence between the object and our knowledge of that object is, in the great majority of cases, only a temporary correspondence. Once consciousness starts delving into the extent of the correspondence, it finds that what appeared to be correspondence on the surface does not appear to be such at a deeper level; consciousness realizes that there is, in fact, a disagreement between object and knowledge, and therefore that both standard and knowledge are inadequate. We can easily see that the process of acquisition of knowledge is endless. It is always possible to enquire into deeper and deeper levels of knowledge. But it is important that this kind of endlessness does not lead to scepticism as in the Cartesian paradigm.

We do not have a gap between the world-for-consciousness and the world-in-itself with these two operating on conceptually different levels, independent of each other with no possibility of a bridge between them. Nor is knowledge obtained by Hegel's method *subjective*. Of course, this knowledge does not possess the apparent objectivity and certainty of traditional epistemology. There are no fixed and immutable pieces of knowledge representing 'something' objective and certain. All knowledge obtained by Hegel's method is relative: it can always be destroyed in the light of a deeper-level discrepancy between the object as it exists for consciousness and the knowledge of that object. It is neither subjective nor 'objective' knowledge. It is knowledge based on *interaction* between the knowing subject and the object of its knowledge. The object as it exists for consciousness and knowledge of it by consciousness form an inseparable unity: sometimes they correspond to each, sometimes they are in *opposition*, to use Hegel's term. But it is through the overcoming of these oppositions that consciousness approaches asymptotically towards the truth. It is, of course, never to be achieved. If it were, there would be no more acquisition of knowledge. It would be the end, it would be death.

The acquisition of knowledge is thus possible only through the reconciliation of oppositions, and the fundamental task of philosophy and psychology is to examine the way in which this is achieved. The oppositions between consciousness and reality can be seen in all sorts of relationships. Taylor (1975, pp. 76–80) summarizes four kinds of oppositions existing between the knowing subject and his world: between nature and freedom, between the individual and society, between finite and infinite spirit, and between the free man and his fate. But as Taylor explains, to overcome oppositions does not mean simply to 'undo' them. There is no possibility of return to the previous, more primitive consciousness any more than it was possible for the romantics to turn the clock back in history. Reconciliation is possible only by a total transformation, or, as Hegel calls it, *negation*, of both factors involved in a disagreement, that is, of consciousness and reality for consciousness. This negation, however, does not lead to destruction. Rather, the negation of the existing states of consciousness and reality results in a new unity of the two.

7.5 Phenomenal knowledge

We have pointed out in Part I that for Descartes the search after truth was also the search for certainty: he examined solicitously one thing after another, the truth of sciences such as physics and mathematics, the existence of the external world as well as the truth-worthiness of his senses and body. Having discounted one thing as lacking in certainty, Descartes started from scratch with something else: everything was rejected in turn and nothing was left of what was discarded for any future consideration. Only finally did he find the only certainty in his own mental activity of doubting, i.e. thinking. And then the old truths were restored unscathed.

Hegel rejected Descartes' method on the following grounds: first, he argued that Cartesian scepticism was not true scepticism because it knew from the beginning what in principle its finished product would be like: it resolved *not* to rely upon any authority, *not* to trust any thoughts of others, but instead 'to examine everything for oneself and follow only one's own conviction, or better still, to produce everything oneself, and accept only one's own deed as what is true' (Hegel, *Phenomenology*, p. 50). But, Hegel says, the substitution of one's own opinion for that of authority does not necessarily alter the *content* of that opinion, or, indeed, replace error with truth. The only difference between the two kinds of conviction is that the latter is based on conceit.

The second of Hegel's objections to the Cartesian method of doubting is that it changes the things rejected into pure nothingness or emptiness; that is, the thing rejected does not and cannot lead the enquiring mind to anything except the examination of something different; the mind itself is not educated in any positive sense; all it knows is that what has been examined will not do. In this sort of scepticism, in which everything examined is independent of any of its alternatives when rejected, one must 'wait to see whether something new comes along and what it is, in order to throw it too into the same empty abyss' (Hegel, *Phenomenology*, p. 51).

What then, does Hegel propose instead?

Hegel's method of doubt is based on the assumption that 'truth' and 'falsity' are not immutable essences existing in isolation from each other and having nothing in common. Truth is not a minted coin which is available in its ready-made form (Hegel, *Phenomenology*, p. 22). Instead, truth is to be approached step by step in a *developmental process* of consciousness which Hegel calls 'the journey of despair'. A proper scepticism has to be directed against consciousness *as such*, that is, against consciousness in any of its forms; it is to be directed against ideas, opinions, and thoughts whether of one's own or of an authority. Just as with Descartes, Hegel's scepticism was based on a complete rejection of previously presumed truth. But in contrast to Descartes, Hegel's rejection was not purely *negative*: it also had a positive content. The rejected form of consciousness gives rise to a new, more adequate form of consciousness. Thus, there is an inseparable unity between the old and the new, between the negative and positive content, and between the rejected and the newly accepted form of consciousness. Discussing this issue with respect to different philosophical systems, Hegel maintains that replacing one philosophical system by another does not mean that the previous system has been shown false while the new one is true. There is an element of truth embodied in each of the systems and each system only represents a step in the development towards truth:

... the bud disappears in the bursting-forth of the blossom, and one might say that the former is refuted by the latter; similarly, when the fruit appears, the blossom is shown up in its turn as a false manifestation of the plant, and the fruit now emerges as the truth of it instead. These forms are not just distinguished from one another, they also supplant one another as mutually incompatible. Yet at the same time their fluid nature makes them moments of an organic unity in which they not only do not conflict, but in which each is as necessary as the other; and this mutual necessity alone constitutes the life of the whole. (Hegel, *Phenomenology*, p. 2)

But what is important is that a bud can be transformed into something else only because the reality is transformed too: the bud uses or takes into itself the reality, that is, it takes nourishment from its environment in order to grow with a resulting transformation of *both* itself and the reality. The final product is a new unity, the blossom in *its* new reality.

Hegel's position concerning truth and falsity must not be interpreted as relativism in the sense that truth and falsity are relative to each other. In other words, Hegel is not saying that what is true in one context may be false in another. Such a position, as we pointed out earlier, was held by the romanticists who, just like Hegel, claimed that every new idea, new creation or social event was a product of certain historical conditions. But the romanticists saw social events as no more than consequences of the contexts in which they occurred. Hegel's developmental or *phenomenal* stages, however, are not just stages in which truth is relative to falsity. Every stage is a step towards a more adequate knowledge or reality and transcends the conditions under which it has arisen. The 'lower' steps in the acquisition of knowledge cannot be said to be false; rather, they are phenomena, that is, *inadequate* expressions of the truth. The truth is obscured in them because it is not revealed in its final form. The acquisition of truth has the character of an ascending process in which Absolute Truth is not to be found in isolated propositions but in the final system as an organic whole (Hegel, *Phenomenology*, p. 11).

The doctrine of the Absolute, one of the most important notions of Hegel's philosophical system of Absolute Idealism, has some similarities with the Christian notion of God. However, there are two important differences. In the first place, in contrast to the Christian God, Hegel's Absolute is wholly immanent in the world. Secondly, the Absolute is above all an endpoint of the process of becoming: 'Of the Absolute it must be said that it is essentially a *result*, that only in the *end* is it what it truly is; and that precisely in this consists its nature, viz. to be actual, subject, the spontaneous becoming of itself' (Hegel, *Phenomenology*, p. 11). To say that the Absolute is wholly immanent is to reject the duality of God and the world; Hegel's Absolute is itself the essence of the world constantly developing and unfolding its potentialities in the search for truth. Since the Absolute is wholly immanent in the world it reveals itself in different ways. The 'spontaneous becoming of itself' has been manifested in the history of nations (Hegel, *Philosophy of History*), in the history of philosophy (Hegel, *History of Philosophy*), and, above all, in the development of the human mind (Hegel, *Phenomenology of Spirit*). Thus, we do not need to dwell upon Hegel's Absolute, and instead we shall be concerned with one of the embodiments of the Absolute, the human mind. Phenomenology is the journey of the mind towards science. It is the process in which the mind gradually appears in various forms as it unfolds all its potentialities in the ascending process towards truth.

Phenomenology is not an expression of science in its definite and final form, but in its phenomena. This statement is of crucial importance because it wipes out the gap between scientific knowledge on the one hand, and non-scientific and pre-scientific kinds of knowledge on the other. According to Hegel, science is already included in the non- and pre-scientific kinds of knowledge in a primitive form. The progressive unfolding of science is Hegel's ever-recurring theme and analogies serve the purpose of clarifying this subject, as in the example of the various stages in the life of a fruit tree, already quoted. Science, in its final form, is related to its first beginnings as the oak tree is to the acorn (Hegel, *Phenomenology*, p. 7) and as the adult human is to the embryo. This last example is important since it contains the basis of Hegel's explanation of the notion of development:

> Though the embryo is indeed *in itself* a human being, it is not so *for itself*; this it only is as cultivated Reason, which has *made* itself into what it is *in itself*. (Hegel, *Phenomenology*, p. 12)

Hegel distinguishes here between two states: potentiality or being-in-itself and *actuality* or being-for-itself. Thus reason, understanding, imagination, and will are present in human beings as potentialities, even in the mother's womb as Descartes had already claimed. However, while for Descartes these potentialities became manifested if the senses were appropriately stimulated, it is not so for Hegel. To say that a child has a potentiality to reason is just the same as to say that he has no reason. 'Reason must become an object to itself. A man must become conscious of himself to study his reason as an object' (Hegel, *History of Philosophy*, I, p. 21). But to become an *object for himself* a human being must struggle through various phenomenal stages (cf. Chapter 8). The fundamental principle guiding the transformation from being-in-itself (potentiality) to being-for-itself (actuality) is not stimulation of the senses but the subject's *activity*. The real being of the mind is thus to act and through acting to become conscious of itself as an object. As Hegel puts it, 'the activity of Mind is to know itself. I am, immediately, but this I am only as a living organism; as Mind I am only in so far as I know myself' (Hegel, *History of Philosophy*, I, p. 32). It is implied that, to be an object for itself, mind has to make a clear division between 'the mind' and 'myself' and thus to establish the mind as external to itself. Hegel points out that this particular feature of mind, to postulate itself as both subject and object, gives the mind a distinctive place in nature.

So the mind, on its journey to knowledge gradually liberates itself from its less adequate forms such as bud-hood, acorn-hood, and embryo-hood, and replaces these potentialities by actual forms that are more adequate expressions of the truth. It is essential, though, that any more adequate expression of the truth follows from its previous form. The fundamental question that remains to be answered is how the mind knows that the new form is more adequate than the previous one. This important problem is the subject of the next chapter.

CHAPTER 8

The Development of Consciousness in Hegel's Phenomenology of Mind

Hegel defined consciousness very broadly. It ranged from such a simple form as the sense-certainty of a human being, on the one hand, to the self-consciousness of Absolute Spirit in its religious, cultural, and historical contexts, on the other. It is, however, only the first three chapters of Hegel's *Phenomenology of Spirit*, concerned with *Consciousness*, and section A of chapter 4 on *Self-consciousness*, that is of the most direct relevance to psychology, and therefore to this book. Moreover, as Taylor says, only the arguments of the first three chapters 'are self-authenticating and stand on their own, because they start from an undeniable beginning '(Taylor, 1975, p. 220). Taylor points out that the rest, that is, the major part of the *Phenomenology*, is based on arguments that are dependent on and interpretive of those included in the first three chapters, and cannot stand on its own. Section A of chapter 4 on *Self-consciousness*, however, is a direct continuation of the first three chapters. If we concentrate upon its *epistemological*, rather than its *historical*, character, then the arguments of Chapter 4A do stand on their own. They are arguments about the social, rather than the *individualistic*, nature of the mind, and about the social nature of the acquisition of knowledge. It is of no consequence for psychologists that these arguments have been inserted into a certain historical period, viz. that of master and slave. Since they are arguments about epistemology, they are basic in many different contexts, both historical and psychological, as we shall see in this and the next chapter.

Taken as a whole, the *Phenomenology* is immensely rich with various important psychological issues such as the fear of death, the problem of guilt, the problem of free will, the social psychology of power and control, human creativity and many others, which await future generations of psychologists who, no doubt, will find a great deal of inspiration in Hegel.

The objective of the present chapter, however, is to give only a limited account of *Consciousness* and *Self-consciousness* while avoiding, as far as possible, Hegel's complex terminology; to examine not only some aspects of the content of this part of the *Phenomenology* but also the *method* Hegel uses to explain the journey of consciousness towards truth; and finally, to highlight

116

the incommensurability of the Hegelian and Cartesian epistemologies so that the consequences of this incommensurability for the psychology of thought and language can be understood.

8.1 Consciousness: sense-certainty

Phenomenology is concerned with the acquisition of knowledge. Hegel shows that we do not acquire knowledge directly, but through an ascending process in which the cognizing mind gradually discards less adequate forms of knowledge and replaces them by more adequate forms. The cognizing mind ascends to more adequate forms by discovering contradictions in the existing forms of knowledge and then resolving them.

According to Hegel, the journey of the mind towards true knowledge starts with immediate apprehension of the object, with *sense-certainty*. The question is why Hegel chose this form of consciousness as the first step in the development of knowledge.

One possible answer might be that Hegel simply did what other philosophers and psychologists before him had always done. Apprehending the world by means of the senses appears, both to the psychologist and to the layman, to be the most natural and the most simple starting point.

Hegel's reason for starting the journey of consciousness with sense-certainty is, however, more complex. He wants to demonstrate the fundamental misconceptions of the traditional epistemology as well as its contradictory nature.

Sense-certainty is characterized by the *appearance* that consciousness is in direct contact with the objects of reality. Consciousness in this form apprehends an entity as soon as the senses are exposed to it. The senses are wholly passive in this process, and the object is known by *intuition*, that is by direct contact without any mediation by concepts. Comprehension and description are not involved because it is simply the *existence* of the entity that is registered. Sense-certainty, because it apparently consists of direct contact with an entity, appears to consciousness to be truth, providing it with the fullest and richest knowledge. In Part I of this book we pointed out that, in Descartes' epistemology, intuition was one of the two ways of apprehending true knowledge, and that the other, deduction, was based on intuition. Only clear and distinct ideas known by intuition provided knowledge that was certain. We had to be passive in order to allow intuitive knowledge of clear and distinct ideas to emerge from within ourselves.

Hegel maintains, however, that no adequate knowledge can be immediate or intuitive. Sense-certainty only appears to be the richest kind of knowledge, but in fact it is the poorest kind of knowledge because it is *unspeakable*. In the *Preface* to the *Phenomenology*, Hegel points out that it is the nature of human beings to be able to communicate and negotiate issues with one another (Hegel, *Phenomenology*, p. 43). However, sense-certainty, because it only relies upon sensory data coming from individual objects, is not communicable. This is for the following reasons.

118

Consciousness, even in the form of sense-certainty, naturally tends to *express* what it knows when it senses an entity. This happens, for example, when one picks up an object and points to it as 'this', or 'here', or 'now'. But pointing to an entity is all that sense-certainty is able to do, because registering the existence of an object, i.e. its *being*, is all that intuition of the immediacy of apprehension allows for.

But what happens if the truth of the 'this', 'here' or 'now' is frozen, for example by writing it down? Nothing can be lost by writing down the truth, says Hegel, because if you can write something down it means that you know it, for example: 'THIS is a tree' or 'NOW it is night'. These truths, however, disappear if we change 'here' and 'now'. We may turn our head and what was 'THIS is a tree' may now become 'THIS is a house'. Or, some hours pass and what was 'NOW it is night' may become 'NOW it is noon'. Thus Hegel says, one truth disappears in the other: if 'THIS is a house' is true, then 'THIS is a tree' (which it *was*) must be false.

It is important to understand that Hegel is *not* concerned in this passage with the triviality of time passing and turning one's head to see something different from a moment before. Hegel is addressing himself to a very important problem which arises from the fact that verbal language is used to refer to both universals and individual entities. Thus, the words 'this', 'here', 'now', and 'I' can apply to any entity or to any situation or to any person. However, when language is used in communication 'this', 'here', 'now', and 'I' are supposed to refer always to particular 'thises', 'heres', 'nows', which are determined by the context at the moment of communication. The problem for sense-certainty is that it is by means of verbal language that we refer to things and identify them. At the same time, however, words themselves represent universals, i.e. concepts that are applicable to many individual things. It is not possible simply to pick up an object and describe it in words that refer to nothing but that particular object. In other words, language has a capricious nature creating a conflict between 'what is meant' and 'what is said'. What is meant is an actual thing, object or individual, such as 'this page'. What is said, however, 'this page' applies not only to this page but to any page in any book. Therefore, the sensuous THIS that is meant *'cannot be reached* by language, which belongs to consciousness'. And consciousness itself is not an individual confined to pure immediacy of sense-certainty. It, too, is inherently universal (Hegel, *Phenomenology*, p. 66).

Hegel's point that the meanings of words refer to universals while when language is actually used words are meant to identify particular entities or situations, has reappeared recently in a slightly different form in the work of Wittgenstein (1953) and Rommetveit (1974). Rommetveit points out that deictic words such as 'this', 'that', 'here', and 'now' remain 'vacuous or at best only arbitrarily defined until the interpersonal speaker-to-listener coordinate of the act of speech has been determined as well' (Rommetveit, 1974, p. 36). For example, the intersubjectively established 'now' may mean either 'now in modern times' used by a history teacher, or it may mean 'now at this moment' as compared to 'a moment ago' or it may even encompass the whole history of mankind on the Earth. Analysing the use of deictic words, Rommetveit points to the social nature of language. 'This' serves the purpose of establishing identifying reference, something that is jointly attended to by both participants in communication. 'That', on the other hand, refers to what is already assumed by both participants at the moment it is uttered.

In the passage on sense-certainty, Hegel is only concerned with the problem created by words such as 'this', 'here', 'now', and 'I'. It is obvious, however, even in this passage, that he sees the problem of universals and individuals as a general problem in language. He implies that the symbolic function of language is reflected in the 'secret meaning of the eating of bread and the drinking of wine' in religious mysteries. These mysteries show that the sensory aspect of eating and drinking does not exhaust the complexity of the meanings of eating and drinking attributed to them by language users.

The passage on sense-certainty highlights Hegel's concern that, in order to have even the simplest kind of knowledge, human beings must have the ability to communicate it. If sense-certainty lays claims to knowledge, and indeed, to knowledge that is supposed to be certain, then it should be possible for this knowledge to be shared publicly. But sense-certainty cannot be shared publicly because it is, as we have seen, unspeakable. 'This, 'here', 'now', and 'I', although they are supposed to mean individuals, actually express universals. And, 'consequently, what is called the unutterable is nothing else than the untrue, the irrational, what is merely meant [but is not actually expressed]' (Hegel, *Phenomenology*, p. 66).

Taylor (1975) points out that Hegel's argument was not concerned only with providing grounds for supposing that it is impossible to have unmediated knowledge of a particular entity. Equally important, Hegel was concerned to demonstrate that it is *human experience itself* that shows that particular entities can be grasped only through mediation of universals.

Sense-certainty thus cannot provide one with adequate knowledge. As Hegel puts it,

If I want to help out language—which has the divine nature of directly reversing the meaning of what is said, of making it into something else, and thus not letting what is meant *get into words* at all—*by pointing out* this bit of paper, experience teaches me what the truth of sense-certainty in fact is: I point it out as a 'Here', which is a Here of other Heres, or is in its own self a 'simple togetherness of many Heres'; i.e. it is a universal. I take it up then as it is in truth, and instead of knowing something immediate I take the truth of it, or *perceive* it. (Hegel, *Phenomenology*, p. 66)

Since language necessarily makes use of concepts, we are, in fact, no longer concerned with sense-certainty but with *objects with properties*, that is, with *percepts*.

But before we move to perception as a higher form of consciousness, let us attempt to discover the precise nature of Hegel's *universals, particulars, and individuals*.

8.2 Universals, particulars, and individuals

Universals were defined in the Cartesian paradigm as common features between objects in virtue of which objects can be classified and categorized (cf. *Encyclopedia of Philosophy*, Vol. 8, pp. 194–206). For example, 'man', 'horse', or 'rose' all represented universals. Identifying objects as 'roses' meant pointing out what is 'common' among roses and distinguishing roses from non-roses. Similarly, Chomskyan linguistics has been concerned to identify universals in languages. This has meant discovering 'common' syntactic or semantic features among languages. For example, all languages can express tenses; all languages can express various grammatical relationships such as subject and predicate, verb and object, or modifier and noun.

Hegel maintains, however, that universals are more than just common features among objects. In fact, Hegel says that universals that are nothing more than common features among objects are 'mere phantoms and shadows' because all they amount to are empty and abstract generalizations. As Hegel puts it,

the universal . . . is not a mere sum of features common to several things, confronted by a particular which enjoys an existence of its own. It is, on the contrary, self-particularising or self-specifying and with undimmed clearness finds itself at home in it antithesis. For the sake both of cognition and of our practical conduct, it is of the utmost importance that the real universal should not be confused with what is merely held in common. (Hegel, *Encyclopedia*, p. 292)

Let us attempt to interpret this rather difficult passage. Hegel claims that the universal is a real universal only to the extent that it realizes itself in a particular. However, the aim of Cartesian science was to identify universals as existing independently of particulars. Universals were stable, common, and relatively unchanging characteristics of things. Particulars, the specific characteristics of this or that individual thing, were ignored. In fact, one of the main aspects of Hegel's criticism of traditional logic was that it ignored particulars. Traditional logic supposed that concepts such as colour, plant, animal, and so on were 'to be arrived at by neglecting the particular features which distinguish the different colours, plants, and animals from each other, and by retaining those common to them all' (Hegel, *Encyclopedia*, p. 292).

Hegel makes a distinction between *universals*, *particulars*, and *individuals* (Hegel, *Encyclopedia*, pp. 291–7, *Science of Logic*, pp. 601–22). Without going into any detail of his complex system, we may say that the difference between a particular and an individual is that a particular is a manifestation of a universal in an individual entity. A universal is real only insofar as it realizes itself in a particular that is characteristic of an individual thing. By saying 'this is a rose' I identify an individual. But in saying 'this is a rose' I am not simply saying that this individual plant has universal features such as *redness, thorniness, a certain kind of scent, a certain kind of texture of the leaves*, and so on, and that it is because of the presence of these features, common to all roses, that I recognize this individual object as a rose. Rather, what I am saying is that 'this is a rose' because I recognize certain universals such as *redness, thorniness, scent*, etc., as revealing or expressing themselves in a particular way in this individual object. Thus, although all roses have certain features in common (those features that appear in the dictionary definition of a rose), each of these common or *universal* features reveals itself in a *particular* way in an *individual* rose. For example, although *redness* is a common feature of many roses, the particular redness of the individual rose differs from all other rednesses, although the naked eye may be unable to perceive any such differences. Commonality of features is expressed in an individual in a particular and unrepeatable way. The particular, as Hegel says above, is the *antithesis* of the universal: there is no universal without a particular and there is no particular without a universal. In forming an inseparable unity they together form an individual object. As for the difference between what is merely 'in common' and what is 'truly universal', Hegel gives the example of Rousseau's Social Contract, in which the laws of the state spring from the universal will, but they need not be the will of each individual person. 'The general will is the notion of the will: and the laws are the special clauses of this will and based upon the notion of it' (Hegel, *Encyclopedia*, p. 293).

The issue of universals and particulars is relevant to theories of *word meanings*. As we have seen earlier, recent theories of meaning based on the presuppositions of the Cartesian paradigm attempt to decompose the meanings of words into semantic markers or semantic features, i.e. into universals (cf. Chapter 4). Particulars were excluded from such theories.

In contrast, Rommetveit (1968, 1971, 1974) argues that isolated words have only *meaning potentialities* rather than full meanings. The only way these universals or potentialities can be brought into action and obtain full meaning is through their use in verbal communication in particular situations. Rommetveit distinguishes between two kinds of meaning potentialities: *core* and *fringe* meaning potentialities. While the core meaning potentialities of the word 'man' refer to such basic categories as *malehood* or *adulthood*, fringe meaning potentialities are those that are contingently associated with the core meanings. For example, *courage* or *size of body* may represent fringe meaning potentialities with respect to *adulthood*. The theory can be represented as in Figure 8.1. Areas *a, b*, and *c* represent the *core meaning* potentialities, which seem to correspond to Katz and Fodor's (1963) semantic markers. The external areas *a', b'*, and *c'* represent *fringe meaning* potentialities. Different contexts activate different meaning potentialities whether belonging to the core or to the fringe. Thus, for example, questions such as

'Who opened the door, a woman or a man?'
'Who opened the door, a boy or a man?'
'Who opened the door, a dog or a man?'

might activate core potentialities such as 'MALE', 'ADULT' or 'HUMAN'

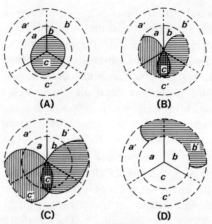

Figure 8.1 Core and fringe meaning potentialities. From Rommetveit (1968), *Words, Meanings and Messages*. Reproduced by permission of R. Rommetveit

respectively (see (B) in Figure 8.1). On the other hand, a question such as

'Can a man open the door?'

might, under certain conditions, activate fringe meaning potentialities such as 'STRENGTH' or 'COURAGE' (see (D) in Figure 8.1). Thus, the meaning of the word MAN is not a collection of semantic markers, i.e. a collection of universals, but a particular context determines which of the meaning potentialities are activated and what their particular expressions are in that particular context.

We can summarize the differences between the Cartesians and Hegelians by saying that, while the focus of attention of the Cartesians is to discover the common features of entities, the Hegelians are concerned to discover the particular expressions of common features in particular situations or in particular individuals. But do not these two focuses eventually amount to the same thing? Consider, for example, Bruner's card experiment discussed in Chapter 4 (cf. p. 48). The task for the subject was to decide in each individual case whether or not that particular individual was an instance of the concept. The Hegelians, however, do not base their decision-making on the counting of perceptual features out of context. A particular context makes it possible to say:

'This man is not an adult'

or

'This woman is a man'.

In such a case we do not have in mind just the size of the body or the sex, but a set of features that have developed in their socio-historical context; in Rommetveit's theory a particular context activates the fringe meaning potentialities and enables one to say things that, *in vacuo*, i.e. without context, would be judged by speakers of the language as semantically anomalous.

But the critic of Hegel is still not satisfied. Does the Hegelian idea of universals, particulars, and individuals amount to anything more than the triviality of saying that all objects of a certain kind have some things in common while some things are different? In fact, the whole idea seems to be rather similar to the old Aristotelian doctrine of *substances* and their *accidental properties*. According to this doctrine, substances such as *a man, horse*, or *rose* are to be distinguished from their accidents such as *qualities, activities, relationships* and so on.

Hegel's universals, though, are more than this. They are dynamic, active, and develop through a constant antithesis with their particulars. In what sense do universals develop through antithesis with particulars?

The development of universals through antithesis with particulars is not restricted to the development of concepts. Darwin demonstrated the same principle in evolutionary biology. The basic idea of Darwin's theory was that particular features that originally characterized an individual and differentiated it from other individuals might, under certain environmental conditions, develop into universal features, i.e. become the features determining a species. For example, when certain animals were changing their diet and became ant-eaters they developed a special kind of a tongue that flicks in and out of the mouth. The Darwinian explanation of the emergence of such a specialized tongue is that only those ancestors of ant-eaters who had a particular feature enabling them to develop the kind of tongue necessary to obtain their food, had survived. Thus, a particular feature eventually became a universal, i.e. a feature common to species.

The importance of particulars is also obvious in the development of the meanings of words. Numerous examples from the etymologies of words could be given. Let us take one example.

The Czech word 'ROBOTA' originally meant 'the dutiful hard drudgery of Czech peasants on noblemen's properties'. The meaning potentialities would include universals such as 'HUMAN', 'ACTIVE', 'UNPLEASANT', 'WILL-LESS', and so on. It was probably the 'WILL-LESS' aspect that led Karel Čapek, a Czech playwright, to associate it with 'AUTOMATIC' or 'MECHANICAL' or both. In his play R. U. R. (Rossum's Universal Robots) Čapek made the Robots mechanical men and women acting automatically without any will of their own. Today the Oxford English Dictionary gives the meaning of the word 'robot' as 'a machine devised to function in place of a living agent; one which acts automatically or with a minimum of external impulse'. Thus 'AUTOMATIC' and 'MECHANICAL' which were particular features of the robots in Čapek's play, became part of the definition of the English word 'robot'. In other words a particular feature, applied for a particular purpose in a particular context, became a universal.

124

It is thus obvious that for Hegel a universal is historically determined or peculiar to a certain historical epoch. Universals are not given once and for ever:

The universal in its true and comprehensive meaning is a thought which, as we know, cost thousands of years to make it enter into the consciousness of men. (Hegel, *Encyclopedia*, p. 293)

Hegel goes on to say that the true recognition of universality did not appear until the arrival of Christianity. Only Christianity created the universal God and only Christianity created a man in his true universality. A truly universal man could appear only when man was recognized to be of infinite worth and to have infinite rights. Hegel maintains that it was recognition of man in this sense that made it possible for slavery to be abandoned in Europe. Only in Christianity did people become equal in a fundamental sense, and therefore recognized as persons. And, as Hegel said, the principle of personality is universality. The master does not look at the slave as a manifestation of this universality in a particular. In other words, the master does not look at a slave as another self. The slave's 'I' belongs to his master.

The transformation of one universal into another one is, according to Hegel, logically determined. The mind of man is never at rest, and his world is a dynamic whole which is constantly renewing itself. In its formation

[the mind] matures slowly and quietly into its new shapes, dissolving bit by bit the structure of its previous world . . . The gradual crumbling that left unaltered the face of the whole is cut short by a sunburst which, in one flash, illuminates the features of the new world. (Hegel, *Phenomenology*, pp. 6–7)

In other words the development proceeds through *quantitative* growth of a particular into a new *quality* of a universal. This idea of the change of quantity into a new quality reminds one of Kuhn's paradigm shifts and scientific revolutions. It is the accumulation of anomalies in the period of normal science that finally leads to a revolution. As more and more cases are found which resist explanation within the existing paradigm, the paradigm collapses, that is, quantity is replaced by a new quality, which manifests itself in the creating of a new paradigm. Such a new paradigm represents, in Hegel's words, a new universal.

8.3 Consciousness: perception

Hegel claims that the starting point not only of our everyday consciousness but also of Kantian epistemology and of the natural sciences, is *perception*. In perception, knowledge of entities is not acquired through immediate apprehension, but is mediated: consciousness observes, compares, reflects upon single apperceptions, and subsumes them under categories in order to obtain universal and necessary truths.

But a difficulty arises again. *What is a thing*? How are we to reconcile the universal and particular properties of things?

There are two basic possibilities as to how to answer this question. First, there is the Lockean answer: a thing is a *collection* of sense data (or ideas). The fact that we perceive such a collection of sense data as a unity is due to our mental activity. For example, *salt* is a simple HERE which is at the same time a collection of properties or universals: it is white, and *also* tart, and *also* cubical in shape, and *also* of a certain specific gravity and so on (Hegel, *Phenomenology*, p. 68), all these existing together in a single HERE. But HERE is the only respect in which all of these properties interpenetrate. Otherwise, they are completely separate and independent of each other. Thus

... the whiteness does not affect the cubical shape, and neither affects the tart taste, etc.; on the contrary, since each is itself a simple relating of self to self it leaves the others alone, and is connected with them only by the indifferent ALSO. This ALSO is thus the pure universal itself, or the medium, the 'thinghood' which holds them together in this way. (Hegel, *Phenomenology*, pp. 68–9)

In other words, the only relationship between universals such as whiteness, tart taste, etc., is their togetherness in the here and now. This togetherness is expressed by the word 'ALSO', i.e. salt is white and also tart and also cubical, etc.

Alternatively, the thing may be assumed by consciousness to be a unity, or, as Hegel says, a *One*. If anything turns up in the process of perception which seems to contradict the one-ness of things, it must be entirely due to our mental activity rather than to the thing. Thus, the thing has a specific colour only to *our eyes*, a specific taste to our *tongue*, a certain texture to our *touch*, and so on. The entire diversity of properties comes not from the thing but from us (Hegel, *Phenomenology*, p. 72). In the process of perception, consciousness is unable to maintain continuously either of these positions but swings constantly from the position of 'Also' to the position of 'One' and back again. Thus, at one moment a thing presents itself as a unity and therefore its essence is one-ness. At the next moment, consciousness in the process of perception becomes aware of the diversity of the thing's properties (bitterness, sweetness, circularity, etc.) which are universal, and which therefore transcend the particularity of the thing. An individual thing certainly is radically different from the universal and unaffected by it, but at the same time is related to the universal. Thus, there is a continuing contradiction between individual things and their particular properties which are objects of perception, on the one hand, and between universals that are supposed to be the essential natures of things, on the other.

So how can the problem of diversity and unity be solved? Consciousness attempts to solve it on its 'journey of despair' by penetrating into the essence of things. Progressing from the pointing and immediate apprehension of sense-certainty, to the perceived contradiction of the essential natures of things, consciousness now attempts to penetrate into their inner being. But this stage no longer has a perceptual character.

8.4 Consciousness: understanding

Understanding (*Verstand*, sometimes translated as 'intellect'), is the next form of consciousness on its journey to truth. Consciousness now attempts to go beyond the sensible characteristics of things. It now believes that the essences of things cannot be grasped by perception, and therefore seeks to penetrate into the inner (unperceived) being of things.

What is perceived is only *appearance*, and consciousness now believes that underlying appearance is an unchanging insensible world which explains all the flux of appearance. It believes it to be the task of science to discover this insensible world. At the level of perception, we find a perpetual play of forces, but these forces are really the manifestation of Force driven back into itself and Force expressing itself. In more modern language we would presumably speak of potential energy and kinetic energy, and say that the purpose of science was to penetrate behind perceptual phenomena and study the nature of Energy itself. But it appears that these manifestations of Force cannot be regarded as a mere flux of appearances, interactions, and effects. Instead these manifestations of Force are governed by *laws*, the *stable* images of unstable appearances (Hegel, *Phenomenology*, p. 90). Thus, the insensible world is an inert *world of laws*. For example, in a single occurrence of lightning we observe the play of electrical forces. But we see this single occurrence as embodying the laws of electricity. Electrical Force (Energy) is so constituted that it expresses itself as opposite electrical charges, but then there is electrical discharge, and force withdraws back into itself. And all this occurs according to law. But what kind of explanation is it? Consciousness finds out that laws do not explain anything; they only *redescribe* phenomena rather than deepen our understanding:

The single occurrence of lightning, e.g., is apprehended as a universal, and this universal is enunciated as the *law* of electricity; the 'explanation' then condenses the *law* into *Force* as the essence of the law . . . *Force is constituted exactly the same as law*; there is said to be no difference whatever between them . . . both have the *same* content, the *same* constitution. (Hegel, *Phenomenology*, pp. 94–5)

In the law of electrical discharge there is no reference to any single occurrence, and the same abstraction from the specific, and therefore disappearance of sensuous content, occurs at a deeper level. Thus, for example, underlying the laws of fall, planetary motion, and the tides is the law of universal gravitation which contains no reference to any of these phenomena. Moreover, a plurality of laws can itself be subsumed under a more general Law which, because it is not concerned with any of these specific laws, expresses no content at all. It is just the bare concept of law. Hegel labours this point because it is here that he finally gets to the crunch of the problem. All that consciousness does in its search after truth is to move in circles. Nothing new is contributed to the understanding of the object. Consciousness only pretends to explain something while explaining nothing; it only pretends to say something different from what it said before while repeating the same thing: 'In the Thing itself this movement gives rise to nothing new; it comes into consideration [only] as a movement of the Understanding' (Hegel, *Phenomenology*, p. 95).

Consciousness finally realizes that it cannot penetrate beyond appearances and that all that it has been doing so far is in fact to experience only *itself* rather than objects outside. This is a new step that consciousness is now taking. It turns its attention upon itself, it itself becomes the object of its study.

8.5 Self-consciousness

The section on self-consciousness starts with Hegel pointing out that so far, in all the modes of knowledge through which consciousness has passed, the truth has been sought outside consciousness itself. In other words, the forms of knowledge discussed so far, sense-certainty, perception, and understanding, have all been concerned with objects outside consciousness, that is, with sensory *data*, the *objects* of perception, and the *objects* of natural science. All of these modes were based on Cartesian epistemology (in our broad sense, including rationalism, empiricism, and Kantianism). But it is through its experience that consciousness now realizes the untrue nature of these 'truths'. It is clear to it now that, passing through sense-certainty, perception, under-standing, force, and law, it has, in fact, been concerned not with alien objects in an outside world, but with *itself*.

But what should we make of this claim? It means that consciousness has realized that the ways in which an object is apprehended are determined not by the object itself but *by the level of the experience of consciousness in relationship to that object*. Although it is not experience in the Kantian sense (cf. Chapter 4), there is something in Kant's subject–object relationship that anticipates Hegel's views. In contrast to other philosophers of the Cartesian paradigm, Kant introduced *activity* into the subject–object relationship. While the senses, because they are passive, only provide us with data, the synthetic unity of apperception is due to 'an act of the self-activity of the subject' (Kant, *Critique of Pure Reason*, B 130), and combines the sensory data into representations of objects. It is through the synthetic unity of apperception that the human mind gives laws to nature. However, we must remember that Kant's synthetic unity of apperception provides us only with appearances, not with things-in-themselves.

But Hegel goes far beyond the Kantian subject–object relationship. The Kantian thing-in-itself completely disappears as Hegel produces a new kind of epistemology. We can divide this process of consciousness into two stages: first, in order to know an object consciousness attempts to identify with it; secondly, this process of identification is only possible if consciousness becomes cons-cious of itself.

Let us take the first step: consciousness has now realized that in trying to comprehend an object it has been analysing its own products and creations, and in order to understand its own products and creations, i.e. *itself*, it now attempts to turn the object into part of itself.

Taylor (1975) points out that for Hegel it is *integrity* that consciousness is aiming at. What is this Hegelian integrity? It is the striving of consciousness for *identification* with the object. This can be achieved by devouring the object, consuming it, penetrating it through and through, or making it part of itself. Integrity, as Taylor points out, cannot be achieved by inner retreat, in which consciousness cuts itself off from the bodily. It means activity, penetrating into the world, making it part of itself, whether in the physical sense (eating, breathing, damaging, destroying, making), or in the mental sense (understanding, reasoning, loving, sympathizing, empathizing).

The importance of this section of the *Phenomenology* is that it is here that a new epistemology begins to emerge: consciousness can achieve integrity, consciousness can identify with the world, consciousness can understand the world, only by *acting* upon it.

Taylor (1975, p. 149) maintains that 'underlying this extremely far-reaching notion of integrity is the Hegelian preoccupation with fate'. It is because of its fear of death that consciousness strives for integrity and makes itself death-less through its creations:

The opposition which is seemingly the most insurmountable of all is that between action and fate, between what men make of themselves which has a certain meaning for them, on one hand, and the seemingly senseless things which happen to them, of which death is the ultimate culmination, on the other. Hegel will not be satisfied until this dualism is overcome, and it is this aspiration which the drive for integrity reflects. (Taylor, 1975, p. 149)

The striving for identification with an object is a process during which consciousness realizes that it is not simply *any kind of object* with which it wishes to identify: *not any kind of identification leads to self-consciousness*. It must be a specific kind of object. Let us take the second step in Hegel's analysis to explain what kind of object leads to self-consciousness.

The striving of consciousness for identification starts with *Desire*. We can see in Hegel's analysis of Desire the twist that his epistemology has taken. Cartesian epistemology has been concerned to discover the nature of things, i.e. the truth about them, by delving into them, contemplating them. But cognitive processes concerned with finding out the truth about objects can never reveal the self:

The man who contemplates is 'absorbed' by what he contemplates: the 'knowing subject' 'loses' himself in the object that is known. Contemplation reveals the object, not the subject. The object, and not the subject, is what shows itself to him in and by—or better, as—the act of knowing. (Kojève, 1969, p. 3)

Such absorption in the object, however, is interrupted by Desire. It could be any physical or biological desire in which the person realizes his own needs. Hegel points out that life is activity and to live means to satisfy one's desires. Life is experienced as Desire: it is through desires that the subject realizes the discrepancy between the world as it is and the world he would like to have. Life can continue only if desires are satisfied and the only alternative to satisfying desires is death. As desires can only be satisfied by acting upon objects, for example, drinking water, eating other organisms, protecting oneself from the cold by wearing clothes, and so on, the unity of the subject and object manifests itself from the very beginning in activity and not in passivity. Objects which satisfy one's desires are not things for contemplation but things to be acted upon. But these kinds of desire, that is desires in the physical or biological sense, are only a necessary part of human activity and are not sufficient. Lower forms of life have these kinds of desire only, and through these they secure the continuation of life, that is, preserve themselves. But biological desires lead only to the maintenance of life, they do not lead to self-consciousness. Self-consciousness does not develop through the transformation of object (food, water) into subject in the biological sense.

8.6 Master and slave

The basis of Hegel's social epistemology is contained in the passage entitled *Independence and Dependence of Self-consciousness: Lordship and Bondage* (Hegel, *Phenomenology*, pp. 111–19).

The main idea of this passage is the following. To become self-conscious one must try to identify with an object that is not inferior to one's consciousness. And physical objects as well as non-human organisms *are* inferior in the sense that they do not have the same power of will and cannot exercise the same kind of control as human consciousness does. In other words, they are good enough to be made use of but not good enough to compete with. It is only another consciousness or, we can now say, self-consciousness, that can fulfil such a task. Self-consciousness can develop only through interaction with another self-consciousness: '*Self-consciousness achieves its satisfaction only in another self-consciousness* . . . 'I' that is 'We' and 'We' that is 'I' . . . they *recognize* themselves as *mutually recognizing* one another' (Hegel, *Phenomenology*, pp. 110 and 112). These statements of Hegel's represent not only an epistemology of action, but also a social epistemology.

Mutual recognition of one human being by another one, however, does not occur naturally in the process of anthropogenesis. It is achieved only through the struggle of one consciousness against another. In the natural relationship of one consciousness towards another, each treats the other as a physical object. Each consciousness, in order to overcome this relationship of mutual inequality, must raise its relationship to the other consciousness from that of inferiority to that of equality. Only in the relationship of equality can consciousness become self-consciousness.

Thus the first attempt of consciousness to deal with other consciousness is in the same way that they have dealt with non-human organisms. They do not recognize each other as self-consciousness, or, to use Hegel's terms, they have not yet exposed themselves as self-consciousnesses. Each is imprisoned in its own self, 'certain of its own self, but not of the other, and therefore its own self-certainty still has no truth' (Hegel, *Phenomenology*, p. 113). At this stage, they attempt to cancel each other, or, in Hegel's words, 'to cancel the otherness', by causing the death of the other, simply by negating him. Thus, a life-and-death struggle for mutual recognition arises first. Each consciousness risks its own life in order to negate the other. This struggle has a most important consequence:

It is only through staking one's life that freedom is won . . . The individual who has not risked his life may well be recognized as a *person*, but he has not attained to the truth of this recognition as an independent self-consciousness. (Hegel, *Phenomenology*, p. 114)

Staking one's life is a recurrent theme in Hegel's writing. For Hegel, it has a purifying value and for this reason he even goes so far as to talk of the importance of wars in human history. Wars shake consciousness, which would otherwise sink 'into merely natural existence', making it aware of the universal. But it would be wrong to interpret Hegel as a warlike philosopher. In talking about the necessity of fear of death, he is concerned with deeply moral and human issues. Seeing others suffering and dying and risking one's own life brings one face to face with the reality of one's own mortality and the inevitability of death. A human being has to go through such disturbing experiences personally in order to grow as a person, to empathize truly with others in such experiences, and thus to become fully self-conscious. Hegel thus expresses his deep psychological insight that if indifference towards others, shallowness of feelings, addiction to immediate pleasures, and easily obtained 'truths' permanently overtake human minds there is not much future left for mankind. Present social psychology, of course, is becoming more and more aware of the essential nature of these problems. Research into bystander apathy (Latané and Darley, 1970; Bickman, 1975), lack of personal responsibility, failure in doctor–patient communication, and weaknesses in the counsellor–counsellee relationship, all point to lack of empathy, the attempt to avoid responsibility for one's actions, and the treating of other human beings as physical objects, and therefore to the inevitable stunting of human personality.

According to Hegel, it is in the life-and-death struggle that two self-consciousnesses recognize each other as equal, and the one who wins expects respect from the other. However, the one who dies cannot recognize the one who stays alive. Therefore, a life-and-death struggle in which one self-consciousness is negated by death does not solve the tension between two self-consciousnesses. In order to achieve mutual recognition, *both* self-consciousnesses must remain alive.

The struggle thus takes a new form, that of master and slave, which Hegel inserts into a definite historical period. The following point is important. Since Hegel has chosen a particular historical epoch to clarify his ideas, it has often been forgotten by both his followers and his enemies that the issue—the struggle for recognition—is a general *human* issue rather than an issue of a particular epoch in human history. It has often been forgotten that the issue is epistemological and psychological rather than historical and political. True, it is

historical, but it is so only in the sense that it has occurred in anthropogenesis—
or in human phylogenesis—and that it appears, in its modified form, in human
ontogenesis.

In the relationship between the master and slave, only the master was free:
he had power, satisfied his need, destroyed, and consumed things. The slave,
however, was dependent on him, having no choice and freedom. He could learn
skills, dominate his physical environment, and create things, but he had to
struggle for the recognition by his master of his human dignity. He lived in
mortal fear of the master (we can see the same theme, the fear of death, coming
up here again). But it was this fear that taught him to value the products of his
work and to discipline and control himself. Through this fear and his own
creations he became conscious of himself as a free human being and demanded
that his master recognize him as such. The master, on the other hand, did not
look on the slave as an equal partner in the battle. He tried to get products from
him to humiliate him rather than recognize him as another self-consciousness.
But because of his inability to recognize the slave as another self-consciousness
he himself could not satisfy the needs of his own self-consciousness: there was
nobody equal to him who would recognize him. His recognition by the slave did
not count because it was only recognition by someone or *something* that, in his
eyes, was lower than himself. The slave, on the other hand, gained, because
there was meaning to his life and an aim: to become free and equal to his
master, and to realize himself in his own activity.

In sum, one cannot achieve self-recognition at the expense of the other.
Recognition has to be mutual if it is to be true and satisfactory recognition in
the sense that it leads to personal growth. And a struggle and conflict between
consciousnesses are for Hegel a logical necessity for the development of
self-consciousness.

The slave's very existence lies in the formation of things and thus humanizing
them. In this process the slave himself changes and realizes his own freedom
with respect to the things he creates and his own fate. It is in his creative power
that he realizes his own value. As Taylor (1975, p. 156) emphasizes, his activity
is the activity of an *embodied subject*. Activity penetrates the whole subject.
Here again we see the essential difference between the Cartesian and Hegelian
accounts of the acquisition of knowledge. Cartesian knowledge is pre-
programmed and except for this pre-programming there is no drive in the
subject. The programme can be separated from its embodiment. Machines
and algorithmic programs do not experience the fear of death, nor do they
experience satisfaction from creativity. However, it is not only personal growth
that one experiences through activity. As Taylor points out, and as we shall see
in Chapter 10 when discussing Rubinstein's work, intellectual and conceptual
development also arise from practical activity:

Conceptual thinking arises out of the learned ability to transform things. We learn to know
the world of material reality, and ultimately our own minds, in trying to bend this matter to
our design. Conceptual thought grows out of this in exchange. (Taylor, 1975, p. 157)

Although in the passage on the master and slave Hegel does not discuss the role of language in the struggle for recognition, he does so in other parts of the *Phenomenology*. It is through language that one recognizes the other as equal to oneself. And, just as important, it is by language that the *ego* is separated from *itself*, and therefore becomes an object to itself.

The Cartesian *pure I*, immersed in its subjectivity and withdrawn into contemplation, can never reach real existence, because it does not exist for others. It is in speech, Hegel says, that self-consciousness as such comes into existence so that it exists for others.

The 'I' is this particular 'I'—but equally the *universal* 'I': its manifesting is also at once the externalization and vanishing of *this* particular 'I', and as a result the 'I' remains in its universality. (Hegel, *Phenomenology*, pp. 308–9)

We can thus see the theme of universal and particular discussed earlier recurring again. One can become a real self only through a universal self and a universal self manifests itself in individual selves. It is through the power of language, revealing itself in culture, ethical order, law, art, and religion, that single self-consciousnesses become aware of themselves as the expression of the universal self.

From the point of view of social psychology there are two main themes in Hegel's analysis of self-consciousness: first, the importance of recognition for human beings, and, secondly, the importance of activity and creativity in the acquisition of knowledge. These two Hegelian themes have been emerging in various forms in social, clinical, and developmental psychology for some time and, quite probably, without the knowledge of the authors concerned that they have been reflecting Hegel's philosophy. In the rest of this chapter we shall briefly point to these Hegelian themes in psychology, while a detailed discussion with respect to thought and language is the subject of the two subsequent chapters.

8.7 Man's search for recognition

We pointed out earlier that according to Hegel self-consciousness achieves satisfaction only in another self-consciousness, i.e. if two self-consciousnesses 'recognize themselves as mutually recognizing one another' (Hegel, *Phenomenology*, p. 112). The same idea has been expressed by Buber (1962) who maintains that two essential features characterize human beings: first, every human being *wishes to be confirmed* by other human beings as what he is and what he can become; and, secondly, human beings have the innate capacity to confirm other human beings in this way. It is speech above all that makes it possible for us either to confirm or disconfirm each other as equal partners. In a genuine conversation, whether aimed at education of both parties or at an increase of emotional closeness, each participant acknowledges the other as equal, they share control over what is being said and what it means. In Buber's words, a genuine conversation is based on the acceptance of the independence and *otherness* of both participants. While animals can call out to others, words and silences in human communication have the function of creating or of adjusting social distances according to situation. Thus, words and silences serve as signs as to whether and to what extent one speaker confirms or disconfirms the listener. Buber maintains that actual humanity exists only insofar as the capacity to confirm and to be confirmed is exercized

The effort for mutual recognition between partners may take different forms and degrees according to the *aims* of recognition. In this respect such apparently diverse activities as love and empathy, on the one hand, and hatred and struggle for power, on the other, are two sides of the same coin.

Concerning the former, the greater the emotional dependence on, admiration or care for a person, the higher the desire to be recognized by him. Thus empathy, one of the essential features of successful human communication, is acquired through one's desire to satisfy another person's desires and needs. Kojève (1969), analysing Hegel's contribution to the psychology of desires, highlights the difference between animal and human desires: while animal desires are based on the physiological and biological needs of the individual, human desires are social desires because they are directed to *the desires of others*. In this sense they transform human reality into a social and historical reality, making human history the *history of desired Desires*:

Thus, in the relationship between man and woman, for example, Desire is human only if the one desires, not the body, but the Desire of the other; if he wants 'to possess' or 'to assimilate' the Desire taken as Desire—that is to say, if he wants to be 'desired' or 'loved', or rather 'recognized' in his human value, in his reality as a human individual. Likewise, Desire directed toward a natural object is human only to the extent that it is 'mediated' by the Desire of another directed toward the same object: it is human to desire others' desire, because they desire it. Thus an object perfectly useless from the biological point of view (such as a medal, or the enemy's flag) can be desired because it is the object of others' desires. Such a Desire can only be a human Desire, and human reality, as distinguished from animal reality, is created only by action that satisfies such Desires: human history is the history of desired Desires. (Kojève, 1969, p. 6)

If, on the other hand, consciousness realizes that there is no chance of achieving recognition and therefore identification in the spiritual sense, love and empathy may be transformed into the more primitive form of desire, 'cancelling the otherness' by destroying it. This, again, can be achieved either spiritually by love being changed into hatred, or physically by killing the other partner, as Othello did.

So how can the other person be disconfirmed? There are a number of different strategies by which disconfirmation can be achieved, ranging from non-respondence at all to responding inappropriately, not to the point. Let us take Laing's (1971) example of a disconfirmatory act characterized by being irrelevant. By relevance, Laing means acting to the point, i.e. responding to the focus of the message rather than to its fringe. Thus a child might communicate to his mother his pleasure at finding a big fat worm, while she might respond by expressing her displeasure at his dirty hands. But it is not the fact that she responds with displeasure to the child's pleasure that makes her response disconfirmatory. It is the fact that she does not respond to the point: the child's focus is the worm, her focus is dirt. This disconfirmatory act is based on *ignoring* the child's focus and thus derogating it as unimportant. Consequently, such an act derogates the person himself as unimportant, as unequal. Laing suggests that disconfirmatory acts might characterize whole patterns of family interactions in schizophrenic families. Moreover, some interaction patterns might be characterized by pseudo-confirmation or pretence of confirmation. This may be a characteristic feature not only of communications in which 'words are not meant' but also of communications confirming a false self. For example, a child may be confirmed by his parents as a non-agent, or led to develop guilt feelings for not loving his parents enough, and so on. More generally, this kind of disconfirmation ignores the other participant's point of view, his opinions, beliefs, and values, and a disconfirmatory act degrades either privately or publicly what is highly valuable in the eyes of the bearer of such mental possessions and spiritual creations.

A continuous failure to be recognized by important others may lead both to deviance and mental illness. Bateson *et al.* (1956) have shown that uncertainty with respect to whether or not one is recognized as a human being, produced by repeatedly being given two contradictory messages at the same time, so called 'double-bind' messages, may lead to schizophrenia. For example, a child may be kissed by his mother but her cold and uninterested face may signal that in fact she does not love the child. In this way the child, who is physically and emotionally dependent, has been given a double-bind message of non-recognition. The constant disconfirmation of maternal love implying a disconfirmation of his humanity may eventually lead to a mental breakdown characterized by a total loss of faith in communication. As Rommetveit puts it,

... the schizophrenic's characteristic withdrawal from 'ordinary reality' is, when viewed in such an ontogenetic perspective, a withdrawal from any kind of temporarily shared social reality. The basic prerequisites for normal human communication seem to have collapsed. His grasp of reality fails in the sense that he has no faith whatsoever that other people share his perspective on states of affairs. (Rommetveit, 1974, p. 53)

Everyone who *feels* dependent, in some respect, or has an inferiority complex of some kind, can be easily disconfirmed. Hegel's slave felt dependent economically and politically. But a person can also feel dependent upon the other because the other has access to information that may damage him, degrade him or bring about shame or embarrassment. Such information may concern the observable parts of his body, something about his mental state or something about his deeds. For example, a person with a physical injury or disability cannot prevent others from perceiving his mutilated body. White *et al.* (1948) point out that since an injury to one's body is an inseparable part of one's body, it may be felt to be a personal matter which one would like to keep private. However, as it is *visible* everyone can stare at it, ask questions about it or express their feelings or evaluations about it. In this case, though, disconfirmation may be imagined rather than real. Goffman, however, in his analysis of *stigma* refers to a real disconfirmation:

By definition, of course, we believe the person with a stigma is not quite human. On this assumption we exercise varieties of discrimination, through which we effectively, if often unthinkingly, reduce his life chances. We construct a stigma theory, an ideology to explain his inferiority and account for the danger he represents, sometimes rationalizing an animosity based on other differences, such as those of social class. We use specific stigma terms such as cripple, bastard, moron in our daily discourse as a source of metaphor and imagery, typically without giving thought to the original meaning. (Goffman, 1968, p. 15)

The one who has already been stigmatized in Goffman's sense cannot, of course, turn the situation back. The stigma has become one of his personal labels, one of the certainties of his life. If he is to continue living he has to accept the label in some way, adjust to it, and make it part of himself. However, Goffman also refers to those who are not actually *discredited*, but are nevertheless *discreditable*. In other words, the derogatory information is not yet publicly known and the person concerned struggles to prevent this information from becoming public. An example of the discreditable is a person suffering from a non-visible physical condition such as haemophilia or epilepsy. The public image of people suffering from such conditions, based on ignorance and prejudice, leads the patient to do anything to conceal his condition. In a recent survey, one haemophilic patient expressed his views as to whether or not to disclose his condition when applying for a job:

Lie like hell when interviewed and pray you have enough time between bleeds to prove you can do the job as well as the next person when you are fit. (Forbes *et al.*, in press)

8.8 Creativity and activity in the acquisition of knowledge

The striving for recognition is one of the forms of consciousness on its journey towards truth (or towards Science). It is thus implied that the acquisition of knowledge is a *social* process. The search for recognition, however, does not manifest itself only through the striving to be recognized by *others*. In discussing the romantic notion of self-consciousness we pointed out that, in striving to recognize others, a human being also recognizes *himself*. He starts seeing himself through the eyes of others because he is able to take the attitudes of others and to empathize with others. Thus, the process of recognition encompasses the recognition of others, the recognition of the self by the self, and the recognition of the self by others.

The striving for recognition reveals itself through *action*, or as Hegel puts it, through *humanizing action*. In the master-and-slave allegory, it is the slave who struggles with things, transforms them and gradually achieves mastery over them, shapes them with his own ideas. He projects himself into his products and creations. In other words, he humanizes things. When a person works on and shapes things he starts seeing in them, not something alien to himself, but his own purpose. Through activity and creativity 'he acquires a mind of his own' (Hegel, *Phenomenology*, pp. 118–19). In this process he not only transforms things but he also changes himself. He acquires knowledge of the things upon which he works; through this activity he also acquires knowledge of himself, and through this self-knowledge he changes both himself and the things:

Man brings himself before himself by *practical* activity, since he has the impulse, in whatever is directly given to him, in what is present to him externally, to produce himself and therein equally to recognize himself. This aim he achieves by altering external things whereon he impresses the seal of his inner being and in which he now finds again his own characteristics. Man does this in order, as a free subject, to strip the external world of its inflexible foreignness and to enjoy in the shape of things only an external realization of himself. Even a child's first impulse involves this practical alteration of external things; a boy throws stones into the river and now marvels at the circles drawn in the water as an effect in which he gains an intuition of something that is his own doing. (Hegel, *Aesthetics*, p. 31)

This conception of human activity is certainly at variance with the conception of 'activity' discussed in Part I with regard to information-processing. The information-processing system does not change as a result of its performance, all that happens is that the empty shelves in the system get filled with more information. This process will continue as far as the capacity of the system permits. Consequently, the theories postulated in information-processing are theories about the performance and the capacity of the system. They are not, however, theories about the performer.

The Hegelian conception of activity presupposes, on the other hand, that the performer himself transforms in the process of performing (=acting). The theory of performing (=acting) is also a theory about the actor himself because there can be no acting without an actor. The *true being* of a man, according to Hegel, *is* his deed, only in his deed is the individual *actual*. For Hegel, an act is not something that is added to a human being, but an act forms the very essence of a human being. It would make no sense to treat an action as a *dependent variable* as was the case in the Cartesian paradigm. In other words, an action in the Hegelian paradigm cannot be treated just as a response to a stimulus, whether external or internal. Some social psychologists have, of course, been presupposing the Hegelian conception of action for some time. For example, Heider's theory of action is based on the assumption that people are agents. In this theory, action is a *primitive concept* and not something that can be decomposed into intentions, bodily movements, and other variables (cf. pp. 94–95). People are agents and perceive other people as agents. Action cannot be other than intentional, and therefore intentions cannot be causes of actions. Actions are the expressions of agents and are *perceived* as such.

In Heider and Simmel's (1944) classic experiment, subjects were requested to interpret a moving picture film of about $2\frac{1}{2}$ minutes duration in which three geometrical figures (a large triangle, a small triangle, and a disc or a circle) were

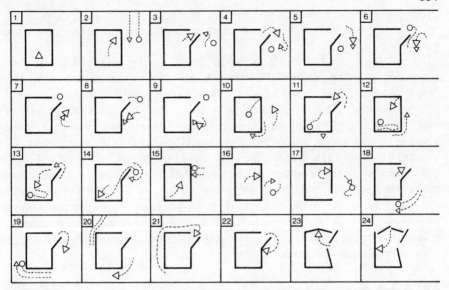

Figure 8.2 Outline of story in a picture film. Broken lines indicate path of movement. From Heider (1967), *American Psychologist*, **22**. Reproduced by permission of the American Psychological Association and the author. Copyright © 1967 American Psychological Association

shown moving in various directions and at various speeds. The only other figure in the field was a rectangle, a section of which could be opened and closed like a door (Figure 8.2). The instruction to the subjects was general: 'write down what happened in the picture'. The outcome of this experiment was that a large majority of subjects perceived the picture in terms of animated beings. Movements were most often interpreted as actions of people.

In another variation of this experiment, subjects were asked questions such as: What kind of person is the big triangle? The predicates used in the descriptions were various, such as aggressive, warlike, quarrelsome, bullying, taking advantage of his size, power-loving, and so on. What this experiment shows is that the *spatio-temporal properties of movements* are certainly not sufficient to explain the fact that people perceive such movements as the actions of agents to whom motives, sentiments, and intentions are attributed. So the attribution of meanings seems to be the distinguishing mark of human perception. From (1971) has made a similar observation:

I see a man putting his hand into the pocket of his trousers to get his matches, after he has just placed a cigarette between his lips. I do not see—and only if I had a very special mental set or attitude would I be able to see—that he moves his hand down along the thigh, then slightly upward in under the edge of his coat and finally downward again into the pocket. What I see is that he puts his hand into the pocket to get his matches.

If we confine ourselves to such a common experience of the behaviour of another person, then the meaning or purpose of the act of behaviour is intrinsic to the perception of the behavioural sequence, i.e., the movements of the hand and arm. We see what people *intend* by the actions they are executing. (From, 1971, p. 5)

From goes on to emphasize that thoughts, ideas, intentions, and purposes are *'all given in and with each other'* in our perception of the actions of other people.

In one of our studies in which children were playing with plasticine, their mothers kept asking them: 'What are you doing?' The children's answer was often: 'Wait and see'. A child finds the handling of plasticine pleasant in itself and he forms his plans while handling it. Even when the child finally decides what it is he is making, an aeroplane changes suddenly into a house, a house into a cake or a kitten, and so on. Vygotsky (1962) makes the same point: 'A small child draws first, then decides what it is that he has drawn: at a slightly older age, he names his drawing when it is half done; and finally he decides beforehand what he will draw' (Vygotsky, 1962, p. 17). As Vygotsky has shown in his work, a child's activity is an interplay of his verbalizations, intentions, and doings, a process in which the child is involved as a whole active being. It is through such a process of activity that he acquires his knowledge about himself and the world he lives in.

8.9 Conclusion

Hegel was the first thinker to break with the dualistic theory of minds and bodies of the Cartesian paradigm. He replaced dualism by the monistic theory of the *embodied mind* (embodiment and mind being separated in the Cartesian paradigm, cf. pp. 77–78). This theory is based on the idea of self-realization as developed by the expressivists:

> It was a basic principle of Hegel's thought that the subject, and all his functions, however 'spiritual', were inescapably embodied; and this in two related dimensions: as a 'rational animal', that is, a living being who thinks; and as an expressive being, that is, a being whose thinking always and necessarily expresses itself in a medium. (Taylor, 1975, pp. 82-3)

Embodiment of the 'spirit' (mind) is not to be understood, as the reader will have appreciated in this chapter, in the sense of two substances (mind and body), one being a tenant of the other. Embodiment of the 'spirit' means, as Taylor points out in the above quotation, that mind and body, mind and medium, are dependent, each upon the other, for their growth and their very existence.

We can see from these ideas of Hegel how much George Mead (1934) owed to Hegel although he hardly ever refers to him. It is obvious, however, from his book *Movements of Thought in the Nineteenth Century* (Mead, 1936), that he not only knew romantic philosophy generally and Hegel in particular, but that he also adopted a great many of their ideas. Mead's (1934) account of consciousness is clearly Hegelian and may help us to clarify the issue of embodiment of the mind. Mead points out that 'consciousness as such refers to both the organism and its environment and cannot be located simply in either' (Mead, 1934, p. 332); it has not simply emerged at a certain point of the phylogenetic development *inside* the living organism and resided in it since. Thus, objects have smells only because there are organisms that have the sense of smell; objects are beautiful or ugly only because there are organisms that *can see* things *as* beautiful or ugly; objects are coloured only because there are organisms that *have* organs of vision. Something becomes food only because there are organisms with a certain kind of digestive system. Similarly, consciousness arises only from the mutual 'interrelationship of the form and its environment and it involves both of them' (Mead, 1934, p. 333).

Therefore, consciousness is not a 'yes–no' matter, something that an organism either *has* or *does not have*. Consciousness is an evolutionary process appearing in various forms, one leading to another. This development occurs because of the mutual interrelationship between consciousness and its world. This development, Hegel claims, is logically determined and proceeds from *abstract* to *concrete*, from less discriminate to more discriminate structures and processes. Hegel points out that according to a common prejudice, philosophy is concerned with abstractions and empty generalizations. On the other hand, sense-perception, natural instinct, and feelings are usually considered as most concrete. As a matter of fact, such assumptions, in Hegel's view, are mistaken. The task of philosophy is to show that truth does not consist of generalities, but of universals. But truth is always determined within the particular, because it is within the particular that development starts. An abstract 'truth' is untrue. 'Philosophy is what is most antagonistic to abstraction, and it leads back to the concrete' (Hegel, *History of Philosophy*, I, pp. 24–5). Hegel goes on to say that a child's thought is more abstract than the adult's because it is less discriminated. The child's consciousness is directed only towards his momentary self and momentary actions: it is unable to project itself into the past and future, that is, into any of his other selves. However, none of the more advanced forms of consciousness is possible without those less advanced. Just as there can be no fruit without a flower, there can be no self-consciousness without perception or sense-certainty.

Hegel's method clearly demonstrates that it is the social activity of the subject that leads to the acquisition of knowledge and scientific progress. In understanding Hegel's method it becomes clear why he uses the phrase 'the world-*for*-consciousness' rather than 'the world-*of*-consciousness'. It is the world that consciousness has created *for* itself.

CHAPTER 9

The Interactive Nature of Mind

The future historian of psychology will have the task of explaining why, after decades of stubborn preoccupation with the *individualistic* nature of the human mind, so much psychological research into the *social* nature of the mind suddenly emerged in the nineteen-seventies. Notions such as 'intersubjectivity', 'interactional synchrony', 'empathy', and 'other-awareness' have a respectable share of the vocabulary of research in social cognition. It is the sheer weight of this research that must be faced by those who have not yet been converted to believing that one has to start with the interpersonal relationships of the dyad in order to come to understand the mind of the individual. But this research does not only aim to prove that the nature of the mind is social. It also seeks to demonstrate that unless the social, i.e. interactive, conditions are successfully fulfilled in the infant's development there is not much chance of his mind unfolding to its full capacities.

The purpose of this chapter is not to review the recent research on social cognition—a task which, in any case, would occupy a whole book. Instead, we shall focus upon the conceptual presuppositions of this research, upon the problems that this research poses for itself, and upon their possible solutions. Although it may not be immediately apparent, the conceptual presuppositions of the research into social cognition are not new. They are based on the ideas of the expressivists generally and on those of Hegel in particular. The reason for pointing to the close relations between recent empirical research and romantic philosophy is not simply to do justice to the latter. Rather, a fundamental examination of the presuppositions of research in this area should lead to the development of the conceptual and theoretical frameworks that are still largely lacking. Moreover, it will reduce the danger of falling back into the Cartesian paradigm; such regression easily happens during paradigm shifts when one's theoretical and methodological positions have not been fully established.

9.1 A conversation of gestures

Although several commentators have recognized Herder's work on language

140

as a magnificent contribution both to philology and the modern philosophy of language (cf. Barnard, 1965, p. 55), Berlin (1965, p. 48) has made an even stronger claim: that it was Herder who founded *social psychology*. It is not simply with respect to the originality of his theory of language that Herder deserves such an appraisal. It was his general conception of what it is to be a human being, his psychological analysis of action, his account of the interaction between man and his environment, and his notion of 'reflexivity', that made Herder's work so modern and timely.

The theories of languages of Herder's contemporaries in the eighteenth century were all based on the Cartesian tradition and assumed either a divine or an individualistic origin of language. They could not cope with a number of problems in language, such as the appearance of new words, the existence of abstract terms, the imperfections of language, and the problem of communication. In order to stimulate the development of new ideas, the Berlin Academy of Sciences set up a competition for the best treatise on the origin of human language. Herder won first prize for his dissertation *On the Origin of Language*.

Herder's treatise was a rejection of both the rationalistic and the empiricist theories of language. His attacks were directed against recent and contemporary authors such as Condillac, Rousseau, and Süssmilch. For example, according to Condillac, human language developed from individuals' expression of emotions, exclamations, and cries, which are also observed in animals. Very much in the style of Locke, Condillac claimed that sounds gradually became associated, in a quite arbitrary way, with certain objects, needs, and states of mind. Through continuous repetition of such associations the sounds started to *signify* objects, states of mind, and so on; they became *words*. In order to support his hypothesis, Condillac presented an example of two children abandoned in a desert before they could speak. Not knowing how to use signs these children started to produce exclamations of their feelings and thoughts. These sounds they repeated endlessly, and they learned to associate them with their feelings and so to use them as signs, and then to combine them into more complex signs and associations. Signs, therefore, became common conventions, which the children learnt to communicate to each other. Thus, they developed language as an arbitrary system of signs.

Herder condemned with irony such an 'unnatural and contradictory' account as an explanation of the origin of 'natural signs' (Herder, *Sämtliche Werke*, V, pp. 18–19). In this account Condillac, just like Rousseau later, was unable to recognize the basic differences between the origin of human speech and the origin of 'speech' in animals. While Condillac identified animals with men, Rousseau identified men with animals (Herder, *Sämtliche Werke*, V, pp. 21–2).

Although Herder does not deny that there is a similarity between onomatopoeic sounds in animals and in humans, there are, nevertheless, essential differences in the *origins* of the two. Animals are equipped with *instincts* by means of which they respond to their environment. They live in a very narrow ecological sphere and adapt themselves to it by developing very complex single-purpose instincts. Herder made the observation that there is a negative relationship between the breadth of the ecological sphere and the complexity of an instinct. For example, spiders can produce highly artistic webs, but live in, and are confined to, a very narrow ecological sphere. The instincts of a bee are admirably fitted to the life of a bee but once a bee gets out of the sphere for which these instincts are fitted, it is lost. The instincts of animals make cooperation and communication wonderfully easy. The narrower the sphere of the animal, that is, the more complex its instincts, the less is speech needed (Herder, *Sämtliche Werke*, V, p. 24).

However, the greater the breadth of the ecological sphere the less well equipped is the animal with respect to its instincts. When we finally consider the case of human beings, we may observe that they have no specific ecological sphere defined for them. In consequence, there is no single and complex activity for which they are particularly well equipped, unlike spiders, bees or ants. Instead, the whole world is spread out in front of them and it is theirs to conquer. They are weak in terms of instincts or other ready-made skills. But instead of instincts human beings have 'other hidden powers' (Herder, *Sämtliche Werke*, V, p. 26). These powers enable people to live in a world they create for themselves (*ibid.*, VIII, p. 252).

Among the most important hidden powers are intellect, reason, and consciousness. But the difference between animals and humans does not lie in the degree to which they possess these powers, or in the addition of these powers to an otherwise animal nature. These powers form the very nature of man and as such are completely distinct from those of animal powers. In contrast to animal instincts, which are instantaneous, humans have reflexion (*ibid.*, V, p. 31). Reflexion is the ability to separate oneself from one's actions. While an animal's behaviour is spontaneous, a human being can stand back and consider possible alternative actions. Reflexion is a specifically human characteristic, and all our human powers are manifested through it.

Human language is a product of reflexion (Herder, *Sämtliche Werke*, V, p. 31). A bird sings because of an inborn instinct and a baby instinctively cries. But a human being does not speak by instinct. It is not the structure of the mouth which makes speech possible; speech is not an expression of our feelings, nor an imitation of animal sounds or a social convention (*ibid.*, V, p. 38). Both speech and reflexion are *expressions* of human nature, which is social.

Herder argues strongly against the claim of Süssmilch that people have language in order to express their thoughts. No pure reason can exist without language, says Herder (*Sämtliche Werke*, XIII, p. 357). Language and reason have both developed from the nature of man and they belong together: *ratio et oratio*. 'Without speech man would have no reason and no reason is possible without speech' (*ibid.*, V, p. 40).

However, Herder's ideas on the origin of language were no more than an admirable expression of the *Zeitgeist*. In other words, Herder was conveying the changing ideas of eighteenth century society concerning human nature, history, and culture, without having any biological, psychological, or anthropological evidence to support these ideas.

George Mead, on the other hand, who wrote about the origin of language more than a hundred years after Herder, had the advantage of being able to support his claims with Darwinian evolution theory, with Wundtian psychology, and with Hegelian philosophy.

Both Herder at the end of the eighteenth century and Mead at the beginning of the twentieth century believed that the root problem of the existing philosophical and psychological theories lay in the fact that their starting point was *the assumption of the existence of a complete and ready-made mind*. Presupposing such a mind, its proponents would ask how language arose, and how people were able to communicate in words and make use of symbols. While Herder's criticism was directed against his contemporary, Süssmilch, Mead raised his criticism against Darwin and Wundt. Thus, for Darwin the expressions of emotions in animals were expressions of the animals' 'states of mind' and animals *communicated these states of mind* to their audience:

Dogs, when approaching a strange dog, may find it useful to show by their movements that they are friendly, and do not wish to fight. When two young dogs in play are growling and biting each other's faces and legs, it is obvious that they mutually understand each other's gestures and manners. (Darwin, 1904, p. 60)

On the other hand, by raising his head slightly, bristling the hairs on his body, pricking up his ears and turning them forward, and so on, the dog may intend the other dog to realize that he is about to attack him.

Such a theory assumes, therefore, that expressions of emotions in the lower animals are substitutes for words: without speech, a lower animal can only express its feelings to the other animal by such actions as erecting his hair, pressing his ears back, looking at him with a fixed stare, and so on. But Mead argues strongly against the assumptions of such a theory. There is no evidence for the belief that an animal has something in its mind that it wishes to communicate to its audience. Again, in his critical analysis of Wundt's contribution to the origin of language, Mead poses the question as to where the mind comes from:

For if, as Wundt does, you presuppose the existence of mind at the start, as explaining or making possible the social process of experience, then the origin of minds and the interaction among minds become mysteries. But if, on the other hand, you regard the social process of experience as prior (in a rudimentary form) to the existence of mind and explain the origin of minds in terms of the interaction among individuals within that process, then not only the origin of minds, but also the interaction among minds (which is thus seen to be internal to their very nature and presupposed by their existence or development at all) cease to seem mysterious or miraculous. *Mind arises through communication by a conversation of gestures in a social process or context of experience— not communication through mind*. (Mead, 1934, p. 50)

This is probably one of the most important claims in Mead's work, but how should it be interpreted? Mead claims that communication is prior to mind, i.e. to consciousness. According to him, there is no evidence to support the supposition that the lower animals *intend* to evoke certain responses in their audience. They are not conscious of the fact that their behaviour may elicit certain kinds of responses in others. In other words, they are unable to take the attitude of the other and to be aware that their behaviour can be interpreted as having meaning. The question Mead poses in this context is what it is that enables two individuals, who originally have nothing in common, to communicate. Mead certainly would reject, as Herder did, Condillac's way of treating language as a system of signs. In fact, Mead is highly critical of what he calls the philologist's approach:

The philologist . . . has often taken the view of the prisoner in a cell. The prisoner knows that others are in a like position and he wants to get in communication with them. So he sets about some method of communication, some arbitrary affair, perhaps, such as tapping on the wall. Now, each of us, on this view, is shut up in his own cell of consciousness, and knowing that there are other people so shut up, develops ways to set up communication with them. (Mead, 1934, p. 6)

The approach of the philologist is typically Cartesian: it starts with the individual consciousnesses and from there it attempts to get communication started. The individual consciousness is prior to what is publicly shared. However, if one accepts Mead's claim that consciousness *arises* from communication, then it follows that it is the public which is prior to the private. This is what Mead actually says:

. . . the whole (society) is prior to the part (the individual), not the part to the whole; and the part is explained in terms of the whole, not the whole in terms of the part or parts. (Mead, 1934, p. 6)

This, of course, is a Hegelian claim and it is commonly misunderstood, often deliberately. The most usual, rather vulgar, misinterpretation of this claim is that the individual's consciousness is not free and must submit itself to the group or mass consciousness, that such views lead to de-personification of a human being and thus support totalitarian regimes where individual freedom does not exist and where the individual cannot develop according to his potentialities and inclinations.

There is no evidence, however, either in Hegel's or in Mead's work, to support this kind of interpretation. It is obvious from an examination of Hegel's and Mead's ideas that the claim does not mean *literally* that society is prior to the individual. Society is not a substance, it is a process in which both participants, the individual and his counterpart (in the broadest sense a society), play an equal role. It is the dyad consisting of the individual and his counterpart, or the subject–object dyad, that is prior both to the individual and his counterpart taken as *isolated existences* (or prior to both the subject and the object). In fact, there is no such thing as a subject or object as *real* separate existences, as has already been pointed out in Chapters 7 and 8. The object exists only for the subject and every act of the subject is an act with respect to the subject–object dyad. Consequently each act of the individual is a *social act* from the very beginning, because it always involves the individual, not *in vacuo* but as an individual acting upon or interpreting the world he lives in.

Let us consider the claim that each act is a social act in more detail. Although, according to Mead, the lower animals *cannot intend* to evoke responses in the audience and are *not aware of the meaning* of their own behaviour for the audience, this behaviour, nevertheless, does have social significance. The behaviour of one animal becomes a stimulus for another animal and evokes a response whether the initiator of the stimulus wishes it or not. Therefore, reactions to such stimuli, although induced by innate biological instincts, are part of a social act.

Let us take Mead's classic example. Two gestures, such as the readiness to attack of the one dog, and the retreat of the other, do not have any shared meanings for the participants. If one dog is ready to attack, there does not have to be anything conscious about his posture. Nevertheless, this dog's posture itself serves as a stimulus for the other dog, who adjusts his own posture to the one of the first dog. These gestures, however, are originally produced, not because they signify something, but because of inborn instincts. They are, as Mead says, *non-significant* gestures. The adjustments to non-significant gestures can be of different kinds. The other dog may simply imitate the gesture of the first dog, or readiness to attack may result in the other running away, himself starting to attack or growling. Such a gesture becomes in return a stimulus for the first dog and evokes a response in him: he himself now adjusts his gesture to the second dog's gesture and this again becomes a stimulus for the first dog. Thus arises 'a conversation of gestures, a reciprocal shifting of the dogs' positions and attitudes' (Mead, 1934, p. 63). But these gestures do not originate in consciousness as Darwin and Wundt assumed, and the beginnings of a social act may be investigated and explained without bringing in consciousness or mind. Biological gestures, however, do serve as social stimuli from the very beginning. Thus this quasi-communicative process has the following parts: the behaviour, the response to this behaviour, and the adjusted behaviour of the former participant. It is not difficult to see that the structure of such a process corresponds to Hegel's 'journey of consciousness towards truth'. Both Mead's non-significant gestures and Hegel's 'journey of consciousness' are continuous adjustments of the existing states (of behaviour or consciousness) of the individual to the state of the environment (the behaviour of the other participant or the object of knowledge). But it is important that in this process both participants transform themselves: it is a two-way process of information-processing rather than the one-way process that was discussed in Part I.

9.2 Synchrony and reciprocity in mother–infant interaction

It is one of the presuppositions of the Cartesian paradigm that the environment of a child only serves the purpose of 'triggering off' and shaping mental structures and functions that have already been innately predetermined. If this were not so, the Cartesians argue, living bodies would develop in a completely undetermined and amoeboid way, one individual organism becoming quite unlike another (cf. p. 44)

For the Hegelians, as for anyone who has adopted evolution theory, the structures and functions of living organisms have an innate basis. As already pointed out in Chapter 7, Hegel's concept of development, defined before Darwin, distinguishes between two states of an organism: first, capacity, power, or *potentiality*; and, secondly, *actuality*:

> If we say, for example, that man is by nature rational, we would mean that he has reason only inherently or in embryo; in this sense, reason, understanding, imagination, will, are possessed from birth or even from the mother's womb. But while the child only has capacities or the actual possibility of reason, it is just the same as if he had no reason; reason does not yet exist in him since he cannot yet do anything rational, and has no rational consciousness. Thus, what man is at first implicitly becomes explicit, and it is the same with reason. If, then, man has actuality on whatever side, he is actually rational. (Hegel, *History of Philosophy*, I, p. 21)

In spite of the similarities with respect to innateness there are essential differences between the two frameworks with respect to the realization of the innate potentialities. First, in the Cartesian framework it is assumed that the whole structure and all the functions of an organism are innately predetermined. The emergence of new structures and new functions is ignored. In the Hegelian framework, although there is an innate basis for the structure and functions of an organism, the emergence of new forms resulting from the organism's functioning as it develops is taken for granted. Secondly, in the Cartesian framework the organism is passive, and its potentialities are actualized when the senses are appropriately stimulated and it finds itself in an environment that triggers off and shapes the development of the structures of the organism, and leads to the unwinding of its various functions. In the Hegelian framework, on the other hand, the organism is inherently active, and its potentialities are not realized unless it actively struggles for actualization:

> Everything that from eternity has happened in heaven and earth, the life of God and all the deeds of time simply are the struggles for Mind to know itself, to make itself objective to itself, to find itself, be for itself, and finally unite to itself. (Hegel, *History of Philosophy*, I, p. 23)

In other words, whatever the potentialities of the organism, they can be actualized not simply by the effect of the environment alone, but only by the mutual effort of the organism and the world in which it lives.

Recent psychological research into social cognition demonstrates that the baby's active struggle for recognition as a human being starts immediately after his birth. Condon and Sander (1974a,b) have observed that as early as twenty minutes after birth an infant responds actively to a human voice and is able to synchronize his bodily movement with it. Microanalysis of filmed movements

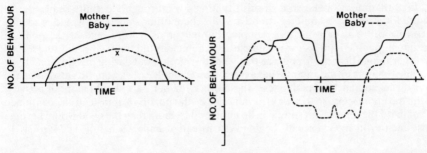

Figure 9.1 Two cases of mother-baby interaction. From Brazelton, Koslowski, and Main (1974), in Lewis and Rosenblum (eds), *The Effect of the Infant on its Caregiver*. Reproduced by permission of John Wiley and Sons, Inc. Copyright © 1974 John Wiley and Sons, Inc

of sixteen newborn infants demonstrated that bodily motion was sustained during the sound of the voice and changed into a new pattern with change of voice. Studies with very young infants demonstrate that reciprocity of interactions and sychrony of actions of the participants in communication are essential for the adequate cognitive and social development of a child. The study by Brazelton *et al*. (1974) is particularly instructive. The authors observed that interaction between mother and infant consisted of cycles of looking and non-looking, or attention and non-attention. The interaction operated on several levels even with infants several weeks old. If the mother responded to the baby in a particular way, the mutual interactional activity of the mother–child dyad increased. If, on the other hand, the mother responded in other ways, the infant turned away and the interactional activity decreased. Moreover, the same applied to mothers' responses to their babies' behaviour. Thus, the participants themselves regulated each others' gestures by increasing or decreasing the activity of their own gestures. But sensitivity to the gesture of the other differed from one mother to another, as can be seen from the graphs shown in Figure 9.1, which is adapted from Brazelton *et al*. (1974). On the left-hand graph, we can see synchronization in mother–baby interaction. The baby looks at the mother and she follows his looks. Then she increases her activity, smiling, vocalizing, touching him. The baby also increases his activity up to the peak X and after reaching this point his activity decreases. The mother follows him and rapidly decreases her activity so that the cycle finishes by decreased activity on both sides. On the right-hand graph, however, the mother is not sensitive to the baby's activities. The baby starts the cycle by looking at the mother and she follows by smiling, touching, and talking. He responds briefly and turns away. The mother, however, continues bombarding him with stimuli without giving him time to reciprocate her activities.

We can see in this study that even very young babies are extremely sensitive to temporal parameters of interaction. The importance of proper timing was also revealed in Richard's (1971) study. In this study, mothers and babies were videotaped when smiling at each other. Frame-by-frame analysis demonstrated, however, that the process of mutual smiling was a complex one. Schaffer describes the results of this study as follows:

... first, the infant's behaviour in this situation goes through a definite sequence: he would, for example, be quietly attentive while the mother smiled, he would gradually become more and more active, pumping himself up as it were, and at the point of maximum 'pumpedupness' he would pause a moment—and then he would smile. And the other thing Richards found was that what the mother did during this time had to be carefully phased to the infant's behaviour. For example, it was important that at the point of maximum 'pumpedupness' the mother for her part should stop all activity, giving the infant time, so to speak, to smile. If she did not do so, if instead she continued to bombard the infant with stimuli in an unphased fashion, then the child would become tense and fretful and eventually begin to cry instead of smile. (Schaffer, 1974, p. 212)

These studies, and many others, show not only that an infant is biologically pre-tuned to communicate with his care-givers (Newson, 1977), but also that the infant is a very active participant in communication, and is sensitive to smooth synchronization and reciprocity of gestures.

The infant has a number of strategies for fighting inappropriate communication on the part of his care-givers. Trevarthen (1977) observed that a baby as young as two months can choose to look at some things with interest while turning away from others. When synchronization and reciprocity of gestures do not proceed smoothly, a young baby attempts to escape further interaction into which he might be forced by his insensitive mother. He may actively increase his physical distance from his mother, e.g. by arching, turning over or shrinking; he may push his hands and feet against her; he may decrease his activity by looking dull, yawning or going to sleep (Brazelton *et al.*, 1974). On the other hand, Trevarthen (1979) observed that when an adult is unresponsive to the baby, avoiding him, or being aggressive, babies as young as two months old show tension or distress by facial expressions of fear, by frowning and grimacing, and by avoiding eye-to-eye contact. Similar distress was observed when the mother suddenly froze her face following a close emotional relationship with the baby.

A number of studies suggest that if an infant is unable to communicate with his care-givers to his satisfaction, and the communication either continues to be asynchronized or disrupted for various reasons, both his social and cognitive development may be affected in the long term (Pawlby, 1981). Asynchrony on the baby's part, on the other hand, may be a sign of brain dysfunction. Thus, Condon (1979) has found that autistic children do not display the synchronized bodily movements which are present in normal children. In his microanalytic study, autistic children displayed multiple delayed responses to the human voice that had no common patterns. Condon also observed various degrees of asynchrony in children with other kinds of childhood dysfunction, such as brain damage and reading disability.

In her study of the communicational patterns of children with Down's syndrome, Jones (1979) found that it was not the quantity of interaction but their quality that distinguished mentally handicapped children from the non-handicapped. The mothers of Down's syndrome children had to work harder to produce responses from their children and thus to maintain dialogues with them. Consequently, the mothers of Down's syndrome children tended to be more directive in their turn, making dialogues more structured and not letting their children experience control in interaction. There were also differences with respect to vocalizations between normal and Down's syndrome children. While the overall quantity and variety of produced sounds was the same the Down's syndrome children did not vary the patterns of production. They produced more isolated, out-of-context vocalizations and fewer 'comment' types of vocalizations. Thus it appears that even at this early stage of language development it is possible to talk about higher or lower communicative competence. Down's syndrome children produced significantly less referential eye contact, as Jones calls it, that is, eye contact with respect to the focus of a dialogue, e.g. a toy or an activity in which both mother and baby are engaged. In this way, the child deprived himself of feedback on his own activities, which the mother could provide. Finally, Down's syndrome children did not show adequate timing pauses; they did not give their mothers enough time to respond and clashed with them more often in turn-taking in interactions than normal children. They were unable to anticipate the responses from their mothers and thus could not establish the general turn-taking pattern that is essential for the development of language.

9.3 Intersubjectivity has to be taken for granted in order to be achieved

It would be wrong to assume that the stress in the struggle for recognition is all that an infant needs to become self-conscious: success between the two parties has to be mutual. As Hegel says in the *Master and Slave* passage, 'A self-consciousness exists *for a self-consciousness*. Only so is it in fact self-consciousness . . . "I" that is "We" and "We" that is "I" ' (Hegel, *Phenomenology*, p. 110). However, the majority of the commentaries on the passage concentrate on the struggle between them rather than on the *mutuality* of their relationship. Unfortunately, this passage has too often been interpreted out of the context of the *Phenomenology* as a whole, and with particular emphasis on its historical and political implications, while its psychological significance has been ignored. And yet, it is clear from the *Master and Slave* that real self-recognition can be achieved only by the mutual cooperation of both participants in communication rather than by the attempt of each individual to achieve his goal at the expense of the other. The one has to be able to see himself through the eyes of the other to become self-conscious.

Mutuality as a precondition for self-recognition is even more explicit in other writings of Hegel. From the point of view of the child's struggle for self-recognition, of particular interest are Hegel's passages about the family. Hegel emphasizes the importance of the family in the development of self-consciousness. The family is a unit in which one consciousness recognizes itself *immediately* in another consciousness. Moreover, all members are aware of this mutual recognition (Hegel, *Phenomenology*, p. 273). This natural recognition of oneself in other members of the family is not guided by any learned ethics. Its unreflexive and spontaneous nature provides security for members of the family and is the guarantee of the continuation of life in children. Thus, the family relationship is characterized by love 'which is mind's feeling of its own unity' (Hegel, *Philosophy of Right*, p. 110). The relationship between two people entering into marriage manifests itself in their voluntary consent 'to make themselves one person, to renounce their natural and individual personality to this unity of one with the other' (*ibid.*, p. 111). This relationship, actualizing itself in a child, is permanently passed on from one generation to another in the history of mankind.

In his concern with possible psychological interpretations of the communicative acts between a father and his daughter, Rommetveit (1980) expresses the same idea as Hegel. In his poem, *Dialectical Lullaby*, the father sings to his little daughter:

> ... so sullelee-lulelee-too
> our boat is drifting ashore
> where one and one don't make two
> but something mysteriously more ...

But both life and psychological research show that this spontaneous and natural recognition of one in the other may become distorted and have sinister consequences. Parental projection onto their children may be one-sided and lead to a conflict between generations. Or pathological self-recognition of mothers in their children may manifest itself in maternal anxiety. This anxiety, whether justified or unjustified, often leads to the symptom of maternal overprotection. Levy (1943) defined maternal overprotection as excessive maternal care of their children which can reveal itself as excessive contact, infantilization of the child, and prevention of the child's independent behaviour. In all cases the mother, perceiving the child as a part of herself, refuses to allow the child to take risks, preserves him from all hardship, and denies him contact with the rest of the world.

But let us turn back to the normal family relationship where spontaneous and natural self-recognition presents no obstacle to the child's independence. The question, though, is how the infant can develop self-consciousness, other consciousness, and finally intersubjectivity.

As we have pointed out already, interpersonal communication starts with non-significant gestures, that is, the gestures of the baby and the mother have no common meaning. So how do the participants arrive at common meanings, or in other words, what makes it possible for significant gestures to emerge? Rommetveit's (1974) answer to this question, and recent empirical research fully supports his claim, is that *'intersubjectivity has to be taken for granted in order to be achieved'*. By intersubjectivity, Rommetveit means a constant oscillation between one's own role as an actor (e.g. as a speaker) and the role of one's counterpart in interaction (e.g. a listener). Such oscillation between the speaking I and listening YOU is possible if, and only if, they each believe in some commonalities concerning their respective interpretations of the social world they in fact share, and each trust in common meanings of words, events, and actions. Total intersubjectivity, of course, is never completely achieved, just as Hegel's absolute truth is unreachable in its totality. We can only approach intersubjectivity asymptotically, under conditions of mutual faith in each other, in a temporarily shared social world.

Rommetveit claims, however, that in order to *initiate* any interpersonal communication one *must* presuppose intersubjectivity. Such a presupposition appears to be a psychologically necessary condition for the actual establishment of intersubjectivity, and, in fact, this is what mothers presuppose immediately after their babies are born. Researchers in mother–infant interaction have repeatedly observed and commented upon the fact that mothers treat their babies as if they already understood words, had intentions and desires, and were responsible for their actions (e.g. Ryan, 1974; Bullowa, 1979; Trevarthen, 1979). As Newson puts it

From birth, a mother interprets her baby's reactions by a process of adultomorphism; in other words, the infant is assumed to have fully human powers of social responsiveness: with wishes, intentions and feelings which can be communicated to others and which must, within limits, be respected. (Newson, 1979, p. 211)

This does not mean, of course, that mothers behave and speak to their babies in the way they would speak to adults. In fact, they have available a number of ways of making themselves understood and are also able to assess what the child can do.

One of the mothers' strategies is repetition. Papoušek and Papoušek (1977) point out that mothers tend to parse their activities into simple repetitive patterns while mothering. Depending on the subsequent development of the mother–infant interaction, these repetitive patterns may either fade away if the infant does not respond to them, or they may become significant if the infant starts associating them with some other activities or happenings. Repetitions are an essential aspect of 'motherese', the language mothers use in talking to their babies. It is characterized by simple syntactic structures, slow parsing, repetitions, higher pitch, and by the use of short and semantically simple words (Cross, 1978; Gelman and Shatz, 1977). Or mothers may endlessly pick up the toys their babies throw from their prams. These actions are at first accidental, then intentional, as they become associated with mothers' repetitive activities signifying their attention to the baby.

Another strategy a mother uses in making herself understood is 'taking turn for her child'. Snow (1977) points out that communication between mother and infant is *conversational* from the very beginning, and changes in the mothers' speech style correspond to changes in the nature of the interaction with their babies. Mothers rarely use monologues when talking to their babies. When babies are too young to reciprocate in speech, the babies' activities, direction of attention, vocalization, and cry evoke speech from their mothers.

Snow demonstrates the changes occurring in mother–infant conversation as the baby becomes more cognitively and socially competent. When the baby is about three months old the mother responds to all of his physiological reactions, such as cries, yawns, burps, and coughs, and to social reactions such as smiles and vocalizing. Her utterances are short and baby-centred, the physiological or social reactions are referred to specifically by naming. The conversation between Ann and her mother went as follows (Snow, 1977, p. 12)

Mother	Ann
	(smiles)
Oh what a nice little smile!	
Yes, isn't that nice?	
There.	
There's a nice little smile.	(burps)
What a nice wind as well!	
Yes, that's better isn't it?	
Yes.	
Yes.	(vocalizes)
Yes!	
There's a nice noise.	

Thus, the mother acts as if the behaviour of the child were intentional and communicative. Snow points out that the common characteristic of infant behaviour is its easy interpretability and that it signifies something about the state of a child. Infant behaviour, such as arm- or leg-waving, which does not have an easy interpretability, does not enter into maternal utterances, unless it is part of some interpretable behaviour. The important aspect of these early conversations is that mothers attempt to maintain a conversation despite the inadequacies of their conversational partners: they do it by being repetitive, asking many questions which they answer for the baby, filling in for the baby, and taking turn for him.

At the age of seven months babies become more active partners in a conversation and mothers no longer respond to all vocalizations but only to 'high-quality' vocalizations such as particularly long babbles, elaborated consonantal babbles, and so on. Such 'high-quality' babbles are imitated by the mother and become turns in a conversation, although these imitations may be mutual failures (Snow, 1977, p. 16):

Mother	Ann
Ghhhhh ghhhhh ghhhhhh ghhhhhh.	
Grrrrr grrrrr grrrrr grrrrr.	(protest cry)
Oh, you don't feel like it, do you.	aaaaa aaaaa aaaaa
No, I wasn't making that noise.	
I wasn't going aaaa aaaaa.	aaaaa aaaaa
Yes, that's right.	

At this stage the mother still has to answer the questions she asks Ann, but at the age of eighteen months Ann was successfully taking her turn. Her mother expected her not only to take turn but also to provide appropriate responses (Snow, 1977, p. 18):

Mother	Ann
Who's that?	Daddy
That's not daddy, that's Dougall	
Say Dougall.	

Sequences of responses, corrections, and corrected responses became an important part of the turn-taking at this stage. Although the mother still had to fill in for the child and Ann still violated the rules of conversation, on the whole it was becoming more effective and really reciprocal.

It thus appears that the way mothers carry out dialogues with their babies reflect their belief that the babies are capable of reciprocal communication. Since the baby is incapable of expressing his message in words, mothers, as Newson (1977) points out, form hypotheses about the meaning of the baby's message. The mother acts on the basis of her hypothesis, and if the hypothesis appears to be wrong she tries another one. For example, if the baby cries she may form the hypothesis that he is hungry. However, if the baby refuses food she may form the hypothesis that he has wetted himself. If that is not true, perhaps that he has a pain, and so on. In other words, the mother believes that the baby is capable of expressing his desires, needs, and wishes in some form. Babies, on the other hand, can also modify their mother's behaviour towards them. A sensitive mother can immediately recognize disapproval of her behaviour by the baby and switch to an alternative.

In this process of constant modification and adjustment of gestures of both participants, a situation eventually emerges in which the child realizes that a certain gesture (vocal or otherwise) on his part evokes a certain response in the other participant (or that the other participant adjusts himself in a particular way to the gesture of the child). The gesture now stands for a certain idea in his mind and the originally *non-significant* gesture becomes *significant* (Mead, 1934). In other words, the gesture (or sound) becomes significant when it arouses the same attitude in both participants, in the one who is making it and in the one who responds to it. It indicates that there is an object common to the attention of both actors. A significant gesture is a more efficient and adequate mechanism of survival than an unconscious or non-significant gesture. Significant gestures, because they are conscious, in the sense of being reflexive, have a much greater adjustment potential: adjustment and readjustment of significant gestures can be negotiated by both participants, that is, the meaning of a gesture, which in its more advanced form becomes a word, is consciously adapted on the basis of the common attitude towards what that gesture represents. The essential aspect of a real conversation of significant gestures is the existence of a shared meaning in the consciousness of both participants; one individual indicates his intentions by his gesture (which now may be a word) and is aware of the meaning of his gesture and knows that the other participant also shares this meaning. In this sense, as gestures become significant, so communication becomes intersubjective.

We have noted already in discussing Snow's (1977) work that pre-verbal dialogue between mothers and babies is originally highly situation-dependent. Thus, a baby's physiological reactions may both serve as stimulus of a dialogue and also serve to maintain it. Anything that becomes the focus of the baby's attention immediately becomes the subject of the mother's speech; she turns her own attention to this part of the environment and elaborates upon it. The context-dependence of stimuli gradually weakens and the word itself finally becomes enough to initiate as well as to maintain the dialogue. In other words, dialogues become *decontextualized*. This process of decontextualization has its parallel in what Hegel calls the *concretization* of an idea. As we pointed out earlier, Hegel assumes that the mind's knowledge is originally abstract, undetermined, and implicit. It is through development that 'healthy human reason goes out towards what is concrete' (Hegel, *History of Philosophy*, p. 25). Similarly, psychological evidence shows that in the acquisition of concepts and meanings of words (cf. also pp. 170–171) the child's knowledge is first immersed in indeterminateness and bound to abstract relationships in context. Gradually he learns to separate concepts and meanings from their contexts and conceive them in their determinateness.

In sum, by acting upon the belief that their pre-verbal babies are capable of reciprocal communication, mothers ensure that their belief will be a self-fulfilling prophesy: by believing that babies can and do communicate, mothers actually give them the chance to communicate and become adequate partners, reciprocating their roles in a dialogue. In this sense intersubjectivity must really be taken for granted in order to be achieved.

9.4   Intersubjectivity in child development

The search for recognition, if successful, has three different aspects: self-consciousness, other-consciousness or empathy, and intersubjectivity. As aspects of a single process, they are mutually interdependent and one cannot be conceived without the other: the use of three different terms to identify them serves the purpose of indicating where either the researcher's attention or the focus of the person involved in an interaction temporarily lies.

To be self-conscious is to see oneself as an object, that is, to see oneself as others do. But to see oneself through the eyes of the other, one must also be able to take the attitude of the other, to empathize with others, or to have other-consciousness. Life, of course, teaches us that many people, just like Hegel's Master, seek self-recognition at the expense of others, that is, without adequate other-recognition. They can, of course, win temporary battles at the expense of others and satisfy themselves with superficial gains, not realizing that they are depriving themselves of personal growth and therefore of a deeper and more permanent gain. Finally, intersubjectivity refers to the ability to switch constantly from one's own to the other's point of view, to modify one's present self-consciousness and other-consciousness, and thus to replace them both by more adequate concepts.

We can easily see that these three notions, self-consciousness, other-consciousness, and intersubjectivity, have their parallel in Hegel's *Phenomenology*. Self-consciousness corresponds to the mind's existing level of consciousness (sense-certainty, perception, understanding, and so on). Other-consciousness corresponds to the mind's experience of physical, mental, and social objects—it is the mind's conceptual framework, within the limitations of the existing level of consciousness, that determines how such objects are experienced. Intersubjectivity then corresponds, in the most general sense, to the process of continuous comparison and mutual adjustment of the mind's existing concept of an object with its experience of that object: it is the way in which knowledge is acquired. At a more specific level, it is the process by which one participant in a communication compares his own self-consciousness with the other-consciousness in order to arrive at more adequate concepts of both consciousnesses. 'More intersubjectivity' then refers to the existence of fewer contradictions between self- and other-consciousness, that is, to more overlap between them.

Questions such as 'at what age does the child develop self-consciousness?', 'at what age is he able to empathize?', and 'at what age is he able to establish and maintain an intersubjective relationship with his care-givers?' cannot be answered in a yes–no manner. One cannot assume that the child has either acquired any one of these accomplishments in its totality or, on the other hand, that he has not acquired them at all. Just as it is assumed that a child starts acquiring knowledge at birth or even prenatally, so we must assume that an infant is endowed at birth with the capacity for at least the rudiments of intersubjectivity (Trevarthen, 1977) and self- and other-consciousness. However, we must also assume that the process of acquiring these accomplishments are inexhaustible, just as the processes of the acquisition of any other accomplishment or concept is inexhaustible. The infant, the child, the adolescent, and the adult only asymptotically approach self-consciousness, other-consciousness, and intersubjectivity. They are able to achieve higher and higher mastery of these accomplishments as their experience and willingness to elaborate upon them is enlarged, but fortunately they never achieve them totally. If they did, would anything be left for the future? The pleasure of the mind is in seeking truth and approaching truth but not in its final and total mastery. People, of course, differ greatly in their accomplishment of self-consciousness, other-consciousness, and intersubjectivity, just as they differ in their mastery of their various concepts. In psychology, these accomplishments have been studied under the names of communicative competence (e.g. Hymes, 1971; Black, 1979; Shields, 1979), interpersonal competence (Cicourel, 1972), and empathy (e.g. Kessler, 1979), with the aim of demonstrating that it is the level of mastery of these accomplishments that makes people more or less socially adequate.

One of the main objectives of Mead's work is to argue that an individual does not become an object to himself through immediate experience of himself, but by readjustment of his gestures and attitudes towards the other. In child development this is learned in three main ways, *play, games*, and *language* (Mead, 1934). With the above discussion in mind, we can take it that these three ways are also the ways of achieving self- and other-consciousness, and intersubjectivity.

Play in its simplest form is little more than a conversation of non-significant gestures. Play in dogs may sometimes be indistinguishable from actual fight. However, the difference between the two lies in the amount of fighting. In play 'there is a combination of responses which checks the depth of the bite' (Mead, 1934, p. 150). Play in children too develops from a reciprocal conversation of gestures. In his analysis of give-and-take play, Bruner (1977) points to the development of such a reciprocity of gestures. While at the age of three months it is the mother who usually initiates give-and-take play, by twelve months it is the child who dominates play. He is able to play for much longer periods, takes the initiative in taking and offering, and expects reciprocal gestures from the other participant. Play like peekaboo, give-and-take, 'round and round the garden', and joint constructing not only teaches the child the rule of turn-taking and anticipating gestures from others, but it also endows him 'with a subtle sense of when to use and when to protest at infractions' (Bruner, 1977, p. 273).

The next step in play is playing *at something*. Once the child is able to play at something it means that the child is able in some simple form to take the role of someone else. To take on the role of someone else presupposes much more than non-significant gestures. Although, as we know, animals do play with one another, there is no evidence that would suggest that animals could take the role of another. To take the role of another presupposes anticipating the actions of another, and therefore *sharing common meanings* with that other. A child is at one moment a mother, then a teacher, a nurse, a policeman. The child addresses himself as if he were a mother; he gives instructions as a teacher does; he puts himself into prison as if he were a policeman; he soothes his non-existent pains as if he were a nurse. In order to be able to take all these roles and switch from one role to another, not only must he have knowledge of what people usually do in such roles, he must also have knowledge of established rules and conventions of the society in which he lives, of the rights and duties of those whose roles he plays, and he must be able to anticipate the actions of those who may become involved with such people.

Another important aspect of play is the child's awareness of time. While non-significant conversation of gestures is characterized only by strings of gestures that emerge and pass away, playing at something presupposes organizing the activities of the role-played other. The child must be able to combine these activities into meaningful wholes and should know which activities come first and which follow so that a particular goal can be accomplished. For example, you must commit a crime first so that a policeman can come and arrest you; you must hurt yourself first so that the nurse can come and attend to your wound. However, in spite of this knowledge of such sequences in activities, play as such does not have any structure. The roles the child takes on change spontaneously with no constraints imposed upon the situations or persons involved.

Play is a social activity in the sense that the child must have social experience in order to be able to take on the roles of other people. The presence of others, however, is not a necessary condition for play to be successful. A child may play at being a mother and address herself as a husband or child would. In other words, the roles of the other are in the child's consciousness and he is dealing with these roles according to his existing perceptions of the world and the theories he puts forward with respect to others.

A *game* is basically different from play because it is an *organized social activity*. In a game the child is not allowed the spontaneity of play. Fantasy and imagination, which are essential to play, are forbidden in a game. A game is formalized and, as Mead points out, the child must now be prepared to take on *any* roles required by the game and not just those he likes. It has rules that have been created for the particular purpose of a particular game. These rules are the focus of the child's attention. As Mead says,

Children take a great interest in rules. They make rules on the spot in order to help themselves out of difficulties. Part of the enjoyment of the game is to get these rules . . . The game represents the passage in the life of the child from taking the role of others in play to the organized part that is essential to self-consciousness in the full sense of the term. (Mead, 1934, p. 152)

A rule makes it possible to exclude from the game someone who is disliked without this being unethical. It also makes it possible to co-opt others. A rule becomes a force in itself, so that the individual avoids responsibility for unpopular decisions: it is the way the community or the generalized other exercises its control over individuals. A fully self-conscious human being takes for granted the organized social attitudes of the group to which he belongs towards social problems of various kinds. These organized social attitudes or rules control the community at any given time and an individual adjusts his conduct accordingly (Mead, 1934, p. 156).

Mead's observations point to the fact that the child's acquisition of other-consciousness is a long-term and complex process. It starts from non-significant gestures, develops into play in the roles of others, and finally leads to games incorporating formalized rules. In contrast to Piaget's claim that young children are primarily egocentric and unable to take the viewpoint of another person until about seven or eight years of age, more and more studies are now emerging to show that children as young as two to three years have the capacity of empathizing with others. Borke (1975) found that there are several factors influencing the child's ability to empathize, some related to the type of task, and others related to the way the child is expected to communicate his awareness of another person's point of view. Borke suggests that if the task given to the child involves conceptual skills which are beyond his ability, then in order to produce some sort of answer the child gives his own perspective and thus appears egocentric. Her research as well as that of others (e.g. Borke, 1971; Levine and Hoffman, 1975) shows that three and four year olds are aware of other people's feelings and can identify situations leading to various emotional states. Research on the child's ability to empathize, however, is on the whole in its infancy, and a number of interesting problems, such as the relationship of this ability to behaviour at play and in games, to sense of guilt, and to altruism, cooperation and competition, await the next generation of psychologists.

The third kind of activity, closely related, according to Mead, to the development of self-consciousness, other-consciousness, and intersubjectivity, is *language*. Just as with games, the use of language is a social activity guided by rules that have to be adhered to. We have already seen that language has its precursors in non-verbal interpersonal communication that starts between an infant and his care-givers immediately after his birth.

Turn-taking in pre-verbal communication starts as early as the age of seven to fifteen weeks (Bateson, 1975). It is the first step in communication in which the one partner recognizes the right of the other to initiate conversation, to respond, to comment, and to make his own point. An infant is thus given the chance both to 'speak' and to listen and he learns that he has to give the other participant the same chance if two-way communication is to be maintained.

Joint action is the next step in mutual recognition. It demands more from the participants than each simply having the same rights in turn-taking. Joint action can take place if and only if one participant endorses the invitation of the other temporarily to accept his own point of view as the focus of mutual attention. In mother–infant interaction, the first joint actions are unreflexive on the part of the infant. It is the mother who brings to their mutual interest a toy, points to it, labels it, elaborates upon its properties, and comments upon them. Or it is the mother who makes the object of the infant's interest one of mutual attention. The mother follows the infant in what he listens to, what he looks at, what he shows interest in. She elaborates upon and endorses his foci of interest so that they become intersubjectively attended to.

The participants in child–adult communication thus have non-identical roles before reciprocity in their joint action is fully established. The child has to learn to become aware of the temporal aspect of joint action contracts. A joint action requires him to interrupt the spontaneity of his own activities and to respect the other's offer of mutual attention. He has to learn to anticipate the actions of the other. Here again, to anticipate the other person's actions, whether verbal or non-verbal, means to have the ability to empathize with that person. Anticipation in communication, of course, has to be mutual. What the speaker says is based on his assumptions concerning the focus of joint speech action. What the listener responds to, once again, is based on his assumptions as to what constitutes a temporarily shared social world. As Rommetveit (1974) points out, *encoding* is tacitly assumed to involve *anticipatory decoding*. The speaker is listener-orientated; and the listener is speaker-orientated and aims to reconstruct what the speaker intends to make known.

We are writing on the premises of the reader, reading on the premises of the writer, speaking on the premises of the listener, and listening on the premises of the speaker. (Rommetveit, 1974, p. 63)

Speaking on the premises of the listener emerges very early in child development. The fact that adults use different speech and communication codes when switching from one dialect to another or when talking to different people is well known (e.g. Fishman, 1969; Erwin-Tripp, 1968). However, Shatz and Gelman (1973) found that four-year olds modify their speech when talking to two-year olds. A similar study by Sachs and Devin (quoted in Gelman and Shatz, 1977) has shown that a four-year old uses modified speech when talking to a doll that has been assigned the role of a two-year old.

In the Gelman and Shatz (1977) study the four-year olds were given the task of explaining the functioning of a toy to both an adult and a two-year old. Substantial differences appeared between these two kinds of communication. When explaining the toy to the two-year olds, the four-year olds focused on demonstrating the toy, and telling the younger ones how to use it. They made no references to mental states such as the speaker's thoughts, wishes or memories, made no suggestions about possible actions to be taken but gave the young ones simple orders, such as 'do this', 'do that'. Since they probably did not expect the younger children to question the veracity of their statements, no modulators (phrases such as 'I am sure', 'I think', 'surely', etc.) expressing degree of certainty were used. The children made clear, simple, and short statements about the topic. They used a great number of repetitive utterances with a variety of demonstrative and attention-increasing devices. Explanations given to adults were very different. Generally, the range of topics introduced in the speech was much wider. There was no need to call for the adult's attention. The children sought information from the adult, used modulators, and made affirmative comments on the speech of the adult.

It is important that in both cases the children made attempts to adjust to listeners, to make themselves understood so that the listener could respond appropriately. Thus, communicative competence, even in very young children, includes not only knowledge of linguistic rules but also the ability to take the role of the other, although in a primitive way, and to reflect upon one's own activity.

9.5 Intersubjectivity in adult communication

An interpersonal interaction between two people can be viewed as a continuum, one end of which would represent the extreme of asymmetry, one-way flow communication, and the other end genuinely symmetrical two-way flow communication. The middle of the continuum would represent varying degrees of asymmetry. That end of the continuum which is labelled as one-way communication at its most extreme is paralleled by the typical Master situation: the master, in his position of power, whether due to status, authority, or knowledge, gives orders to the other participant with respect to what the other should believe or should do. The other is given no chance of expressing his own view of the matter. He has no choice with respect to his response and the only responsibility left to him is to fulfil his master's orders. The master, on the other hand, is alienated from the actual content of his speech because it is not the content that is at issue in this interaction; what is at issue is the expression of power. The content serves only as an opportunity for the master to further his goal, and to seek self-recognition at the expense of the other. In such an exercise, neither the master nor the slave can grow as persons, nor can they acquire any real knowledge. True, the slave may obtain facts or quasi-facts but these do not lead anywhere, since they cannot be discussed, elaborated upon or creatively moulded. Moreover, there is no possibility of growth of inter-subjectivity. The master, the politician, the propagandist or bureaucrat degrades the other person to the level of a physical object. The only satisfaction he himself can achieve in return is the sense of having obtained something by force.

A less extreme form of one-way communication is *persuasion*. In persuasion, too, the master is alienated from the content of the communication. However, in contrast to the situation in which the master simply gives orders and expects them to be fulfilled, the persuader's goal is actually to produce changes in the other's mind. And, in fact, this is how success in persuasion is defined. However, just as in the former case, the persuader does not grow as a person because the communication is highly asymmetrical and he is not prepared to take on the attitude of the other because he is not genuinely interested in the other.

A necessary condition of communication in which both participants acquire knowledge and grow as persons is *sharing of control*. It does not mean that such communication has to be symmetrical. Thus education is an asymmetrical process in the sense that there is one who knows more and has control over the content and methods of theorizing about the subject. However, the person who is being educated is given the chance of sharing that control. He can comment, elaborate, disagree, and argue his point of view. Education is not something that is done to the student but both the teacher and the student actively participate. It is a two-way process in which both participants change and grow. In such a process, one participant recognizes the other as an equal and respects his rights in turn-taking and expressing his point of view.

Psychological evidence, in particular that in psychotherapeutic situations, illustrates this point well. In his review article of psychotherapy, Eysenck (1952) has argued that both counselling and psychotherapy are ineffective in the treatment of mental disorders. Truax and Carthuff (1967) endorse Eysenck's claim insofar as *average* counselling and psychotherapy as *currently practised* are ineffective, which, of course, does not mean that if well practised they are ineffective. Truax and Mitchell (1971) point out that average coun-selling is no better than non-professional help, and in their own work they were concerned to identify the therapeutic factors, both in the counsellor and in the counsellee, that lead to effective counselling. In effective counselling both the patient and the 'helper' change for the better, that is they grow as persons. In agreement with Rogers (1961), Truax and Mitchell emphasize the importance of accurate empathic understanding of the client on a moment-by-moment basis, of non-possessive warmth, and of genuineness in the helping relation-ship. By empathic understanding on a moment-by-moment basis, they mean the ability to oscillate between self-consciousness and other-consciousness; by non-possessive warmth, preparedness to recognize the patient as an equal partner in communication; and by genuineness, a person's authenticity, the presenting of himself as he really is rather than putting on a mask. Truax and Carthuff (1967) point out that these factors have a significant effect on various kinds of mental disorder and are related to constructive changes in patients. They have been shown to hold with a wide variety of therapists and counsellors regardless of their training and theoretical orientation, and with a wide variety of clients and patients.

In this chapter we started with a simple conversation of non-significant gestures and after passing through more complex processes we have reached a level at which both participants interact intersubjectively or can exercise their power over each other symbolically by various means. A Cartesian one-way model of information-processing appears to be appropriate in cases where one of the participants, the one who does not share control over communication, is reduced to the level of a physical object. For any other kind of information-processing a one-way model is unsuitable and the Cartesian paradigm breaks down. It has to be replaced by a Hegelian two-way model in which control in communication is shared. This does not mean, though, that communication has to be fully symmetrical with respect to control for it to lead to the personal and intellectual development of the participants. It is important, nevertheless, that communication is reciprocal and that each participant has some means of expressing his power. The speaker, as Rommetveit (1980) points out, has the privilege of deciding what constitutes an answer or whether the listener's response actually is a response to the speaker's question. The listener, on the other hand, can exercise his power by a variety of means, by silence, by choosing to respond tangentially, by not responding to the point, by disagree-ment, by elaboration of the issue, and so on. Nevertheless, both the speaker and the listener must recognize the other as an equal self-conscious human being if communication is to have the 'change for the better' effect.

CHAPTER 10

The Activity of the Knower in the Acquisition of Knowledge

In the previous three chapters we have identified various aspects of the activity of the knower in the Hegelian framework. However, in order to highlight Hegel's approach to this subject, we shall re-examine, from the Hegelian point of view, the following epistemological issues which we discussed in terms of the Cartesian paradigm in Part I: the laws of thought, the compartmentalization of the mind and the limits of its capacity, the algorithmic nature of the acquisition of knowledge, and the separation of cognition from its embodiment.

10.1 The laws of thought in the Hegelian framework

The laws of thought in the Cartesian framework, i.e. the laws of identity, of non-contradiction, and of the excluded middle (cf. Chapter 3), were *purely formal*. They were not concerned with the identity and non-contradiction of things but with the identity and non-contradiction of the variables in formal logic. This point is easily misunderstood because identity and non-contradiction are, of course, illustrated inevitably in concrete terms: the tree is the tree $(P \equiv P)$, or it is not possible to give something away and keep it at the same time $(-(P \& -P))$, and so on.

Hegel's objections to these formalistic laws of thought are expressed in the section on Reason in the *Phenomenology*, but above all, in the *Encyclopedia* and in *Science of Logic*. The formal laws of thought, Hegel says, lie *outside* reality. Although they are not supposed to represent the whole truth, they are, nevertheless, supposed to represent *formal truth* (Hegel, *Phenomenology*, p. 180). But what is such a formal truth? It is a mere empty tautology that leads to nothing.

If, for example, to the question 'What is a plant?' the answer is given 'A plant is—a plant', the truth of such a statement is at once admitted by the entire company on whom it is tested, and at the same time it is equally unanimously declared that the statement says *nothing*. If anyone opens his mouth and promises to state what God is, namely God is—God, expectation is cheated, for what was expected was a *different determination*. (Hegel, *Science of Logic*, p. 415)

162

What Hegel objects to most, however, is not that the laws of thought are formal and therefore have no content. What he objects to, on the contrary, is that their content is particular, highly specific, and fixed, and that on the other hand they have no form. What he means is that since the laws of thought are supposed to be universally true their 'content', which is totally abstract, is absolutely determined and immutable. On the other hand, they have no form because what is fixed cannot be true but is only a 'figment of thought' (Hegel, *Phenomenology*, p. 180). The laws of thought are only an instant of truth just as a photograph is not a truth of a person but only an abstraction catching that person in a particular moment; and just as a photograph does not represent a person in his movement and activity, so the laws of thought do not represent the actual process of thinking. The formal laws of thought have been torn out from the context of the movement of thought and stated separately. Thus the traditional formal laws of thought treat identity, difference, and contradiction as though they occurred independently and separately from one another in human reasoning.

So does Hegel suggest that the laws of thought should be abandoned as totally useless? Not at all. These laws, however, are given a new meaning by Hegel. They are no longer static, but are immanently active. Concepts such as identity, difference, opposition, and contradiction are, in Hegel's terms, the *categories of reflexion*. They are characterized by the following:

First, the categories of reflexion are the *manifestation* of the underlying Essence. For our purpose it is enough to say that every entity has its essence. The essence of an entity is what that entity is *in its absolute truth*. But we know already that absolute truth is not something that is immediately available. What is wrong with the formal laws of truth is exactly that they seem to offer absolute truth as something that is given immediately. Truth is a process and can be reached only by penetrating under the surface of things, behind their appearances. It is clear, therefore, that it is not the essence of things that is presented to the senses: 'things really are not what they immediately show themselves. There is therefore something more to be done than merely rove from one quality to another' (Hegel, *Encyclopedia*, p. 208). We have seen already (Chapter 8) that, in order to penetrate into the essence of things, consciousness has to go beyond the senses, beyond understanding to reason and self-consciousness. It is on this journey of penetration, Hegel now tells us, that essence reveals itself as, at the same time, identical with itself, different from itself, and self-contradictory.

Secondly, by 'reflexive' Hegel (and the romantics generally) meant 'interacting with something' (cf. note 2). It could be interaction with itself or with something else. Just as universals develop through particulars (cf. Chapter 8), so identity develops through self-differentiation. For example, a man remains the same man in spite of the changes he undergoes. But these changes, which interact and conflict with his identity, all reflect his human nature (his essence). Thus, everything in the world is inherently contradictory: identity is conditioned by difference, the positive is conditioned by the negative. Hegel uses a number of examples to clarify this point: a magnet has a north and south pole, and if it is cut in two, each of the two pieces has a north and south pole. The nature of electricity, too, consists of two opposite powers, the positive and negative.

And, finally, the world does not consist of abstract identities that are expressed in the formulae of the formal laws of thought. Instead, the world consists of concrete things, and therefore abstract identity must be replaced by *the concrete identity of things*. 'Whatever exists is concrete, with difference and opposition in itself. The finitude of things will then lie in the want of correspondence between their immediate being, and what they essentially are' (Hegel, *Encyclopedia*, p. 223).

What can we make of Hegel's claim that identity, difference, and opposition all exist together in a concrete thing?

While in the Cartesian paradigm the most important law is the law of *non*-contradiction, for Hegel it is the *law of contradiction* that is the essence of all activity and self-movement. The formal law of non-contradiction, stating that a thing cannot be both A and not A at the same time, is a sheer abstraction. If anything is to develop it *must* have internal contradiction. 'Contradiction is the very moving principle of the world: and it is ridiculous to say that contradiction is unthinkable' (Hegel, *Encyclopedia*, p. 223).

Let us consider the organism in its ontogenetic development in order to demonstrate what Hegel means by his reflexive law of contradiction. Ontogenetic development of a living organism can be said to be based on the assumption that an organism is both one thing and something different, which exactly violates the formal law of non-contradiction. If an organism is to grow and to develop, then, while being what it is, it must also be something different in the sense that it must have an inner capacity for change. It is in its development that the *potentiality* of an organism changes into *actuality* (cf. also Hegel, *History of Philosophy*, pp. 20–3). Every biological change, including breathing and the growth and decay of a single cell, and every experience, makes the organism different from what it was a moment ago. Let us consider again the example chosen earlier in the book in our discussion of universals and particulars. The Darwinian theory of phylogenetic evolution can also be seen as a manifestation of the reflexive law of contradiction. Thus, each organism, although a member of a particular genus, has its own individual characteristics that differentiate it from other members of the same genus. These individual characteristics, although they may be minimal at the time, may grow and develop and finally lead to the emergence of a new genus. However, if we did not presuppose that the organism is both the same organism and something different at the same time, any possibility of development would be eliminated. The whole essence of evolution is that it is based on sameness and difference at the same time. Thus, as Hegel says, 'contradiction is the root of all movement and vitality' and something is active only because it embodies an inherent contradiction:

Something is therefore alive only in so far as it contains contradiction within it, and moreover is this power to hold and endure the contradiction within it. (Hegel, *Science of Logic*, p. 440)

Therefore, contradiction is not something lying peacefully within a thing but it is something that the thing has to endure. If a thing is unable to withstand contradiction within itself, it dies.

The categories of reflexion are the manifestations not only of the essences of *things* but also of *thought*. In this context Hegel opposes speculative thinking to ordinary thinking. Speculative thinking, which in today's terms could be called scientific thinking or philosophical thinking, *is* able to endure contradiction, it can see different aspects of things, their potentialities and actualities. Speculative thinking, Hegel says, sharpens 'the blunt difference of diverse terms' into *opposition*, and

. . . only when the manifold terms have been driven to the point of contradiction do they become active and lively towards one another, receiving in contradiction the negativity which is the indwelling pulsation of self-movement and spontaneous activity. (Hegel, *Science of Logic*, p. 442)

Ordinary, or non-speculative thinking, on the other hand, is unable to consider the contradictions in things and terms. For ordinary thinking, the relationships between things and terms are strictly determined: if something is *below* then it is not *above*, and if something is *right* then it is not *left*, and so on. Thus, these opposite determinations are held one against another, are separated one from another rather than seen in their unity. Ordinary thinking 'abhors contradiction, as nature abhors a vacuum' (Hegel, *Science of Logic*, p. 442); it is one-sided, can see only one aspect of things and is unable to recognize the positive aspect of contradiction.

Perhaps we would not be too wrong to draw a parallel between Hegel's notions of speculative and ordinary thinking, on the one hand, and the notions of cognitive complexity and cognitive simplicity in recent psychology of personality, on the other. A cognitively complex person is characterized by a high degree of cognitive discrimination and by extensive bonds of relationships between the elements of his cognitive system. Both the discrimination and the number of bonds are taken in a relative sense, and cognitive complexity is a characteristic of a person in comparison to other persons. Thus, depending on the relative degree of cognitive discriminations and the extent of the bonds, cognitive systems have been labelled as cognitively complex or cognitively simple (Crockett, 1965). Empirical evidence has demonstrated that people with relatively complex cognitive systems are more flexible in their attitudes towards others, they seek out variety of information when solving problems, interpret the same information differently in different contexts, and make finer differentiations among people and events. Cognitively simple people, on the other hand, have relatively little tolerance in judging others and in extreme cases they may use only one dimension, that of good–bad, when referring to others. Moreover, people with relatively complex cognitive structures seem to have a greater capacity for tolerating contradictory information and integrating it into meaningful formations. Thus experiments have demonstrated that cognitively complex subjects are able to integrate contradictory information about others when forming impressions of them (Nidorf, 1961; Mayo and Crockett, 1964; Rosenkrantz and Crockett, 1965). It appears that it is the ability to consider information from different aspects, both positive and negative, as well as developed relationships among the fine elements in the structure of the mind, that is related to the tolerance for contradictory information which cognitively complex persons commonly display.

10.2 Formal logic and Hegelian logic in psychology

It has become obvious in the above discussion that Hegel's laws of thought, on the one hand, and the traditional formal laws of thought, on the other, are two completely different matters. By his criticism of contemporary logic, Hegel created a gulf between himself and whole generations of logicians. Hegel's criticism of logic is most commonly interpreted as a rejection or at least an unfair criticism of *formal logic as such*. However, such interpretations are unjustified. When making claims about Hegel's criticism of formal logic we must not overlook that he objected to two things. First, he objected to Kant's version of formal logic based on the syllogism conceived as a completed system to which nothing could be added. As we know, the development of symbolic logic in the nineteenth century started after Hegel and along completely different lines from traditional logic (cf. pp. 27–28). Secondly, and more important, he objected to the claim of formal logic that the laws of formal logic were ranked

as *the universal laws of thought* that lie at the base of all thinking, that are absolute in themselves and incapable of proof, but are immediately and incontestably recognized and accepted as true by all thinking that grasps their meaning. (Hegel, *Science of Logic*, p. 409)

Hegel's objection was not to the system of logic as such but 'to this alleged experience of the logic-books' that the law of identity, for example, was a law of thinking, or that it in any way regulated our thinking. He emphatically argued that 'no mind thinks or forms conceptions or speaks, in accordance with this law', and that nothing that exists in the world conforms to it:

Utterances after the fashion of this pretended law (A planet is—a planet; Magnetism is—magnetism; Mind is—mind) are, as they deserve to be, reputed silly. That is certainly matter of general experience. The logic which seriously propounds such laws and the scholastic world in which alone they are valid have long been discredited with practical common sense as well as with the philosophy of reason. (Hegel, *Encyclopedia*, p. 214)

A contemporary formal logician, on the other hand, is not concerned with whether the laws of formal logic and the formal logical systems are the laws of human *reasoning* or whether there is any relationship between the two. He is concerned with the finished product of the thought process, that is with a system of propositions, and with the application of the rules of logic to these. Such a system of propositions is completed and fixed, and presupposes that the logical meaning of the propositions is the one given to them by the logical calculus. Given such a system of propositions, the formal rules of logic offer no account of the *process* of thought, that is, of the process of working something out. In fact, given such a system, no change, no development, no self-movement or variety is allowed except for inferences based on the rules of logic.

We can thus say that the formal laws of thought are not the laws of thought as a process but the laws of a *fixed product* of the process of thought. Every attempt to use formal logic except to test the perfection of the finished product is a misuse of formal logic.

Bearing in mind that thought is a dynamic process and not a static system, the following question remains to be answered. What do we learn from the psychological experiments in which the subject is presented with propositions and required to draw a conclusion, or in which he is expected to evaluate a conclusion or a set of possible conclusions? To answer this, consider what we learn from a study in which a child is given the task of completing a sentence, or of completing a story, or of evaluating whether a story makes or does not make sense. From such studies, we do not learn about the child's *productive use* of language but about his *comprehension*. Similarly, from a subject's answers to tasks in deductive reasoning (see Chapter 3) we do not learn about his reasoning but about his comprehension of reasoning tasks. We learn something about the extent to which people untutored in formal logic are able to comprehend logical riddles and thus solve them. A problem of this kind is the same as if someone untutored in mathematics was given a mathematical task, or someone untutored in physics given a task in physics, and so on.

What is involved in these tasks is not, then, simply the solving of logical riddles, but the encoding of tasks in language, which may be done differently by different people. The experimenter, intending a task to be a logical riddle, must give the subject the instructions: 'Please ignore the content', or 'Please ignore the meaning', or 'Please ignore the context' and 'Concentrate solely on the structure of the propositions, not on what they mean', in order to force the subject to think according to the formal laws of thought. This is because under normal circumstances the human mind thinks according to the reflexive laws of thought which do not ignore content, meaning or context. As Hegel said, 'no mind thinks or forms conceptions or speaks, in accordance with these [formal] laws' (Hegel, *Encyclopedia*, p. 214).

Success in formal logical tasks, of course, has little to do with success in tasks in which a developing process or movement of reasoning is required. For example, a doctor's diagnosis or prognosis about a patient is not based just on a ready-made list of propositions describing the illness. The patient's immunity, his state of mind, and a number of other variables are all brought into play at different stages of the reasoning process. While inferences based on the propositions of a logical calculus are based on formal identity and formal non-contradiction, a diagnosis and prognosis must presumably be based on reflexive identity and reflexive contradictions.

In conclusion, perhaps we could say that both kinds of identity and contradiction play a part in human thought, although in very different ways. On the one hand, we unreflexively take it for granted that a tree is a tree and that if something is white it is not black. But these unreflexive truths lead nowhere, as Hegel said. In reflexive thought the developing power and creativity of the human mind consist precisely in the fact that it can recognize that sometimes trees are not trees and that something that is white is also black.

Rubinstein (1959) explicitly accepts Hegel's principle of contradiction and incorporates it into his assumptions about the nature of thought. According to him, everything, including both physical and mental phenomena, exists in various systems of connections and relationships. The clue to answering the question concerning the relationship between consciousness and reality is to be found in Hegel's claim that *one and the same thing is both itself and something else*' (Rubinstein, 1959, p. 9). According to Rubinstein (1957) the use of *logic* in human thought must be taken for granted. This point, of course, is similar to the one made by Smedslund and already mentioned in Chapter 3. As a Hegelian, however, Rubinstein goes far beyond Smedslund. Rubinstein claims that if a thought did not correspond to the 'logic' of things, that is, of cognized things, there could not be any logic in the thought itself. This is so both in ontogenetic and in phylogenetic development. In the ontogenetic development of thought, a constant mutual relationship is maintained between the logic of the objects of thought and the logic of thought, and it is because this relationship is maintained that the child's thought becomes more and more logical. We should not understand this process simply in Piagetian terms of the growth of logicality with respect to formal operations. What is so important and is implied by both Hegel and Rubinstein is that the child's thought proceeds from non-reflexive to reflexive thought. A young child cannot cope with contradictory information and with contradictions in things: for him things cannot be both good and bad, he cannot fear and hope at the same time. It is only with the development of reflexive thought that he is able to withstand contradiction, and to see an identity in a difference.

The same applies to phylogenetic development. The science of logic, like other sciences, is a historical process, and in its historical development human thought has proceeded more and more in accordance with reflexive thought. We could say that Aristotelian logic, like child logic, was based on unreflexive laws of thought and could not admit non-identity and contradiction in things. This logic was as far as public knowledge had gone in ancient Greece.

It thus appears, as Rubinstein points out, that both in ontogenetic and phylogenetic development human thought became reflexive before people had realized the existence of the reflexive laws of logic and become conscious of them. Once people become aware of the reflexive laws of logic, their thinking simply proceeds according to the logic of the objects of thought; they do not need to practise their logic in logical exercises to know how to use this or that logical formula.

Similar points seem to apply to the relatively finished products of the mind, to systems of propositions. As Rubinstein says, people learn grammar while using language rather than learning it through special exercises in grammar. Grammar as a system of rules serves the purpose of correcting one's deviations from the public norms. Similarly, knowledge of the formal logical rules only serves the purpose of checking one's logic rather than being something to be learned in its own right.

It follows from the above discussion that people do not use any special logical processes that are in a 'pure' form and separated from the other, non-logical processes. The processes of the acquisition of knowledge are not only the processes of the individual but also involve the historical development of knowledge by society. The historical development of knowledge consists basically of the processes of the acquisition of knowledge in which the reflexive laws of logic have become embedded.

10.3   The nature of language and concepts

Herder argued that if language were of God's rather than of man's creation, it would be based on and constructed from contemplative rather than active elements: the subjects of sentences would be more important than the predicates. But, as Herder goes on to point out, this is not so. A child does not call a sheep 'a sheep' when he first learns to speak. He refers to a sheep as 'baaaa', he refers to it by the kind of sound it produces. Sounds are connected with activities; things that are active produce sounds. A human being is primarily a hearing and a noticing creature and cognizes objects through their activities and changes rather than by contemplating them as entities. Thus, for a human being, predicates are more important than subjects, and are learned earlier than subjects. It is not true that verbs developed from nouns as previously believed, but verbs were the first words in language and nouns developed from verbs (Herder, *Sämtliche Werke*, V, pp. 48–54).

Herder's claims about the primary role of verbs in language acquisition were, of course, no more than a naive attempt to express the active nature of language and communication. Nevertheless, modern philosophy and contemporary psychology of language do not seem at all remote from Herder's naive position.

Thus, Wittgenstein has pointed out that where the learning of language was concerned, mediaeval philosophers like Augustine did not distinguish between various kinds of words. The learning of language was conceived to be simply the learning of the names of objects and people's names, i.e. of subjects, while the learning of words expressing actions and properties of things, i.e. of predicates, was only of secondary importance (Wittgenstein, 1953, §1). The rest of the words were considered 'as something that will take care of itself'. But Wittgenstein maintains that even modern empiricists commit the same mistake. They believe that we learn the names of words by sheer ostension, i.e. naming an object by a certain word. According to them, labelling or naming is attaching ready-made labels to ready-made objects: objects are decomposable into their elementary characteristics, such as colour, shape, sounds produced, and so on, and the child learns which colours, shapes, and sounds go together to compose a particular object (see Chapter 4). Wittgenstein emphatically argues against such simplifications. Learning a language is not a process in which the pupil simply repeats words after the teacher. The child learns words in various *language-games*, which means that language is learned in *'the actions into which it is woven'* (Wittgenstein, 1953, §7). Labelling is a complex process which occurs in various activities in a social context. For example, the child does not learn the word 'pain' by repeating the word when his mother points to the various sensations he experiences, saying 'this is pain'. He learns the word in various language-games: the child is hurt and cries, the parent talks to him, offers help, cuddles him, and soothes his pain; the child also observes others in pain and seeking help. The word 'pain' refers to all of these activities but cannot be identified with any of them (Wittgenstein, 1953, § 244).

Empirical evidence, given by the developmental psychology of language and communication, supports the intuitive and analytic claims of Herder and Wittgenstein. Research into mother–infant interaction has demonstrated that ostension is only one of the activities leading to reference. Prerequisites of reference are to be found in shared activities between the parent and infant long before an infant starts talking. Visual co-orientation, i.e. focusing of the eyes on the *same* object at the *same* time by both mother and infant, seems to be essential for the development of reference. Schaffer's studies (Schaffer, 1974; Collis and Schaffer, 1975; Schaffer *et al.*, 1977) demonstrate that the mother continuously follows the direction in which the child is looking in her attempt to discover the focus of his attention and so engage in mutual activities with him; to recognize his demands, interpret his intentions, share an object of attention, anticipate his subsequent activities. Scaife and Bruner (1975) found that from the age of four months up to nine months the child learns to turn his head in the same direction as the adult and is thus able to follow the same object visually. Bruner (1978) makes the point that what is important about joint focus of attention is not simply the fact that the eyes of the child and the mother are *focused on the same object*; in fact, it is this kind of emphasis that has been the shortcoming of all theories of naming. What is important is that,

What has been mastered is a *procedure* for homing in on the attentional focus of another: learning where to look in order to be tuned to another's attention. It is a discovery routine and not a naming procedure. (Bruner, 1978, p. 30)

But a whole set of more complex procedures acquired by shared activities between the parent and child is required before the child actually learns to refer to objects. Rommetveit (1968) has examined the way a simple noun like 'cup' is acquired by a child. The reference of such a word does not emerge through repeated ostension (pointing of the parent to the object named 'cup') but through a set of events involving such activities as: drinking from a cup, washing up a cup, pouring from a cup, requests for a particular cup, pointing to a cup, finding a cup, and so on (Rommetveit, 1968, pp. 124–7). This is a stage in which the child does not have a precise definition (i.e. an adult definition) of a cup, but has what can perhaps be called a 'pseudo-concept' of a cup. He has mastered a chain-complex of activities (Vygotsky, 1962) in which a cup plays a role but the object 'cup' is not as yet singled out. The singling out of an object, i.e. the distinguishing of it from glasses, bowls, pots, pans, and other kinds of container, is a later part of the process of word acquisition. It is the stage of *decontextualization* (Werner and Kaplan, 1963; Rommetveit, 1968; Bruner, 1978) during which an object is gradually separated from the set of activities in which it was originally embedded. It is only now, in the decontextualization process, that ostension with regard to objects and the individual properties of objects (e.g. the kind of material from which a cup is usually made, its handle, shape, etc.) become important and 'the child may then get on with the Augustinian business of learning to refer—but in no sense can it be taken as claimed by St Augustine (cf. Wittgenstein, 1953) as learning language through naming *ab initio*' (Bruner, 1978, p. 32).

This procedure of decontextualization in which the object is gradually singled out from the set of activities in which it was originally embedded appears to be a very good example of what Hegel meant by development from the abstract to the concrete (cf. 139). For the child at first an object is not discriminated from other objects with which it shares some functions and some perceptual properties. In other words, it is abstract. However, in the course of the child's activities involving an object, his apprehension of the object becomes more and more concrete. Not only does he distinguish it and other objects more and more from one another, but he increasingly discriminates its various functions, uses, and perceptual properties.

The essential presupposition of researchers working within the Hegelian framework is that the outstanding general characteristic of the child's early words is not his reference to static perceptual features but their expressive nature. Thus, Nelson (1974, p. 268) finds that the child's first words serve 'to regulate relations between people but do not have stable identifiable referents'. This claim of Nelson sounds like an echo of Herder: 'Words do not just refer, they have expressive power, they are learned because they have personal relevance for a person. Words are filled with passion' (Herder, *Sämtliche Werke*, XIII, 357). Nelson argues that early words are acquired in dynamic relationships between actions, changes, and all kinds of variation. Perceptual similarity between objects is only one kind of similarity. Similarity of functions, of actions associated with objects, and of the effects these objects have are much more relevant if a child is to generalize from one object to another. What is important for the child is not static but dynamic information: 'The world of the young child is composed largely of *complex dynamic events*, and this characteristic is therefore basic to an understanding of the natural concepts of children' (Nelson, 1974, p. 269). The child's concepts are not acquired in a yes–no manner (cf. pp. 76–77) but develop with the child's experience. Nelson, like Rommetveit, assumes that the first namings with a particular word are context bound: all the relational information, such as actions, and relations to other objects and events, are required to produce the name. At an early stage the name is not used independently of these relations; it is only when the child is able to go beyond Vygotsky's chain complexes, or, to use Werner's and Rommetveit's words, it is only when decontextualization has taken place, that he can detach the object from the totality of its various relationships.

Nelson's example concerning the development of the concept of BALL is most instructive. Nelson argues that the concept of a ball is originally known to a child only as a totality of various kinds of relationships. This totality of relationships gradually becomes separated into a set of *functional core relationships* (rolls, bounces) which are obligatory for acquisition of the concept and a set of *non-core relationships* (actions which can be performed on small rigid objects, set of places where ball can be used, etc.). The non-core relationships are shared with a number of other objects. Differentiation (or decontextualization) proceeds even further, and as the child detaches the object from the various relational specifications, he becomes able to name the object outside the original definitional context. For example, the child would be able to recognize the object in a picture, or in a new environment, etc. When this happens, i.e. when the child is able to name an object independently of its definitional relationships, he becomes actually able to start forming two-word utterances.

According to Nelson (1974, p. 280) the structure of the concept BALL can be represented as follows:

$$
\text{BALL} \begin{bmatrix}
\text{Functional core relationships: rolls, bounces} \\
\text{Non-core implicit relationships: actor } (X_j), \\
\text{action } (A_k), \text{ location } (P_1, L_i) \\
\text{Optional relationships: possessor } (O_m) \ldots \\
\text{Descriptive features: shape (round } \ldots), \text{ rigidity} \\
(\ldots), \text{ texture } (\ldots), \text{ size} \\
(\ldots), \text{ colour } (\ldots) \\
\text{Names: 'ball', 'baseball', } \ldots
\end{bmatrix}
$$

The structure also represents the set of procedures which might be used when the child identifies a new instance of a concept. Information from top to bottom, i.e. from functional to descriptive information, is most reliable for new identifications. It is the functional relationships that determine what counts as an instance of a concept, not the descriptive features. Nelson makes the interesting observation that when a child starts making two-word utterances he is unlikely to say 'ball round' or 'ball roll' because these are functional core relationships and so defining characteristics, and therefore utterances which included them would be redundant. The child is much more likely to say 'daddy ball', 'throw ball', etc., which include optional relationships. Characteristics which are part of the definition, and therefore taken for granted, are not worth commenting upon unless there is a special reason for it. Thus, if a child says 'ball roll' it is likely to be in a situation where, for example, the ball is actually rolling away out of the child's reach and he is expressing his displeasure. But in this case he does not point to the defining, i.e. dispositional characteristic of the ball, but to an episode (Marková and Farmer, 1978). As Nelson says, 'children in the early stages of talking do often comment on changes in the state of objects (e.g. 'open', 'hurt', 'broken', 'all gone') but not on their invariant attributes' (Nelson, 1974, p. 281).

Herder's claim that the first words of language were verbs was obviously a rather naive reflection of his conviction of the active and expressive nature of language. It certainly is not true that the first words of child language are verbs though more and more studies support Nelson's claim that 'the outstanding characteristic of children's first words is their basis in dynamic or functional relations' (Nelson, 1974, p. 279).

So if the claim that language is acquired in the course of a child's activities is true, why is it that verbs are not the first words to be acquired? One possible explanation might be sought once again in reflecting upon *what is taken for granted*: since functions and changes *are* among the defining characteristics of objects, there is no need or incentive for a child to use verbs as first words. We usually do not comment upon what is taken for granted. It is only when decontextualization takes place that verbs obtain their role *as verbs*: and this is at the stage when the child starts forming sentences. Once this stage is reached, the function of the verb in a sentence seems to obtain a more important role. Some researchers have pointed out that the verb is much more important for the comprehension and interpretation of a sentence than is the noun, i.e. the subject and object of the sentence (Healy and Miller, 1970; Abelson and Kanouse, 1966; Marková and Farmer, 1978).

10.4 The reflexive nature of thought

We pointed out earlier that many of the psychologists who are applying Hegelian ideas in psychological theory and method have perhaps never read any of Hegel's works. An important exception, already mentioned, is S. L. Rubinstein, who not only explicitly refers to Hegel and uses some of his terminology, but also applies Hegel's ideas in both his empirical and theoretical studies of human thought.

Rubinstein calls the reflexive theory of knowledge stemming from Hegel 'the Copernican revolution' (Rubinstein, 1957, p. 38), implying obviously that Kant's theory of knowledge (cf. pp. 52–53) does not deserve this label. Rubinstein criticizes the traditional theories of knowledge, in particular Locke's representationalism and the presentationism of Berkeley and Mach. The representational theory of knowledge of Locke is based upon the assumption that the objects of knowledge are our ideas that represent objects in the world. Presentationism, on the other hand, claims that the objects of the external world consist of sense data, and therefore are given to us directly through the senses.

For Rubinstein, just as for Hegel, knowledge and truth are neither immediate nor representative, but are reflexive processes:

Thought in its real sense is penetration into deeper levels of the essence of things, bringing to light what has so far been hidden in the unknown depths; it means setting up and solving the problems of being and life; it is both a search for and the answer to the question 'what is reality?', both being necessary if one is to find out how to live truly and how to act. (Rubinstein, 1959, p. 53)

This is clearly not only a Hegelian theory of knowledge but is also formulated in Hegelian terms. 'Penetration into deeper levels of the essence of things' is particularly important since it is the active process of thought that Rubinstein emphasizes. In order to highlight the activity of thought in his theory, Rubinstein (1958) submitted Gestalt psychology to critical discussion. According to Gestalt psychology the process of thinking consists of transformations of problem situations. Thus, when, in solving a problem, new aspects of the situation take priority, Gestalt psychologists do not interpret this as the discovery of previously unknown properties of the problem situation but as a change in focus of what is being attended to in perception. Problem-solving thus consists of gradual switches from one focus to another, to 'seeing' different aspects of the problem situation, the solution of a problem being the final correct 'seeing' of that situation. In such a theory, thinking is reduced to the mutual relationships between a succession of situations, while the thinking subject is no longer actively involved in the task.

Just as for Rubinstein, so for Mead (1934) thought is reflexive and arises in a problem situation. When learned processes are carried out automatically, there is no need for reflexive thought; thought occurs only when such automatic processes are for some reason interrupted. Under such circumstances conscious reflexion is mobilized and reflexive thought becomes 'an imaginative rehearsal, a comparison and evaluation of alternative routes to consummation' (Mead, 1938, p. 79). It is when automatic action has been checked that reflexive thought starts testing the various means and alternative routes available to the actor. The inhibition of an action invites a person to invent hypotheses as to how the action could be continued, gives him opportunities for the creation of images, and so mobilizes his activities. The process of reflexive thought enables the person to reconstruct his environment in such a way that he can act in a different fashion, using knowledge that lies inside the process itself.

10.5 The mind as a dynamic whole

Just as Herder and Mead argued that the mind develops through the activity of communicating subjects, so Rubinstein claims that thought develops through practical activity. There is, in fact, nothing new about this claim. We know already that the journey of consciousness towards knowledge starts with non-reflexive activity and only turns into reflexive activity when consciousness reaches self-consciousness. Activity, of course, is never considered as some-thing private to the subject, but is interaction between the subject and his world. He is always acting upon the world, and by acting getting to know it:

Knowledge and action are mutually related. Knowledge is originally directly interwoven with practical activity; only then it detaches itself and forms itself into a special cognitive 'activity'. It is not correct to oppose action and knowledge and treat them as external to each other. It is not correct, therefore, to imagine that in genetics matters have pro-ceeded in such a way that originally there was action without knowledge (and then, accordingly, knowledge without action). (Rubinstein, 1959, p. 59)

What Rubinstein means is that there is no phylogenetically and ontogenet-ically predetermined *external* relationship between activity and knowledge, with the activity of the highly specialized 'mental organs' being 'triggered off' by the environment. The relation between the two is immanently internal. Moreover, 'mental organs' such as thought, speech, perception or conscious-ness can develop only in mutual relationship with one another. Although the high specificity of these mental organs is recognized by Rubinstein, the isol-ation of the Cartesian compartments of the mind is rejected. The mind is a dynamic whole in which thought, language, consciousness, and activity are all intimately related. What happens in the process of phylogenetic and ontogenetic development is that these 'mental organs' gradually become decontextualized. While initially thought and language are interwoven with activity, in the process of development the child starts thinking without acting at the same time and can speak without acting at the same time. The experi-ments of Rubinstein and of his students demonstrate this mutual relationship between thought and activity.

Žukovova (Rubinstein, 1958) carried out a series of three experiments. In her study three- to six-year old children were required to get a sweet out of a container by means of 'a tool'. Several kinds of tool were presented to the children. Some of them were suitable for the task, some unsuitable. The tools were little hammers, big hooks, small hooks, and curved hooks. The tools were of different colours. The sweet could be removed from the container only by means of a small hook.

The task demanded of the child that he analyse the tools and find out which of the tools were appropriate for obtaining the sweet.

In the first experiment a group of children were individually presented with tools of different kinds with random colours. In the second experiment another group of children were presented with tools of different kinds but of the same colour. The third group of children were presented with tools of different kinds, but in one variant the 'correct' tool had a bright and attractive colour and in the other variant the 'wrong' tool had a bright and attractive colour.

The first experiment was closest to a real-life situation. In this experiment the features of the tool essential for the solution (the *kind* of tool) were presented together with irrelevant features (the *colour* of the tool). Thus, the demand put on the child was to analyse the tools of different kinds and colours and then to separate the *kind* as a relevant feature from the colour as an irrelevant feature. The task had two steps for the child: *analysis* of the tool and *abstraction* of the relevant and irrelevant features.

In the second experiment the colour of the tool was the same in every case, and therefore it was not necessary for the child to abstract the kind from the colour. Only one step was thus necessary.

In the third experiment, the bright and attractive colour indicated either 'correct' or 'wrong' tool, so that the child, immediately attracted by the colour, did not have to analyse the kind of tool as the colour indicated its utility. Again, only one step was required for the solution. The difference between the second and the third series was that in the second series it was not necessary to separate the kind from the colour, while in the third series it was not necessary to analyse the kind of tool.

In all three experiments, irrespective of age, the children initially solved the problem by practical effort. They tried one tool after another to find out the one that was appropriate for the solution of the problem. Later on, after a number of trials, the children stopped solving the task practically, but only compared the shape of the tool *visually* with the container. Finally, many children stopped even the visual comparison of the tool with the container. Instead, when an inappropriate tool was presented to him, for example, a tool without a hook, or hooks of inappropriate sizes, the child said: 'Sticks without hooks will not get the sweet out'.

The final result for all age groups was that the children started with practical trials. But by their practical experience they were able to transform their problem-solving activity into a perceptual comparison of tool and container, and eventually they solved the problem purely theoretically, without the use of practical trials.

The number of practical trials for the above three series was different: in the first series where the child had to carry out a two-step analysis (the kind and the colour), nearly twice as many practical trials were needed to solve the problem as in the second and third series. Once the child was able to carry out the task intellectually, he was also able to generalize from one task to another of a similar kind because he was now able to analyse the problem.

Rubinstein is concerned to emphasize that the task for psychologists is not only to describe the external manifestations of such a generalizing process but also to discover its internal nature. The study of thinking is not reduced to the study of practical activities. That the child can generalize means that he is able to discover the essential relationships of a problem situation, and the study of generalization is therefore very important from the educational point of view. Rubinstein is quite emphatic that practical and theoretical analysis in the process of thinking form a unity, and that it would be wrong to talk about practical and pure thinking separately.

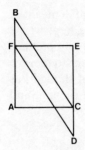

Figure 10.1 Geometrical patterns in
Mansurov experiment. From
Rubinstein (1958)

Just as, according to Rubinstein, practical activity and reflexive thought are interrelated in the development of a human being, so is language and thought. Thought in its proper sense is impossible without language. 'Abstract thought is *thought in language*, it is *thought in words*' (Rubinstein, 1958, p. 162). Rubinstein and his students are particularly concerned to demonstrate the interrelationship between language and thought in problem-solving. In problem-solving the way the task is formulated in words partially determines the way the task is encoded by the subject. As Rubinstein puts it, the formulation of the problem in words is the 'living witness of the unity of thinking and language'. One and the same problem can be formulated in different ways, different formulations directing the subject's attention upon different aspects and relationships between the elements of a task. In fact, the formulation of the task not only represents the beginning of the analysis of the problem but also determines the way the analysis will be carried out. Every verbal formulation of the problem is an act of thinking at the same time, and therefore is an act of *analysis through synthesis* (cf. later).

Let us consider an experiment by Mansurov (Rubinstein, 1958), in which the subjects were given a task in two different formulations. The pupils were presented with a geometrical pattern (Figure 10. 1), and in one case were given this instruction: Compute the sum of the areas of the parallelogram FBCD and the square AFEC. In the second case the instruction was as follows: What is the sum of the areas of the two triangles ABC and FED? In both cases the pupils were given the lengths of AB and AC.

Given the former formulation of the problem, all the pupils computed the areas of the parallelogram and of the square and added them together. In the latter case, the pupils only had to compare the two triangles together perceptually. Then they added their areas together. We can thus see that the formulation of the problem determined the way the problem was analysed and, moreover, that different formulations already *contained* different levels of analysis of the problem.

One of the 'secrets' of the difficulties of puzzles is, as Rubinstein points out, that the words in which the task is expressed direct the subject's attention upon inessential features and mask the real essence of the problem. Of course, any kind of insincere communication is an attempt to disguise, through the choice of words, the real issue of the communication and to mislead the listener into understanding 'what is not meant'. Attempts to discover what Kafka meant in his novels or what Kant or Hegel meant in their writings have kept whole generations of literary specialists and philosophers preoccupied. Thus, puzzles, insurance application forms, or literary works all require the reader to remove the veil created by the choice of words, those *fixed* products of thought, as Rubinstein calls them. This all means that the compartments of thought and language must be interconnected by a very wide opening indeed.

10.6 Knowledge is acquired through a 'circle returning within itself'

It will by now have become clear that one of the most important differences between the Cartesian and Hegelian frameworks lies in their different conceptions of the acquisition of knowledge. The Cartesian search for certainty, both in rationalism and empiricism, has led to the algorithmic approach to knowledge. The process of acquisition of knowledge is decomposed into elementary steps that can be represented by hierarchical decision trees, so that progress in knowledge is dependent on whether the previous step was right or wrong.

There is no such thing as a 'yes–no' approach in the Hegelian framework. The manner of acquisition of knowledge in the Hegelian framework has been given different descriptions by Hegel's followers and named as a 'hermeneutic circle', or a 'spiral' or a 'circle of understanding'. Hegel himself talks about a 'circle returning within itself'. Discussing the nature of the development of mind he maintains that a succession of processes in development must be represented not as a straight line drawn out into a vague infinity, but as a circle returning within itself, which, as periphery, has very many circles, and whose whole is a large number of processes in development turning back within themselves (Hegel, *History of Philosophy*, p. 27).

There is nothing mysterious about Hegel's 'circle returning within itself'. It can be understood as follows: the acquisition of knowledge is an active subject–object process. But Hegel is not simply saying that the Cartesians were mistaken in supposing that man is wholly passive in the acquisition of knowledge, that there are certain important respects in which he is active, and that they should not be overlooked. Nor is he just engaged in conceptual analysis, valuable as this can be. He is concerned with the *interaction* in the process of coming to know an object in which both partners in the interaction, *both the knowing subject and the object of his knowing*, are gradually transformed. Let us look at what Hegel is saying more closely.

Every process of the acquisition of knowledge starts with the subject grasping what is in the reach of his senses or his understanding. For example, a baby may grasp a transistor radio as a box of different colours producing some noise. What the baby perceives is something that is immediately accessible to his senses; but what is accessible is an undistinguished and incomprehensible whole; or perhaps we can say, it is comprehensible but only on a superficial level of understanding. By means of practical manipulation and experience the child may discover various knobs on the radio set, these having various effects upon the quality and quantity of the sound, or stopping the sound completely. In Hegel's words, what the child does is to transform the *object as it is*, i.e. the box of different colours producing some noise, into the *object for himself*. Both partners have changed. The child's mind transformed as he manipulated the various controls on the transistor radio. Consequently, the child's concept of the radio set has changed too as he is now able to understand more of the cause–effect relationships of the parts of the set. Well, someone might argue, but the object, the transistor radio, has not changed, it is still the same as it was before. Such a person might bring in witnesses to demonstrate that the object in itself is unchanged: but this would only show that the object for the adult was unaltered. We know already that in the Hegelian framework there is no point in talking about things-in-themselves but only about things for consciousness. And in the light of his practical activity, the object has certainly changed for the child's consciousness. It would certainly be a different object for a mediaeval person, as it will be a different object for a future scientist.

But let us follow Hegel's 'circle returning within itself' a bit further. Having acquired his new knowledge about the transistor radio, the child now stands again at the same place of the spiral or 'circle returning within itself', where he started. The difference is that the child-knower has changed because his mind has developed through his experience obtained in the process of practical activity; and his concept of the radio has changed too. As he grows older and learns something about science, he may now start looking inside the radio and discover various causal relationships intermediate between the operation of the controls and the appearance of the programme. Again, in the process of this manipulation, the transistor radio—or the transistor radio as conceptualized by him, that is the transistor radio for him—changes again. So he returns to the same place of the circle again but with a more developed mind and with a more complex concept of a transistor radio. Thus we see that although the transistor radio was originally grasped as a whole, there has been a gradual transformation of that whole on the basis of attention to a detail and from the detail back to the whole again.

Two things are important in this process. First, the initial grasping of the object in the process of the acquisition of knowledge is vague, or *abstract*, to use Hegel's term. The process of the acquisition of knowledge is the process of concretization. This process is not one of simply adding more detail to what the person already knows. For example, the child's acquisition of concepts or meanings of words cannot be conceived as a process in which the child adds new attributes of a concept or new semantic markers to those he has acquired already. Changing some elements while others are left untouched in the acquisition of knowledge was the case in the Cartesian paradigm. For example, as mentioned in Chapter 5, Hamlyn has criticized Piaget on the grounds that Piaget assumed that the child had already attained the adult concept of water and that what was missing was the concept of conservation. Clark's semantic theory assumes that the child gradually adds new semantic features to those he has already and thus his overextension of the meaning is gradually reduced to the adult meaning.

The Hegelian framework assumes, on the other hand, that in the light of every new detail the whole of the knowledge changes too, nothing remains stable and unchanged. In literary criticism this idea of the acquisition of knowledge has been expressed by Wellek. According to him, too, the acquisition of knowledge should not be conceived of as a straight-line process carried out in a 'yes–no' manner, but it proceeds through a movement from the whole to a detail and from the detail back to the whole by a gradual reconstruction of the previously held 'truths':

In reading with a sense for continuity, for contextual coherence, for wholeness, there comes a moment when we feel that we have 'understood', that we have seized on the right interpretation, the real meaning ... it is the main source of knowledge in all humanistic branches of learning, from theology to jurisprudence, from philology to the history of literature. It is a process that has been called 'the circle of understanding'. It proceeds from attention to a detail to an anticipation of the whole and back again to an interpretation of the detail. It is a circle that is not a vicious, but a fruitful circle. (Wellek, quoted by Rommetveit, 1974, p. 89)

It would not be difficult to demonstrate that the majority of cases of the acquisition of knowledge can be viewed as circles returning within themselves, and therefore as *indirect* processes of obtaining truth. In spite of this, however, as Kosík (1963) points out, human beings have been trying throughout the whole process of history to grasp the world in its entirety immediately and to obtain the truth directly. And very often the truth appears to be obtainable directly and in its concreteness. Kosík maintains, however, that under such circumstances the world presents itself to human beings not in its concreteness, that is, in its truth, but in its *pseudo-concreteness*, that only appears to be truth; superficial properties of objects appear to be the essential properties; insincere relationships present themselves as genuine ones; the world of manipulations presents itself as a non-possessive relationship; the possession of objects gives one the appearance of status and power.

The world of pseudoconcrete is the twilight of truth and deception. Its root is ambiguity. The appearance discloses the essence and it conceals it at the same time. The essence manifests itself through its appearance but it manifests itself in an inadequate manner, either as a part or through some of its aspects only. (Kosík, 1963, p. 11)

The second characteristic of the acquisition of knowledge is the *creative* nature of the process. The acquisition of knowledge is not conceived simply as obtaining something that is already in existence, accepting what is available, but as also creating it. Every constructive process is a creative process. We can observe young children creating words, and giving meaning to the words they have just created. It is self-expression and self-growth through creativity.

Kosík points out that there are two aspects of human consciousness: its reflexiveness and its projective function. Reality is not only a reflexion or expression of human consciousness, but is also created by it. The penetration of nature is feasible only because a new, *human* reality is created. The achievements of modern technology demolish the view that the acquisition of knowledge is based on contemplation. The arts are also a part of this process of the creation of human reality. The mediaeval cathedral is not only a reflexion or expression of the existing world but it is also a new creation of that world; not only a reproduction but a production. As Hegel said—and in this the productive aspect of the acquisition of knowledge becomes obvious—man humanizes nature, he makes it for himself. He learns to know it by working upon it and by creating it.

In experimental psychology the principle of the 'circle returning within itself' has become part of Rubinstein's work. Rubinstein (1957, 1958) claims that human cognition generally and thought in particular can be understood on the basis of 'the principle of determinism'. This principle claims that every cognitive process is determined by the external conditions that function through internal conditions. He postulates four cognitive operations through which the principle of determinism is realized: analysis, synthesis, abstraction, and generalization. By analysis is meant breaking the problem situation down into what appear to be the known and unknown elements. It starts with the formulation of the problem situation, the importance of which we have already seen. Synthesis is the process of conceptual reconstruction of the object. Rubinstein also points to the importance of comparison in analysis and synthesis. Comparison is an operation by means of which a person considers what has been analysed with respect to its synthesis. Abstraction occurs during analysis and it is an operation that enables a person to separate details from the whole and thus concentrate on essential aspects of the problem. Generalization is an operation enabling one to perceive common features between different objects and thus to apply the experience obtained in one problem to another problem.

A human being never solves a problem *in vacuo*, that is in isolation from the context in which the task occurs or from his past experience. Instead he compares the given task with tasks he has already solved in the past, and attempts to use his previous knowledge and experience to deal with the present problem. This is how the process of analysis through synthesis starts off.

Analysis through synthesis occurs in different kinds and qualities, but the most important is the one which is essential to all thinking activities. In this form

... in the process of thinking the object is continuously being put into new relationships, and therefore, manifesting itself in new qualities. These new qualities fix themselves in new concepts. It is as if the object supplied the thinker with new content all the time; as if it was constantly turning different faces towards the subject, and disclosing new properties. (Rubinstein, 1958, p. 85)

This certainly is a Hegelian formulation of the relationship between subject and object. We are not faced with the Kantian thing-in-itself that remains impenetrable, but through the mutual relationships of subject and object the truth is asymptotically discovered. Rubinstein's operation of comparison reminds one of Hegel's process of comparison of one's consciousness of an object with one's concept of the object. A concept is obtained through the process of constructive synthesis while practical activity enables one to analyse the problem. Abstraction, the method of focusing upon a detail again, is indispensable in the 'circle returning within itself'. It is through abstraction of a detail that the whole can be reformulated at a higher conceptual level.

Let us consider another of the experiments of the Rubinstein school. Ancyferova (Rubinstein, 1958) was concerned to investigate problem-solving in technical and scientific tasks in which the pupil was expected to discover the cause–effect relationships between certain events. In one of her experiments, subjects were given the following task. They were required to put a chemical balance into a state of balance in such a way that after a lapse of time the balance was upset without any external interference. The subjects were provided with various objects that might be useful for putting a balance into balance, among them a candle and a box of matches. The solution of the task consisted of putting a candle on each side of the balance and lighting one of them. A lighted candle, of course, slowly decreases in weight, so that the original balance is upset without any interference on the part of the experimental subject.

The task proved to be a difficult one. The main difficulty appeared to be due to the fact that the subjects perceived the objects provided for the solution of the task in terms of their well known properties and uses. Thus, a candle is an object that gives out light rather than an object that loses weight while alight. In order to solve the problem the subjects had to overcome the difficulty of perceiving the objects in terms of their most obvious characteristics and uses. In other words, it was necessary for them to carry out an analysis of the properties of these objects and insert these properties into new cause–effect relationships, that is, to reconstruct the objects using different concepts. As we know, such a conceptual reconstruction was described by Rubinstein as a synthesis. Moreover, the verbal formulation itself determines the beginning of the analysis. The original formulation of the problem was 'to upset the balance of the scales'. Only as a result of an analysis of the properties of the objects could the subject reformulate the problem as 'to change the weight of the objects'.

In the process of solving the task, the subjects usually started by trying substances that evaporate, such as ether. Secondly, they attempted to use wet objects, the weights of which decrease as they dry. Finally, a candle was seen not as an object that gives out light, but as an object that when alight decreases in weight. In sum, it was the realization of new cause–effect relationships between objects that led to the solution.

Rubinstein emphasizes that cognitive operations such as analysis through synthesis and abstraction lead to reformulation of the task for the subject. Language itself is a system of fixed analyses, syntheses, and abstractions. Therefore, the reformulation of the task is a verbal expression of the relationships between analysis and synthesis; reformulation of the task creates a new synthesis and depends on the analysis that has already been achieved. The act of analysis can be manifested as a verbal act.

And, of course, because language often functions as a fixed system, it freezes the activity of the subject–object relationships. As Rubinstein puts it

Human knowledge is a historical category. It cannot be reduced to a momentary act in which knowledge emerges in order to be extinguished again. Knowledge in a proper sense presupposes a continuity of obtained knowledge and its fixation by means of a word. (Rubinstein, 1959, p. 102)

CHAPTER 11

Paradigms and Scientific Method in Psychology

11.1 Cartesian and Hegelian science

The reaction of the expressivists against the scientific rationalism of the Enlightenment was not a reaction against Science as such. It was a reaction against a particular kind of science, against Newtonian science based on a mechanistic conception of the world. The expressivists objected to this science for the following reasons: it reduced the world to a conglomeration of particles in endless motion; it separated body from mind and excluded values and human experience from the field of scientific investigation; values were made irrelevant to scientific activity; the intelligible and mathematical world of science was supposed to have nothing to do with morality and freedom of judgement; and finally, the object of truth was assumed to exist out there in the objective world and was to be discovered solely by means of scientific activity, independent of any personal experience.

The expressivists generally and Hegel in particular were very interested in scientific achievements. However, their basic presuppositions concerning the physical and social world differed from those of the Newtonians. Thus we mentioned earlier that in the eighteenth century the ideas of dynamics and evolution started emerging in various forms both in philosophy and in science. Also the influence of Leibniz's conception of self-unfolding monads upon the German expressivists was considerable.

While the main body of physical science was still based on mechanics, the new discoveries of Franklin, Priestley, and others opened up the new area of the physics of electricity and dynamics. These new developments, which were in full agreement with the *Zeitgeist*, attracted the attention of the *Stürmer and Dränger* and provoked their enthusiasm. Pascal (1953) comments upon their interest in physical dynamics and their metaphoric use of physical terms:

They [the Stürmer and Dränger] are fond of the term 'elasticity'; Herder and Bürger both use the phrase 'elasticity of the spirit'. Most of all they delight in electrical images, in this period when Franklin and Priestley were carrying out their experiments in electricity, and when Merck's acquaintance Lichtenberg was measuring the electric charge in the atmosphere. Wieland calls Herder 'an electric cloud', Lenz speaks of the 'spark of God', probably a reference to the charge of the Leyden jar. Goethe wrote to a girl friend: 'Happiness of the soul and heroism are as communicable as electricity, and you have as much of them as the electric machine contains sparks of fire'. Herder uses such symbols over and over again. 'We electrify ourselves to activity . . . that is the wondrous creative power to set souls alive, like the electric spark, perhaps, in blood and sun'. Genius speaks to genius, he writes, as an electric spark sends out its energy; he even speaks of Prometheus fetching the 'electric spark' from Heaven. In such terms as these, 'irritation', 'energy', 'elasticity', 'electricity', the Stürmer and Dränger link up the dynamic principle of matter with the creativeness of spirit. Herder's *On Knowledge and Perception in the Human Soul* is the systematic exposition of this relationship, an attempt to define the dynamic nature of being. (Pascal, 1953, p. 182)

For the expressivists, scientific activity does not consist just of ordering of the impressions made by Nature upon the scientist's mind. The mind is neither a Lockean *tabula rasa*, passively accepting impressions, nor does knowledge arise from innate ideas as Descartes and Leibniz suggested. The scientist is himself a creator of Nature and the world. His scientific activity cannot be separated from his deep personal experience. Knowledge *is* activity and it changes both the scientist and the world he lives in. Coleridge expressed his views upon the subject as follows:

My opinion is this—that deep Thinking is attainable only by a man of deep Feeling, and that all Truth is a species of Revelation. The more I understand of Sir Isaac Newton's works, the more boldly I dare utter to my own mind, and therefore to *you*, that I believe the Souls of 500 Sir Isaac Newtons would go to the making up of a Shakspere or a Milton . . . Newton was a mere materialist—*Mind* in his system is always passive—a lazy Looker-on on an external World. If the mind be not *passive*, if it be indeed made in God's Image, and that, too in the sublimest sense—the Image of the *Creator*, there is ground for suspicion, that any system built on the passiveness of the mind must be false, as a system (Coleridge, to Thomas Poole, 23rd March, 1801)

Moreover, mechanistic science could offer no explanation for the occurrence and development of new forms except for the quantitative redistribution of physical elements in terms of their separations from previous structures and associations in new ones.

Hegel expressed his criticism of Newtonian science in a systematic manner. According to him, science is the process of continuous penetration into the essence of things. The Newtonian approach to scientific exploration, Hegel says, is defective because it relies upon the principle of quantity, and searches for evidence based on mathematics only rather than upon philosophy. What Hegel means is that science should be concerned with the qualitative analysis of concepts because the qualitative and not the quantitative analysis of concepts is essential to knowledge. Newtonian science, on the other hand, being pre-occupied with quantitative, and therefore, *non-essential* relationships within and between things, can never reach adequate knowledge. Its 'process of knowing proceeds on the surface, does not touch the thing itself, its essence' (Hegel, *Phenomenology*, p. 25) and thus fails to comprehend it. The material that mathematics provides with such a 'gratifying treasury of truths, is space and the numerical unit'. Since mathematics is concerned with the non-actual, its truths are rigid and dead. The *actual* cannot be expressed as something moving forward 'along the line of *equality*' (Hegel, *Phenomenology*, p. 26). Mathematical equations based on abstract identity of the right and left sides cannot explain anything about the concrete nature of things that are filled with inner self-movement.

Newtonian time, too, Hegel says, constitutes only a counterpart of space and is reduced to pure mathematics. Mathematical equations 'dealing with numerical units cannot, moreover, 'cope with that sheer unrest of life and its absolute distinction' (Hegel, *Phenomenology*, p. 27). Within such a conception, life appears only in a paralysed form in which the self-movement of life is reduced to lifeless unity. What is essential in being is not expressible in terms of fixed numerical units. True reality, Hegel says, is a Bacchanalian revel where nobody is sober; it is self-movement which must be the subject matter of true science.

The expressivists were also critical of the Cartesian conception that organisms are machines, decomposable into elements related to each other as causes and effects. For Hegel, living organisms are characterized by their undividedness (Hegel, *Phenomenology*, p. 160). Organisms are wholes that can be understood only as purposefully functioning unities, and their parts can only be explained in terms of the purposes of the wholes to which they belong. Hegel's position, of course, is not without its predecessors. Hegel himself acknowledges his debt to Aristotle. Aristotle was one of the first to comprehend Nature as a unity and as alive. For Aristotle Nature was purposive activity, and in this sense 'purpose is what is immediate and *at rest*, the unmoved which is also *self-moving*' (Hegel, *Phenomenology*, p. 12). Thus we can see that Hegel's notion of contradiction expressed in his 'at rest' and 'self-moving' appears in this context again as a principle of life and a purpose in Nature. Nature *or* life is *entelecheia*, a transformation of potentiality into actuality. This self-maintaining activity of life brings out the unity in all relationships, and in living beings 'cause and effect are identical, since all individual parts are related to this unity of end' (Hegel, *History of Philosophy*, II, p. 159). But then Hegel points out that this Aristotelian conception of Nature as purposive activity became lost in the history of thought in two ways: first, through a mechanistic philosophy that substituted the self-productive action of Nature by the principles of mechanics such as those of pressure, impulse, and chemical and physical relationships; and, secondly, through theology which has sought the causes of natural phenomena in forces outside Nature itself.

For Hegel, purpose is not an entity, but a set of basic underlying laws relating the organism and its environment. There is no separation into an outer and inner world and an organism must be considered as a whole, and from the point of view of the genus, as Kant himself pointed out. Like Kant, Hegel recognized the crucial role of reproduction in securing the unity of the organism, whether of parts of itself in growth, or of its whole in new individuals: 'Reproduction, taken in the sense of *self-preservation in general* ... is ... the real organic Notion or the *whole*, which returns into itself, either *qua* individual by producing single parts of itself, or *qua* genus, by bringing forth individuals' (Hegel, *Phenomenology*, p. 161). Hegel, as a genuine evolutionist, was not confronted with the Kantian problem as to how the system starts working. According to Hegel, any kind of *being* is charged with an internal tension which is necessary and essential for the development of the contradiction on which life depends. This inner tension results in the opposition between what a thing potentially is and what it actually is, which we have already discussed with respect to the development of consciousness. The development of an organism thus proceeds through its activity, and it is the character of its activity that defines a living organism. It is through its activity that the organism transcends what is fixed in itself, that is, what is inorganic, and by consuming it converts it into itself. It develops through the negation of its earlier forms, it reproduces itself as an individual and as a genus (Hegel, *Phenomenology*, pp. 161–2).

In order to demonstrate his point concerning the wholeness and activity of the organism, Hegel discussed the methods and practices of the observational psychology of his time. In their studies of human consciousness, psychologists had recounted a great many sorts of faculties, inclinations, and passions which were treated like a collection of things in a bag. While these individual characteristics of the mind could not be treated in isolation one from the other, neither could they be mingled together into an undistinguished unity. The mistake of observational psychology, according to Hegel, was that it tried to understand psychic faculties as laws which were constituted in terms referring on the one hand to the individual and on the other to the environment. He argued strongly against expressing the relationship between the individual and his environment in terms of the kind and amount of influence the environment has on the individual. The relationship between the individual and his environment cannot be taken as fixed or given. The laws of psychology should express the dynamic relationship between the individual and his environment resulting in the mutual unfolding of both. Psychology at Hegel's time (and, to a great extent, at the present time), however, assumed that the external world influences the individual and manifests itself in the individual, so that the individual can be comprehended from these influences. Such psychology, once again, assumed a dual inner and outer nature of the individual:

We should have a double gallery of pictures, one of which would be the reflection of the other: the one, the gallery of external circumstances which completely determine and circumscribe the individual, the other, the same gallery translated into the form in which those circumstances are present in the conscious individual: the former the spherical surface, the latter the centre which represents that surface within it. (Hegel, *Phenomenology*, p. 184)

This mistaken conception, tearing the individual apart between his inner and outer natures, cannot account for the expression of activity and creativity. What actually influences the individual, and in what sense, depends solely on the individual in question. The individual is what his world is as a world which is specifically *his*. It is through the individual's activity that being-in-itself and being-for-itself achieve unity. A truly scientific approach would take for granted this unity of the *actual* individual and the world he has created for himself, 'a unity whose sides do not fall apart'. In the above conception of psychological law, however, the world falls on one side *in itself*, as something already given, and the individual, on the other hand, is supposed to exist *on his own*. Having established such a duality between the two, psychology then attempts to discover the effect of the one upon the other.

Finally, for the expressivists, science is a *social* activity. Values and personal experience, excluded from scientific activity as irrelevant since Galileo, have an important role to play. The kinds of problems science attempts to solve are very often determined by historical circumstances. Historical experience of the culture in which the scientist lives also enters into his scientific activity. His understanding of the world, which is a world socially created, affects the methods he chooses for exploration.

We can thus see that the presuppositions of the Hegelian framework led to a quite different conception of the world and of the scientific enterprise from that arising from the presuppositions of the Cartesian framework. However, it was the Cartesian framework that became established in the seventeenth century, and has been taken for granted by both the natural and social sciences ever since. Because of its universal acceptance, it has also been taken for granted that its scientific and methodological principles are universally valid. Hegelian ideas have certainly *not* attracted the natural sciences and their influence on the social sciences has been doubtful and definitely not universal.

It was partly due to the obscurity of Hegel and the Hegelian writers that their writings came to be considered 'not worth reading'. There is, however, little doubt that the time is becoming ripe for a thorough investigation of Hegel's work and that Hegelian ideas are beginning to penetrate the minds of the social and even the natural scientists. This fact brings us back to Kuhn's and Hanson's problem of the theory-ladenness of observation and scientific method.

11.2 Theory-ladenness and the neutrality of scientific observation

Kuhn's and Hanson's ideas that all our perceptions and conceptualizations are theory-laden, referred to at the very beginning of the book, have not been accepted with universal applause. Some philosophers, in their search for objectivity in science, still argue that in order to obtain knowledge that is certain one must start from *neutral data* and *neutral observations*. Examining and challenging the doctrine of theory-ladenness in science, Scheffler (1967) claims that the ideal of objectivity would be threatened if the attack on 'the notion of a fixed observational given', on a 'constant descriptive language', and on 'a shared methodology of investigation' were taken seriously. Moreover, he is concerned at what he sees as the consequence of the extreme position of the doctrine that 'data are manufactured by theory', that is that there is no possibility of evaluating rival hypotheses, indeed, no possibility of communication about them because there is no common and neutral ground from which to start.

The search for neutral and therefore objective data and facts in psychology has also been well documented. Let us take for example, the long debate between the behaviour therapists and dynamically orientated therapists concerning the symptom substitution hypothesis. According to this hypothesis, set up by the dynamically orientated therapists, the removal of the symptoms of a mental disease, as practised by behaviour therapists, that is without attention to the hypothetical underlying causes of the disease, will result in the appearance of new symptoms, or the return of the old ones. The behaviour therapists, however, from the position of learning theories, deny that their treatment is at all inadequate. Although it may appear that the question is empirical and could therefore be easily resolved, this is not so, because the behaviour therapists are not treating *symptoms*, and the psychotherapists are. In his attempt to resolve this controversy, Cahoon (1968) complains that definitions of the term 'symptom' have tended to be loaded with the framework of the psychodynamists. To make communication possible between the two sides, the *facts* must, Cahoon argues, be released from the frameworks with which they are loaded: a common ground should be found from which a discussion could be started. Thus, he suggests that everyone agrees that a symptom 'refers to behaviour troublesome to the individual or his culture' while any more complex definition would preclude communication between dynamic and behavioural therapists.

The search by psychologists for a theoretically neutral immediate data language demonstrates the above point even more clearly. The authors of the book *Modern Learning Theory* (Estes *et al*., 1954) praise Hull, Tolman, and Skinner for defining terms in, and for their use of, a theoretically neutral data language. Data language, although it conforms to the rules of English syntax, is restricted to the use of expressions that are supposed to contain only 'neutral' information. The words of data language are derived from an 'uncodified psychological vocabulary more or less common to experimental psychologists (e.g. "reaction", "habit", "bar-pressing habit", "extinction", "learning curves", "threshold")'. Words such as 'hear', 'intention', 'in order to', 'feel' or 'try' that supposedly are loaded with redundant and biasing information should not be used. They may, however, be translated into neutral terms. Lewin, whom they also include among modern learning theorists, is not praised in the same way. The 'lack of any explicit consideration of the data language appears as a rather striking omission' in his writings. And 'this apparent blind spot' is complemented by the fact that since he has neither defined nor used a data language he could not provide the basis for any adequate communication.

However, in spite of all the attempts to establish neutral data, neutral observation, and neutral language, evidence shows that implicit presuppositions and conceptual frameworks do determine what is observed, even for researchers working in the same framework. Turner gives this example from behaviouristic psychology:

190

Recall the cat in the Thorndike puzzle box. It claws, bites, struggles, strikes and finally escapes. Simple facts it would seem. Yet to Thorndike it was a random trial and error sequence of responses supported by an initial, instinctive, response-repertory; whereas to Tolman, such a sequence of events could be seen as demonstration of persistence and 'docility' culminating in the subject's responsive orientation towards its goal-objects (Tolman, 1932). Something in this behavioural situation is identical for the two observers and something is very different. (Turner, 1967, p. 190)

Turner points out in this context that scientific observation is much more than just bringing data into the focus of awareness. Rather, the observer sees the data that fit into his prevailing conceptual system.

Studies into the acquisition of the meaning of words in young children also demonstrate the theory-ladenness of observation. Clark (1973) has observed that acquisition of the meanings of words in young children is based on perceptual features such as similarity, shape, size, texture, movement or sound. In the process of the acquisition of meanings, according to this theory, the child first overextends meanings and applies a word to a referent lying outside the semantic category of the adult language (cf. pp. 50–51). Nelson (1974), on the other hand, observes that young children acquire new words on the basis of functional rather than perceptual similarity (cf. pp. 171–173). Bowerman's (1978) observation of the spontaneous speech of her two daughters, Christy and Eva, presents strong evidence against Nelson's theory that functional similarity predominates over perceptual similarity in the acquisition of child language. Bowerman claims that children often disregard functional similarity and classify objects purely on the basis of perceptual similarities. Bowerman offers a number of cases to illustrate her claim. For example, Eva used the word 'moon' for a ball of spinach she was about to eat. Moreover, Bowerman makes the following observation of the use of words by her two children:

Most of their first object words (e.g., 'ball', 'bottle', 'dog', 'dolly', 'cookie') were initially uttered *not* when the children (or others) were acting upon the objects in question (or, for animate objects, watching them act) but when the objects were static, seen from a distance ranging from a few feet to across a room ... This suggests that the role of function ('actions' and 'relationships') in the child's early formulation and naming of concepts is less crucial than Nelson proposes. (Bowerman, 1978, p. 267)

This argument, of course, highlights Bowerman's Cartesian presuppositions: that the naming of stationary objects serves to prove that their functions are not as important as their perceptual properties. A supporter of the functional approach, however, might interpret this very observation in a completely different way: naming stationary objects can serve the child the purpose of rehearsing what he has learned when playing, eating or acting upon those objects. There would not seem to be much point in saying 'ball' while the child is actually playing with the ball. The child is not a machine churning out the names of objects in order to remind himself and others what he is eating, or playing with, or acting upon. The acquisition of words is a complex social process and cannot be reduced to the occasions when the object in question is present in front of the child and the child actually names it. People usually say things for particular purposes, whether to give information, to express their emotions, to share information with someone else, and so on. On most occasions, therefore, they do not comment upon their act of eating or what they are eating or that they are playing with a doll, unless there is some special purpose for doing so. Not only are such activities obvious to everyone around and taken for granted, but commenting upon them would disrupt the flow of those very activities.

Bowerman also points out that there is not much support for Nelson's functionalist approach in the work of other researchers. This, of course, is not surprising. Since the majority of research workers have been working so far within the Cartesian framework, most of the evidence is Cartesian in character. Not only are these studies based on the assumption that the meanings of words are decomposable into semantic features and that physical objects are collections of perceptible properties, but, in addition, the majority of the words explored by such studies refer to physical objects, and feature analysis can be applied to such words with relative success. In other words the conceptual framework once again determines the kind of material used for empirical exploration. Virtually no research has been carried out within the Cartesian framework with words for which the functional approach would show its clear advantage, for example with words such as 'good', 'kind', 'hope', and so on.

But examples of this kind certainly do not convince the opponents of theory-ladenness. Kordig (1971) maintains that theory-ladenness of observation leads to absurdities; the acceptance of theory-ladenness would prevent scientists working within a particular tradition from revising their theories and traditions, and so progress in science would be totally obstructed; it would make it impossible to judge, compare, and verify theories and traditions; and no theory or tradition could be tested by observation.

Kordig argues as follows: Let us assume that experience E_1 is laden with theory T_1 which explains it. An alternative theory T_2 would be concerned with an experience E_2 differing from E_1. Given this, how could a scientist ever revise his theories and essential beliefs so that they would still be theories about what he experiences? The very moment he changed his theory, experience itself would change too. Thus, if a scientist revised his theory T_1 and substituted it by a new theory T_2, this new theory T_2 would no longer be about experience E_1 but about experience E_2, which is absurd. Similarly, since a theory T_1 refers to experience E_1 and theory T_2 refers to experience E_2 it would be impossible for two scientists, holding different theories, to communicate with each other because they would be experiencing different worlds, each scientist talking about his own specific experience. Consequently, their theories would not be rivals or alternatives.

Kordig's objections to the theory-ladenness of observation are not, of course, launched from a neutral battlefield as he seems to assume. They are already laden with particular kinds of assumptions, that is that scientific data and scientific method are independent of each other, and that the scientist can be an independent and passive observer of his own experiences and of the data. These are assumptions of the Cartesian framework with which we are already familiar. Let us consider Kordig's two main objections from the point of view of the Hegelian framework.

Concerning the first objection that theories could not be revised if the thesis of theory-ladenness were accepted, we know already that revisability of theories is a fundamental aspect of Hegelianism. Consciousness continuously revises both itself and its concepts. And, in fact, it is consciousness's *experience* that leads to the revision. The scientist is not an idle observer of the world around him, recording his experiences and then devising concepts and theories to fit them. On the contrary, he is always actively conceptualizing and theorizing, and his experience is laden from the beginning with concepts and theories which determine the form which it takes. Some elements in his experience may, of course, resist his conceptual and theoretical activity and so lead to contradictions in his experience. This in turn will force the scientist to revise the concepts and theories with which his experience is laden, and therefore the experience itself changes. But we should not picture the process of devising theories as an active conceptualizing and passive recording of experiences. Experience itself is activity, it delves into the essence of things, searching for difficulties and seeking contradictions in things and thoughts as Hegel claimed. This is looking for trouble, but it has an important feature. The process of revision of theories is a continuous and ascending process as we have seen in the case of Hegel's conception of the development of consciousness. Previous theories and experiences are not simply thrown away as useless, as in the Cartesian paradigm. Instead, previous theories and experiences are *transformed*: the bud changes into a flower, the flower changes into a fruit. The process is an ascending one, it is not an arbitrary switching from one theory to another as in Gestalt psychology. Kordig's problem is that he actually substitutes the position of Gestalt psychology for the position of Kuhn and Hanson. Both Kuhn (1962) and Hanson (1958) use Gestalt pictures to illustrate their point that perception is theory-laden and our presuppositions determine what we actually see. However, the analogy ends here. The changes in scientific theory are not just reversible Gestalt switches happening arbitrarily. Kuhn himself points out that the new paradigm *grows* from the old one. The replacement of one scientific theory by another one happens in a systematic and determined manner as knowledge progresses.

Kuhn's position is similar to that of Hegel. Whatever Kordig may say about the consequences of unrevisability in theory-ladenness thesis, the fact remains that, in Kuhn's account, theories *are* revised and necessarily so. Revisions within a particular paradigm occur in order to accommodate contradictions. It is only when these contradictions have reached such an extent that they can no longer be accommodated in a particular paradigm that the paradigm eventually breaks down. We pointed our earlier that this process corresponds to Hegel's notion of transformation of quantity into a new quality.

But what about Kordig's second objection that if theory-ladenness of observation is accepted, alternative theories within a paradigm could not be compared? The answer to this question depends of course on the meaning of the word 'compared'. Up to a point alternative theories cannot be compared just as personal experiences, up to a point, cannot be compared. We all live in partially shared social worlds, our concepts of things and meanings of words overlap to a great extent but are not identical. We can, however, communicate and negotiate our discrepancies and disagreements and asymptotically approach identity of our concepts and meanings. The partial identity of our different theories makes communication worthwhile, but if our experiences and theories were totally the same there would be nothing to argue about and little to communicate about. Fortunately, such cases are extremely rare and in most cases, as Hegel says, it is contradiction that is 'the root of all movement and vitality'.

The question, though, is how different our different theories are. Members of different cultures, religious beliefs or political parties often find it impossible to compare their theories. Thus, it may prove impossible to take a part of one theory and compare it with a part of the rival theory because each part is a part of a different whole. To use, once again, the Gestalt picture analogy (see Chapter 1, p. 9), there is not usually much point in saying 'look at this, it's a duck's beak' when the opponent sees the ears of a rabbit. But while in ordinary life it is taken for granted that what we perceive is influenced by our attitudes, presuppositions, and expectations, science is supposed to be based, at least by some, on completely different principles.

11.3 Research methods in psychology

By adopting a paradigm, the research worker accepts not only theoretical commitments but also methodological commitments to that paradigm (Kuhn, 1962, p. 41). While theoretical commitments are statements about the supposed nature of the phenomena and their mutual relationships, the methodological commitments specify what the fundamental explanations must be like. Thus, methodological commitments determine not only the formulation of problems but also what count as acceptable solutions, and the successions and kinds of steps to be taken in order to arrive at such solutions. The steps to be taken are specified by rules that follow from the methodological commitments.

The methodological commitments of the Cartesian psychology are best illustrated by the laboratory experiment. As a number of researchers have repeatedly claimed, the laboratory experiment in psychology faithfully follows the rules and commitments of the physical experiment developed in the Cartesian paradigm (e.g. Harré and Secord, 1972; Harré, 1979; Joynson, 1974; Shotter, 1975). Both kinds of experiment, physical and psychological, are based on the same assumptions. As Meyerson says,

It is rightly assumed that, in order to study a phenomenon, we are obliged to set it apart artificially from the great whole, to isolate it, to make it as 'pure' as this may be done; we only follow as far as possible the variation of a single element at a time, while we suppose that, during this time, all others remain without change . . . If in mechanics *m* appears constant, that only means that we are studying the motions of bodies, assuming that during the duration of the phenomena in which we are interested the mass will not vary, or what is the same thing, assuming that purely mechanical phenomena exist. We are not occupied with the thermal, electric, or chemical state of the bodies we are dealing with; we lay this down as invariable. But really we do not doubt for a single instant that the mechanical phenomenon is accompanied by thermal, electric, or chemical phenomena. It in no way follows that, when we study these phenomena in their turn, *m* must remain constant. Were it otherwise one could directly prove the conservation of mass by mechanics. (Meyerson, 1908, pp. 431–2)

This kind of experiment, which allows us to postulate the invariability of some factors and variability of others, is essential for the traditional manipulation of independent and dependent variables. Although, as Meyerson points out, 'we do not doubt' that one change is also accompanied by other changes, this belief does not preclude one from studying these variables in their turn. In other words, although a psychologist does not doubt that the changes he observes while studying language are accompanied by changes in thought, memory, the emotional state of a person, and so on, the above experimental design not only allows him but *forces* him to study the psychological phenomena independently of each other.

However, it has been exactly this kind of experimental design that has proved to be fatal for the psychology of the Cartesian paradigm. It has become apparent that the 'purity' of variables only appears to be a purity; and that the assumption of the immutability of variables cannot reasonably be applied in experimenting with human beings who under no circumstances are immutable, as physical objects are. As a result of these realizations, it has been *with respect to its research method* that the Cartesian paradigm in psychology has broken down first.

It became obvious early in the nineteen-sixties that both the experimenter and the experimental subject considerably 'obscure' the data. Since the subject acts upon his own interpretation of the experimental situation, instead of responding to the stimulus as defined by the experimenter, he introduces unwanted variables into the experiment and thus 'ruins' it. The experimenter, in the same vein, may unwittingly convey to his subjects unwanted information which, once again, leads to experimental 'artefacts'. Since there is numerous literature on the subject, it is unnecessary to labour this issue any further. For important references see, for example, Farr (1978), and Brenner and Bungard (1981).

Problems of this kind and uncertainty with regard to their solution first became apparent in social psychology. In his influential paper Gergen (1973, p. 310) argues that social psychology can never achieve the status of a science because 'the facts on which [it is] based do not generally remain stable'. According to Gergen it would seem misguided to establish any general laws of social behaviour because social psychology reflects contemporary affairs rather than accumulates knowledge in the manner of the natural sciences. While social psychology utilizes scientific methodology, its 'results are not scientific principles in the traditional sense' (Gergen, 1973, pp. 316–17). Social psychology cannot be a science because scientific methodology is not equipped to deal with the changing and unfolding phenomena of human social life. The facts of science should be invariable with knowledge quantitatively cumulating

However, not everyone has reached the kind of conclusion that Gergen has. In Kuhn's (1962) account of the process by which a paradigm collapses, the first attempts to solve anomalies are sought within the paradigm. This is precisely what we find in present psychology. Thus, several ways of eliminating or minimizing human influence in laboratory experiments have been suggested. It has, for example, been proposed that the medical placebo model should be followed and double-blind experiments carried out (Aronson and Carlsmith, 1968); that deception should be used and the subject provided with a plausible hypothesis unrelated to the experiment (Aronson and Carlsmith, 1968; Miller, 1972; Freedman, 1969; West et al., 1975); that tape-recorded instructions should be used (McGuigan, 1963; Johnson, 1967); that the number of experimenters should be increased (Terris and Milburn, 1972); and so on. However, none of the remedies within the paradigm have been found satisfactory (Brenner and Bungard, 1981).

The next attempts to solve the methodological problems have been much more revolutionary. They have called for the abolition of the traditional experiment in which the human subject is treated as a mere physical object (Harré and Secord, 1972; Shotter, 1975; Bannister and Fransella, 1971) and its substitution by experiments in which people are treated as they really are, as active and meaning-searching beings. Experiments should be reconceptualized in social and human terms, involving the recognition of real human powers and capacities (Brenner and Bungard, 1981). Psychologists should learn that experiments with people can be carried out because of their human powers rather than in spite of them. Once reactivity is accepted and taken for granted, it will become possible to interpret the findings of psychological experiments in terms of the psychology of action. Experiments should be based on attribution theory, which takes into consideration intentions and reasons (de Charms and Shea, 1976). Traditional experiments based on deception should be substituted by role-playing (Ginsburg, 1979; Mixon, 1979).

Finally, some researchers have suggested that none of the traditional research methods will do and completely new research methods should be established (de Waele and Harré, 1979; Harré, 1979). For example, accounts people give of their own actions and of actions of others should replace the traditional experiment (Harré, 1978; Brown and Sime, 1981).

All of these attempts to solve these methodological problems, either by means of 'saving' them within the old paradigm or by proposing new research methods to be used in a new paradigm, demonstrate impatience and misconceptions as to what paradigms are about. As if it were possible to establish a new paradigm overnight by the conscious effort of this or that individual!

The conceptual framework of the Cartesian paradigm, with its research methodology, has been developed during the last three hundred years; research methods in psychology within this paradigm have been refined for more than one hundred years. Minute details of these methods have been carefully considered and even the most severe critics are in some ways committed to it simply because they have been educated within this paradigm whether they like it or not. We cannot dispose of it as easily as a pile of useless rubbish.

Claims that human beings are active and meaning-searching form only the beginning of a new story and, if the story is to be successful, a rigorous conceptual analysis must follow. Once a new conceptual framework has been established and research problems within this framework formulated, the appropriate research methods will follow. However, any attempts to postulate a new research methodology prematurely, without the existence of a clear conceptual framework, will only lead opponents to claim that 'the approach of physics is rejected in favour of activities more akin to literature, biography or journalism' (Argyle, 1978, p. 238).

11.4 Universals, particulars, and research methods in psychology

We have demonstrated in Part I that the psychology of the Cartesian paradigm is based on the assumptions that the nature of cognitive processes is individualistic, static, and passive, that these processes are decomposable into elements, and that elements of these processes can be conceived of and investigated in their pure form unaffected by other elements. These commitments to the Cartesian assumptions are reflected in a research methodology. The best example of this methodology is the laboratory experiment, the aim of which is to discover cause–effect relationships or correlations between dependent and independent variables. Such experiments should have external validity, that is, cause–effect relationships and correlations should be generalizable from the sample studied to the relevant population, or to other conditions. The assumptions of a Cartesian experiment thus reflect the idea of a *Cartesian universal*. Just as a Cartesian universal specifies what is *common* among the objects in question, so a Cartesian experiment, if it has external validity, makes claims as to what is common between the samples studied and their conditions, on the one hand, and the relevant populations and their conditions, on the other.

Obviously, if a laboratory experiment is to be acceptable in some form as a research method in the psychology of the Hegelian framework, it should be based on Hegelian assumptions. In particular, it should be based on the assumptions that the nature of cognitive processes is social, developing, and active, that cognitive processes are wholes that cannot be decomposed into discrete elements, and that cognitive processes can be studied only in their relationships to one another. Moreover, the assumptions of a Hegelian experiment should reflect the idea of the Hegelian unity of universal and particular. But then, it should also follow that a factorial design with manipulation of variables would contradict these assumptions and, therefore, would be an inappropriate tool of exploration. The question, thus, is whether the Hegelian framework can have anything to offer with respect to a laboratory experiment that would also have some external validity.

The answer is YES. In fact, it was Mead (1938) who vehemently defended the laboratory experiment against those who claimed that all psychological phenomena should be explored and could be understood only in terms of individual experience. Arguing against phenomenologists and positivists at the same time, he claimed that it was wrong to overemphasize the artificiality of the experimental apparatus and technique of the psychological laboratory (Mead, 1938, p. 35). They are a necessary part of a psychological investigation because they enforce a specific and exact kind of human conduct which otherwise would not be available for investigation. One's experience is dependent upon one's relation to the world and laboratory techniques are traps in which individual experience can be tested against social reality in its amplified form.

Before taking this further, let us recall our earlier discussion of the unity of a universal and particular. As we pointed out earlier (cf. Section 8.2), a universal is real only insofar as it realizes itself in a particular that is characteristic of an individual thing. A Hegelian experiment, therefore, should reflect this kind of unity between a universal and particular. There is nothing new about this, it could be argued: psychology has long been aware that individual differences should not be overlooked, nor situations ignored (Forgas, 1979) or subjectivity disregarded. If *this* is the problem, it can be easily remedied. Moreover, who *does* claim that human beings are passive and static? *Every* psychologist would agree that human beings are active, that they develop, that there is a constant interaction between people and their environments, and that the whole is more than a sum of its parts.

Admitting and agreeing to something, however, is not the same as embodying what is admitted and agreed to in one's conceptual framework. One can agree to something in science simply because of the sheer weight of the evidence of the issue or because the logic of the thing makes it apparent. In spite of that, one's own conceptual framework, and theoretical and methodological commitments may remain unaffected.

But there is more to the Hegelian unity of a universal and particular than simply paying attention to individual differences and admitting that people are active, meaning-searching, and self-developing beings. If that was all there was to it, the remedy to the methodological problems indeed would be easy. Activity, individual differences, meanings, and other factors would simply be added to the other variables. That this is not so and could not be so follows from the very nature of a universal and particular. Their relationship is immanent in things, it is a dynamic relationship, and therefore Cartesian assumptions can in no way accommodate it.

An experiment within the Hegelian framework must be designed to explore the manifestation of the universal in subjective internal conditions, and the conditions under which something is interpreted in a particular way. Michotte (1946) was concerned to find out the minimum conditions under which physical causality is perceived by adult subjects. In his well known experiment, a small object A glides and touches another stationary object B. A stops and B immediately begins moving in the direction A would otherwise have taken. People perceive the movement of B as caused by A. If, on the other hand, the movement of B is delayed or if B changes colour rather than moves, causation is not perceived. Heider and Simmel's (1944) experiment, mentioned earlier, is concerned with demonstrating the minimum condition under which intentionality is perceived in adult subjects. In these experiments, statistical analysis is not necessary. Nothing is established with a thousand experimental subjects that isn't established with one.

The research of Luria (1961) and his students on the regulatory function of speech is based on the assumption that a young child is capable of actively modifying the environment influencing him, is able to change the relative strength of the stimuli acting upon him, and is capable of adapting himself to the stimuli he has himself modified. In a series of simple experiments, Luria's students have demonstrated the effect that speech has upon the perception of physical objects. The research method, of course, incorporates commitments to Luria's conceptual framework.

In the first series of experiments, conducted by Martsinovskaya, children three to five years old were asked to squeeze a balloon with their right hand when a red circle appeared on a grey background. If a green circle appeared on a yellow background they were supposed to squeeze a balloon with their left hand. After several trials the children learned to squeeze balloons as instructed. Having learned the task, the children were presented with a picture with a red circle on a yellow background (Figure 11.1). Since the circle appeared to be the stronger element in the compound stimulus for a child, the child squeezed the balloon with his right hand. By means of verbal instructions, however, it was possible to reinforce the weaker element, that is, the background, in the compound stimulus. In her experiments, Martsinovskaya instructed the child to squeeze the balloon with his right hand in the case of a grey background and with his left hand in the case of a yellow background. While children three to four years old still had difficulties in responding to the background rather than to the circle, children aged five years and over were able to modify the natural strength of the stimuli.

In the second series of experiments, Abramyan was able to demonstrate that if an instruction that is more meaningful for a child is used then the child is able to modify the relative strength of stimuli much earlier. Thus, Abramyan replaced the circles by coloured aeroplanes and, once again, the child was asked to squeeze a balloon with his right hand in the case of an aeroplane on a yellow background because 'the plane can fly when the sun is shining and the sky is yellow'. In the case of an aeroplane on a grey background the child was supposed to squeeze the balloon with his left hand because 'when it's rainy the plane can't fly and has to be stopped'. With this kind of instruction even children three to four years old responded to backgrounds (Luria, 1961, pp. 4–6). Rommetveit's (1978) experiments on identifying reference in adult–child communication demonstrate the same point. Eight-and-a-half year

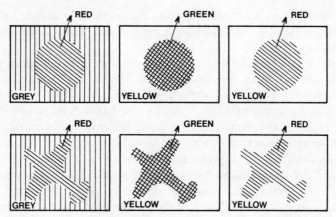

Figure 11.1 Pictures used in 'squeeze a balloon' experiment. From Luria (1961), *The Role of Speech in the Regulation of Normal and Abnormal Behaviour*. Reproduced by permission of Pergamon Press, Ltd. Copyright © 1961 Pergamon Press Ltd

old children were presented with a series of formally identical tasks in which bipolar pairs of adjectives, BIG/SMALL, HIGH/LOW, and LONG/SHORT, were used. Success in the tasks depended very much on whether the objects in the tasks were identified by the experimenter as a SNOWBALL or a WHITE circle, a BLACK-clothed man or a FIREMAN, a BOY or a SHORT man, and so on.

Leontyev (1967) defines psychology as the study of activity, and psycholinguistics as the theory of verbal activity. What is important about his work is that psycholinguistics is an integral part of the general theory of activity rather than just a particular application of it. Verbal processes are not studied in isolation and experiments are designed so that the mutual relationships of action, thought, and language are demonstrated. For example, Belous (1978) found that verbalization of a problem by a child has a considerable effect on his performance in deductive reasoning tasks. He carried out a series of experiments using a seriation problem. He has shown that when children, who according to Piaget were still at their pre-operational stage, actually verbalized what they were doing, they were able to solve seriation problems. In addition, if they were given the opportunity of taking the role of the experimenter, they were capable of understanding oppositions such as 'bigger–smaller' earlier than claimed by Piaget.

Bilkhugov (1979), in a similar vein, demonstrated that formal logical operations can be performed by children who, according to Piaget, are still at the pre-operational or concrete-operational stage. Thus, if a child is given an opportunity *to analyse* a Piagetian problem in detail so that he discovers the essential aspects of the task and their relationships, and if he verbalizes his analyses, then, again, he can grasp the rules of propositional logic while at the stage of concrete operations.

Zaporozhets (1948) argues and gives evidence that the logical thinking of a pre-school child develops in close connection with his play and practical activity and with more general changes in the child's life. His logical ability unfolds as he gradually obtains knowledge of the purposes of things and masters their relationships.

All of these tasks can be interpreted as attempts of the children to reflect upon their own activities. The children thus become self-aware as a result of verbalization, and learn to see themselves as they see other social objects.

Finally the experiments carried out by the Rubinstein school should be mentioned again. These experiments embody Rubinstein's theoretical assumptions that the child is taking an active role and learning to think whenever he experiences something. The problems he sought to solve were formulated on the basis of these assumptions; for example, how a task should be presented to the child, what kind of instruction he should be given, what kind of initial analysis he uses in the formulation of the problem for himself, in what way he reformulates the task for himself. All of Rubinstein's problem-solving tasks are educational, and education should take an active part in developing the child's imagination and ability to generalize the methods he has developed to solve other tasks. If the child is unable to transfer a solution from one kind of task to a similar task, then it means that he has not carried out an adequate analysis. To be able to generalize one must discover the essential relationships in the task so that this analysis can be applied to other tasks of the same kind.

These studies demonstrate how a conceptual framework determines the kind of experiments that the experimenter designs. While the experimenter of the Cartesian paradigm, because he assumes that processes are decomposable into elements, carries out experiments based on stimuli consisting of a single word or sentence, and devises problems in deductive reasoning with no content and free from any context, the Rubinstein school conducts experiments that are holistic, in which various processes are mutually interrelated and in which the child plays an active role.

The research methods of those concerned with studies into mother–child interaction reflect other Hegelian assumptions, those of concretization and the circle returning within itself. Let us compare the method of traditional research with the Hegelian method. In traditional research based on observation of interactions, the researcher postulates categories and counts their instances. The same applies with respect to content analysis. The experimenter must formulate his hypotheses and develop the categorization of items for observation or content analysis in advance. If this is not done, and the psychologist devises his content analysis and categories only after the experiment has been carried out, a special statistical (post-dictum) test has to be used to allow for unexpected results. The same argument, of course, applies to one-tail and two-tail tests in statistics. But what justification is there for imposing predetermined structures upon self-unfolding interactions?

Condon (1977) points out that Nature does not discriminate events in the way experimental psychologists do, separating various pieces and putting them together again. Events are not at one moment isolated from one another, at another put together:

We analyse Nature into bits and pieces and then believe that we have discovered original elements which were somehow combined to become what Nature *is* in her encompassing unity. (Condon, 1977, p. 155)

Such an approach, Condon says, is paradoxical. The inquirer is originally part of that natural unity. However, he went to school and was educated and became an investigator rather than a poet, and now he has learned how to separate the various bits and pieces of the natural unity of which he himself is still part.

The problem for the investigator remains how to deal with the complexity of the human mind in the process of exploration and how to deal with the intricate subtleties of human behaviour without analysing it into bits and pieces, for example, the frequency with which participants look at each other, the frequency and length of their utterances, frequency of smiles, and so on, which supposedly can then be added together again to reform the total communication. Condon and Newson both offer some insight into one way of dealing with the problem. Both have been concerned with the analysis of mother–child interactions using videotapes. Condon points out that one of the most difficult tasks is to discover *natural subforms* of the total behaviour. On the first viewing of films, as Condon says, one is not usually aware of subtleties of interaction. We could say, using Hegel's term, that our observation on the first viewing is abstract. All the researcher has is just an overall picture of what is actually going on in the interaction, which may be reasonably accurate, or may be mistaken. Only subsequent and repeated viewing allows him to discover the details of the interaction, to see it from the point of view of the whole, and to re-interpret the whole and see the detail differently. Such a process corresponds to Hegel's notion of concretization. As Condon puts it:

The method has primarily been that of viewing sound films of human behaviour and interaction again and again until a variety of forms of order begin to emerge. The 'units' or 'categories' in terms of which the analysis is to proceed are themselves the result of intensive analysis and are not postulated arbitrarily in advance. To a certain extent the most arduous and time-consuming task is the discovery of what might constitute the natural 'units' or 'sub-forms' within the process being investigated. This continues to remain the primary method. In this approach the investigator is required to continually question and often change his views about the structure of the process. In essence, the 'units' are discovered and modified during the inquiry as a function of the inquiry itself. Even the notational categories, in terms of which the data are described, emerge during this inquiry process. (Condon, 1977, pp. 155–6)

Thus interactions are viewed over and over again, frame by frame, until forms of order begin to be seen, the analysis starting at a relatively macrolevel, gestures and word sequences of natural speech being examined in mutual relation. As Condon (1979) says, there are always gestures detectable at minor levels which at first viewings were not noticed. The process of human interaction is inexhaustible. The truth, once again, is reached through the circle returning within itself.

Rubinstein (1957) makes the same point. He analyses the process of perception. At the beginning, perception is global, the reality is given immediately as a totality, more or less, of various kinds of interactions. Mental analysis discovers their essential features, and then through examination of their mutual relationships reconstructs the reality. Thinking and perception are mutually related, it is impossible to study one without the other. This is the path of every science, whether of political economics, or of classical or modern physics. But analysis through synthesis is not only characteristic of thinking, it is characteristic of every process of knowing.

Newson (1979) characterizes the method by which he studies mother–child interaction as one that does not involve manipulation of 'subjects' but observation of spontaneous behaviour and recognition of its biological and evolutionary basis. Such studies involve repeated observation of the same mother–child pair, and also, in his case, 'systematic and finegrained analysis of episodes of mother–infant interaction preserved on video tape and capable of being re-run as often as required' (Newson, 1979, pp. 216–17). In the study by Jones, reported by Newson, videotapes were first analysed without predetermined categories. It was not simply an analysis of sequences of the type 'response follows stimulus' because such analyses again result in artefacts. Instead,

. . . within the acting dyad, each partner is continuously aware of the other's behaviour—whether it be passive or active. In a study of interaction it is therefore essential that the investigator is aware of the cues being received by both partners at any one time. Observable 'listening' behaviour in the other is as important to the currently active partner as the act itself. (Newson, 1979, pp. 217–18)

There is a gradually increasing awareness that the study of change and the evaluation of change in human beings should be part of research in psychology. Designs for single subject research begin to appear, discussing different methods of examining single subject data and evaluating results statistically, elaborating specific experimental designs, examining problems in data evaluation and interpretation, and considering the validity of such studies (Kratochwill, 1978; Hersen and Barlow, 1976; Petermann and Hehl, 1979). Similarly, new strategies are appearing for the study of interaction. Cairns and Green (1979) point to the importance of studies of behaviour which are not concerned just with reliable observations. They point out that the occurrence of 'unreliability' of child behaviour in repeated observations is due to the child's ability 'to adapt to changing demands of the social and nonsocial environment'. In other words, 'unreliability' of child behaviour should be the focus of analysis because it may constitute the active and adaptive regulatory principles in human development:

Washing out these adaptive capabilities, either by controlling them through statistical transformation on the obtained data or by requesting 'raters' to control for them in the first stage of analysis, precludes an understanding of how accommodations are made and how behaviors change over time and space. (Cairns and Green, 1979, p. 223)

All of these examples show that, if problems are adequately defined and a conceptual framework adequately developed, Hegel's philosophy provides methods for research. These examples also show that the alternative that is offered by those maintaining that accounts, biographies, and self-reports should be the research methods of the new framework are, in fact, mistaken. Their methods are concerned with particulars only and there is no possibility of true universals and, therefore, no science. All these methods deny universals and are therefore counterparts of the Cartesian methods that overthrow particulars.

11.5 Not a conclusion

Is psychology as a whole going to adopt the Hegelian framework? Certainly not in the immediate future. There are areas in psychology in which the Cartesian framework will appear more convenient at least for some time, just as the Newtonian framework in physics is still more convenient than the Einsteinian in some areas of engineering. This will be the case where the anomalies produced by the existing framework are not sufficiently serious to necessitate a change. In psychology it applies, for example, to those fields in which all that is required of a person is the performance of a machine or computer, and to some aspects of psychophysiology and psychopharmacology. In addition, there may be cases in which the experimenter for some reason wishes to disregard human agency or in which human agency does not count because a person is reduced to behaving like a physical object.

In all other areas of psychology the Hegelian framework will undoubtedly be the one with the future, and Hegel's philosophy will prove to be a deep source of inspiration. Finally, a word of caution. There is no doubt that people must be treated in psychology and in all the social sciences as creative, self-unfolding, and immanently active. But action can be sinister if based on non-recognition of the other person as a human being. The future of mankind depends on taking actions in which human beings mutually recognize each other *as* human beings.

Notes

1. Works originally published in this century are referred to in the text by author and date, and earlier works by author and a (shortened) title. The editions or translations used are given in the References. Where no English translation is mentioned, a translation is mine except in the case of the translation of Herder by Berlin (see note 6).
2. Page references in the case of Kuhn are to the first edition of his book. For the second edition, add 1 to the page number except for the quotations from pages 12 and 41 which are on the same page in both editions.
3. I have used the different spellings of the this word in order to distinguish its different meanings in the two traditions. In fact, the *Oxford English Dictionary* does give somewhat different meanings for 'reflective' and 'reflexive', though it does not distinguish between 'reflection' and 'reflexion'.
4. In Adam, C., and Tannery, P. (eds), (1964 and 1971), *Oeuvres de Descartes*, Vol. VIII–1 (Latin) and Vol. IX–2 (French), Paris: J. Vrin. This Principle is not available in English translation.
5. No distinction is made for the purposes of this book between the terms 'purposive' and 'teleological' (on this issue, cf. Taylor, 1964, p. 6n).
6. This translation of Herder is by Berlin (1965, p. 80).

References

Abelson, R. P., and Kanouse, D. E. (1966), Subjective acceptance of verbal generalizations. In Feldman, S. (ed.), *Cognitive Consistency*, New York and London:
Academic Press.

Alexander, P. (1963), *Sensationalism and Scientific Explanation*, London: Routledge
and Kegan Paul; New York: Humanities Press.

Allison, H. E. (trs. & ed.), (1973), *The Kant–Eberhard Controversy*, Baltimore and
London: The Johns Hopkins University Press.

Alston, W. P. (1974), Conceptual prolegomena to a psychological theory of intentional
action. In Brown, S. C. (ed.), *Philosophy of Psychology*, London and Basingstoke:
The Macmillan Press.

Argyle, M. (1978), An appraisal of the New Approach to the study of social behaviour.
In Brenner, M., Marsh, P., and Brenner, M. (eds.), *The Social Contexts of Method*,
London: Croom Helm.

Aristotle, *Analytica Posteriora*, trs. Barnes, J., *Aristotle's Posterior Analytics*, Oxford:
Clarendon Press, 1975.

Aristotle, *Analytica Priora*, trs. Jenkinson, A. J. In Ross, W. D. (ed.), *The Works of
Aristotle*, Vol. 1, London: Oxford University Press, 1928.

Aristotle, *Metaphysica*, trs. Kirwan, C., *Aristotle's Metaphysics, Books* Γ, Δ *and E*,
Oxford: Clarendon Press, 1971.

Aristotle, *Topica*, trs. Pickard-Cambridge, W. A. In Ross, W. D. (ed.), *The Works of
Aristotle*, Vol. 1, London: Oxford University Press, 1928.

Aronson, E., and Carlsmith, J. M. (1968), Experimentation in social psychology. In
Lindzey, G., and Aronson, E. (eds.), *Handbook of Social Psychology*, 2nd edn, Vol.
II, Reading, MA: Addison-Wesley.

Aydin, O., and Marková I. (1979), Attributional tendencies of popular and unpopular
children, *British Journal of Social and Clinical Psychology*, **18**, 291–298.

Bannister, D., and Fransella, F. (1971), *Inquiring Man*, Harmondsworth: Penguin
Books.

Barnard, F. M. (1965), *Herder's Social and Political Thought*, Oxford: Clarendon Press.

Bateson, G., Jackson, D. D., Haley, J., and Weakland, J. (1956), Toward a theory of
schizophrenia, *Behavioral Science*, **1**, 251–64.

Bateson, M. C. (1975), Mother–infant exchanges: the epigenesis of conversational
interaction. In Aaronson, D., and Rieber, R. W. (eds.), *Developmental Psycholinguistics and Communication Disorders*, New York: New York Academy of
Sciences.

Beck, L. J. (1965), *The Metaphysics of Descartes*, Oxford: Clarendon Press.

Begg, I., and Denny, J. P. (1969), Empirical reconciliation of atmosphere and conversion interpretations of syllogistic reasoning errors, *Journal of Experimental Psychology*, **81**, 351–354.

Belous, V. P. (1978), On the importance of conditionality in the formation of ways of logical thinking in pre-school children, *Voprosy psikhologii*, **4**, 36–45.

Berdyaev, N. (1936), *The Meaning of History*, New York: Scribner; reprinted London: Geoffrey Bles, The Centenary Press, 1945 and 1949.

Bergson, H. (1889), *Time and Free Will*, trs. Pogson, F. L., London: Swan Sonnenschein; New York: Macmillan, 1910.

Bergson, H. (1922), *Durée et Simultanéité*, Paris: Félix Alcan.

Berlin, I. (1965), Herder and the Enlightenment. In Wasserman, E. R. (ed.), *Aspects of the Eighteenth Century*, Baltimore: The Johns Hopkins Press.

Bickman, L. (1975), Bystander intervention in a crime: the effect of a mass-media campaign, *Journal of Applied Social psychology*, **5**, 296–302.

Bierwisch, M. (1970), Semantics. In Lyons, J. (ed.), *New Horizons in Linguistics*, Harmondsworth: Penguin Books.

Bilkhugov, S. Yu. (1979), The formation of elements of formal logic in children of pre-school age, *Voprosy psikhologii*, **4**, 56–65.

Black. J. K. (1979), Assessing kindergarten children's communicative competence. In Garnica, O. K., and King, M. L. (eds), *Language, Children and Society*, Oxford and New York: Pergamon Press.

Bobrow, D. G., and Collins, A. (1975), *Representation and Understanding*, New York and London: Academic Press.

Boden, M. A. (1978), *Purposive Explanation in Psychology*, Hassocks: The Harvester Press.

Boole, G. (1847), *The Mathematical Analysis of Logic*, Cambridge: Macmillan, Barclay & Macmillan.

Boole, G. (1854), *An Investigation of the Laws of Thought*, New York: Dover.

Borke, H. (1971), Interpersonal perception of young children: egocentrism or empathy? *Developmental Psychology*, **5**, 263–269.

Borke, H. (1975), Piaget's mountains revisited: changes in the egocentric landscape, *Developmental Psychology*, **11**, 240–243.

Bourne, L. E. (1966), *Human Conceptual Behavior*, Boston: Allyn and Bacon.

Bower, T. G. R. (1967), The development of object permanence, *Perception and Psychophysics*, **2**, 411–418.

Bower, T. G. R. (1971), The object in the world of the infant, *Scientific American*, **225**, 4, 30–38.

Bower, T. G. R. (1974), *Development in Infancy*. San Francisco: Freeman.

Bowerman, M. (1978), The acquisition of word meaning: an investigation into some current conflicts. In Waterson, N., and Snow, C. (eds), *The Development of Communication*, Chichester and New York: Wiley.

Braithwaite, R. B. (1953), *Scientific Explanation*, Cambridge: Cambridge University Press.

Brazelton, T. B., Koslowski, B., and Main, M. (1974), The origins of reciprocity: the early mother–infant interaction. In Lewis, M., and Rosenblum, L. A. (eds), *The Effect of the Infant on its Caregiver*, London and New York: Wiley.

Brenner, M., and Bungard, W. (1981), What to do with social reactivity in psychological experimentation? In Brenner, M. (ed.), *Social Method and Social Life*, London and New York: Academic Press.

Brett, G. S. (1912–21), *History of Psychology*, ed. and abrgd. by Peters, R. S., *Brett's History of Psychology*, London: Allen and Unwin; New York: Macmillan, 1962.

Broadbent, D. E. (1958), *Perception and Communication*, Oxford: Pergamon Press.

Broadbent, D. E. (1973), *In Defence of Empirical Psychology*, London: Methuen.

Brown, J., and Sime, J. (1981), A methodology for accounts. In Brenner, M. (ed.), *Social Method and Social Life*, London and New York: Academic Press.

Bruner, J. S. (1977), Early social interaction and language acquisition. In Schaffer, H. R. (ed.), *Studies in Mother–Infant Interaction*, London and New York: Academic Press.

Bruner, J. S. (1978), From communication to language: a psychological perspective. In Marková, I. (ed.), *The Social Context of Language*, Chichester and New York: Wiley.

Bruner, J. S., Goodnow, J. J., and Austin, G. A. (1956), *A Study of Thinking*, New York and London: Wiley.

Brunswik, E. (1952), *The Conceptual Framework of Psychology*, Chicago and London: The University of Chicago Press.

Buber, M. (1962), *Werke*, Vol. 1, Munich and Heidelberg: Kosel Verlag and Verlag Lambert Scheider. Engl. trs. in Buber, M. (1965), *The Knowledge of Man*, ed. Friedman, M., trs. Friedman, M., and Gregor-Smith, R., London: George Allen and Unwin.

Bucci, W. (1978), The interpretation of universal affirmative propositions, *Cognition*, **5**, 55–77.

Bullowa, M. (1979), Introduction. Prelinguistic communication: a field for scientific research. In Bullowa, M. (ed.), *Before Speech: The Beginning of Interpersonal Communication*, Cambridge and New York: Cambridge University Press.

Cahoon, D. D. (1968), Symptom substitution and the behavior therapies: a reappraisal, *Psychological Bulletin*, **69**, 149–156.

Cairns, R. B., and Green, J. A. (1979), Appendix A. How to assess personality and social patterns: observation or ratings? In Cairns, R. B. (ed.), *The Analysis of Social Interactions: Methods, Issues, and Illustrations*, Hillsdale: Lawrence Erlbaum.

Carswell, E. A., and Rommetveit, R. (eds), (1971), *Social Contexts of Messages*, London and New York: Academic Press.

Cassirer, E. (1942), Giovani Pico della Mirandola, Part II, *Journal of the History of Ideas*, **3**, 319–346.

Chapman, L. J., and Chapman, J. P. (1959), Atmosphere effect re-examined, *Journal of Experimental Psychology*, **58**, 220–226.

de Charms, R., and Shea, D. J. (1976), Beyond attribution theory: the human conception of motivation and causality. In Strickland, L. H., Aboud, F. E., and Gergen, K. J. (eds), *Social Psychology in Transition*, New York and London: Plenum Press.

Chase, W. G., and Clark, H. H. (1972), Mental operations in the comparison of sentences and pictures. In Gregg, L. W. (ed.), *Cognition in Learning and Memory*, New York and London: Wiley.

Cherry, C. (1953), Some experiments on the reception of speech with one and with two ears, *Journal of the Acoustical Society of America*, **25**, 975–9.

Chomsky, N. (1957), *Syntactic Structures*, The Hague: Mouton.

Chomsky, N. (1965), *Aspects of a Theory of Syntax*, Cambridge, MA: MIT Press.

Chomsky, N. (1966), *Cartesian Linguistics*, New York and London: Harper and Row.

Chomsky, N. (1962), Exploratory models in linguistics. In Nagel, E., Suppes, P., and Tarski, A. (eds), *Logic, Methodology and Philosophy of Science*, Stanford, California: Stanford University Press.

Chomsky, N. (1968), *Language and Mind*, New York: Harcourt, Brace and World.

Chomsky, N. (1977), Conditions on rules of grammar. In Cole, R. W. (ed.), *Current Issues in Linguistic Theory*, Bloomington and London: Indiana University Press.

Chomsky, N. (1980), Rules and representations, *The Behavioral and Brain Sciences*, **3**, 1–61.

Cicourel, A. V. (1972), Cross modal communication: the representational context of sociolinguistic information processing. In Shuy, R. (ed.), *Monograph Series on Language and Linguistics, Twenty–third Annual Round Table*, Washington: Georgetown University Press.

Clark, E. V. (1973), What's in a word? On the child's acquisition of semantics in his first language. In Moore, T. E. (ed.), *Cognitive Development and the Acquisition of Language*, New York and London: Academic Press.

208

Clark, H. H. and Chase, W. G. (1972), On the process of comparing sentences against pictures, *Cognitive Psychology*, **3**, 472–517.

Coleridge, S. T., to Thomas Poole, 23rd March, 1801. In Griggs, E. L. (ed.), *Collected Letters of Samuel Taylor Coleridge*, Vol. II, 1801–1806, Oxford: Clarendon Press, 1956 and 1958.

Collins, A. M., and Quillian, M. R. (1969), Retrieval time from semantic memory, *Journal of Verbal Learning and Verbal Behavior*, **8**, 240–247.

Collins, A. M., and Quillian, M. R. (1972), Experiments on semantic memory and language comprehension. In Gregg, L. W. (ed.), *Cognition in Learning and Memory*, New York and London: Wiley.

Collis, G. M., and Schaffer, H. R. (1975), Synchronization of visual attention in mother–infant pairs, *Journal of Child Psychology and Psychiatry*, **16**, 315–320.

Condon, W. S. (1977), A primary phase in the organization of infant responding. In Schaffer, R. H. (ed.), *Studies in Mother–Infant Interaction*, London and New York: Academic Press.

Condon, W. S. (1979), Neonatal entrainment and enculturation. In Bullowa, M. (ed.), *Before Speech: The Beginning of Interpersonal Communication*, Cambridge and New York: Cambridge University Press.

Condon, W. S., and Sander, L. W. (1974a), Neonate movement is synchronized with adult speech: interactional participation and language acquisition, *Science*, **183**, 99–101.

Condon, W. S., and Sander, L. W. (1974b), Synchrony demonstrated between movements of the neonate and adult speech, *Child Development*, **45**, 456–462.

Copi, I. M. (1965), *Symbolic Logic*, New York and London: Macmillan.

Coplestone, F. (1964), *A History of Philosophy*, Vol. IV, London: Burns and Oates.

Crockett, W. H. (1965), Cognitive complexity and impression formation. In Maher, B. A. (ed.), *Progress in Experimental Personality Research*, Vol. 2, New York: Academic Press.

Cross, T. G. (1978), Mothers' speech and its association with rate of linguistic development in young children. In Waterson, N., and Snow, C. (eds), *The Development of Communication*, Chichester and New York: Wiley.

Darwin, C. (1904), *The Expression of the Emotions in Man and Animals*, London: John Murray.

Dennett, D. C. (1978), Why you can't make a computer that feels pain, *Synthese*, **38**, 415–456.

Descartes, R. (1641), *Arguments Demonstrating the Existence of God*. In Haldane, E. S., and Ross, G. R. T. (trss & eds), *The Philosophical Works of Descartes*, Vol II, London and New York: Cambridge University Press, 1911.

Descartes, R. (1637), *Discourse on the Method of Rightly Conducting the Reason and Seeking for Truth in Sciences*. In Haldane, E. S., and Ross, G. R. T. (trss & eds), *The Philosophical Works of Descartes*, Vol. I, London and New York: Cambridge University Press, 1911.

Descartes, R., Interview with Burman, 16th April, 1648. In Adam, C., and Tannery, P. (eds), *Oeuvres de Descartes*, Vol. V, Paris: J. Vrin, 1974.

Descartes, R., Letter for [Arnauld], 29th July, 1648. In Kenny, A. (ed. & trs.), *Descartes: Philosophical Letters*, Oxford: Clarendon Press, 1970.

Descartes, R., Letter to ? August, 1641. In Anscombe, E., and Geach, P. T. (eds & trss), *Descartes*, London: Nelson, 1954.

Descartes, R., Letter to Mersenne, 16th June, 1641. In Kenny, A. (trs. & ed.), *Descartes: Philosophical Letters*, Oxford: Clarendon Press, 1970.

Descartes, R., Letter to Regius, May, 1641. In Kenny, A. (trs. & ed.), *Descartes: Philosophical Letters*, Oxford: Clarendon Press, 1970.

Descartes, R. (1641), *Meditations on First Philosophy*. In Haldane, E. S., and Ross, G. R. T. (trss & eds), *The Philosophical Works of Descartes*, Vol. I, London and New York: Cambridge University Press, 1911.

Descartes, R. (1647), *Notes Directed Against A Certain Programme*. In Haldane, E. S., and Ross, G. R. T. (trss & eds), *The Philosophical Works of Descartes*, Vol. I, London and New York: Cambridge University Press, 1911.

Descartes, R. (1644), *The Principles of Philosophy*. In Haldane, E. S., and Ross, G. R. T. (trss & eds), *The Philosophical Works of Descartes*, Vol. I, London and New York: Cambridge University Press, 1911.

Descartes, R., Private thoughts. In Anscombe, E., and Geach, P. T. (trss & eds), *Descartes*, London: Nelson, 1954.

Descartes, R. (1628), *Rules for the Direction of the Mind*. In Haldane, E. S., and Ross, G. R. T. (trss & eds), *The Philosophical Works of Descartes*, Vol. I, London and New York: Cambridge University Press, 1911.

Descartes, R. (1642), *Seventh set of objections with the author's annotations thereon*. In Haldane, E. S., and Ross, G. R. T. (trss & eds), *The Philosophical Works of Descartes*, Vol. II, London and New York: Cambridge University Press, 1911.

Descartes, R. (1641), *Third set of objections with the author's reply*. In Haldane, E. S., and Ross, G. R. T. (trss & eds), *The Philosophical Works of Descartes*, Vol. II, London and New York: Cambridge University Press, 1911.

Descartes, (1662), *Treatise on Man*, ed. & trs. Hall, T. S., Cambridge MA: Harvard University Press, 1972.

Deutsch, J., and Deutsch, D. (1963), Attention: some theoretical considerations, *Psychological Review*, **70**, 80–90.

Duncker, K. (1945), *On Problem-solving*, Washington: The American Psychological Association.

Encyclopedia of Philosophy, Edwards, P. (ed.), New York: Macmillan and Free Press; London: Collier-Macmillan, 1967.

Erikson, J. R., and Jones, M. R. (1978), Thinking, *Annual Review of Psychology*, **29**, 61–90.

Erwin-Tripp, S. (1968), An analysis of the interaction of language, topic and listener. In Fishman, J. A. (ed.), *Readings in the Sociology of Language*, The Hague: Mouton.

Estes, W. K., Koch, S., MacCorquodale, K., Meehl, P. E., Mueller, C. G., Schoenfeld, W. N., and Verplanck, W. S. (1954), *Modern Learning Theory*, New York: Appleton-Century-Crofts.

Evans, J. St B. T. (1977), On the absurdity of being an anti-psychologist: a reply to Bannister, *Bulletin of the British Psychological Society*, **30**, 341–42.

Evans, J. St B. T. (1978), The psychology of deductive reasoning: logic. In Burton, A., and Radford, J. (eds), *Thinking in Perspective*, London: Methuen.

Eysenck, H. J. (1952), The effects of psychotherapy: an evaluation, *Journal of Consulting Psychology*, **16**, 319–324.

Farr, R. M. (1978), On the social significance of artifacts in experimenting, *British Journal of Social and Clinical Psychology*, **17**, 299–306.

Ficino, M. (1576), *Opera Omnia*. In Kristeller, P. O. (ed.), *The Philosophy of Marsilio Ficino*, trs. Conant, V., New York: Columbia University Press, 1943.

Fishman, J. (1969), The sociology of language. In Miller, G. A. (ed.), *Communication, Language and Meaning*, New York: Basic Books.

Fodor, J. (1972), Some reflections on L. S. Vygotsky's 'Thought and Language', *Cognition*, **1**, 83–95.

Forbes, C. D., Marková, I., Stuart, J., and Jones, P. (in press), To tell or not to tell: haemophiliacs' views on their employment prospects, *International Journal of Rehabilitation Research*.

Forehand, G. A. (1974), Knowledge and educational process. In Gregg, L. W. (ed.), *Knowledge and Cognition*, New York and London: Wiley.

Forgas, J. P. (1979), *Social Episodes*, London and New York: Academic Press.

Foster, M. B. (1935), Christian theology and modern science of nature, *Mind*, **44**, 439–466.

Franks, J. J. (1974), Towards understanding understanding. In Weimar, W.B., and

210

Palermo, D. S. (eds), *Cognition and the Symbolic Processes*, Hillsdale, NJ: Lawrence Erlbaum Associates.

Freedman, J. L. (1969), Role playing: psychology by consensus, *Journal of Personality and Social Psychology*, **13**, 107–114.

From, F. (1971), *Perception of Other People*, New York and London: Columbia University Press.

Galilei Galileo (1623), *The Assayer*. In Drake, S. (trs. & ed.), *Discoveries and Opinions of Galileo*, New York: Doubleday, 1957.

Galilei Galileo (1615), Letter to the Grand Duchess Christina. In Drake, S. (trs. & ed.), *Discoveries and Opinions of Galileo*, New York: Doubleday, 1957.

Galilei Galileo (1613), Letters on Sunspots. In Drake, S. (trs. & ed.), *Discoveries and Opinions of Galileo*, New York: Doubleday, 1957.

Gelman, R., and Shatz, M. (1977), Appropriate speech adjustments: the operation of conversational constraints on talk to two-year-olds. In Lewis, M., and Rosenblum, L. A. (eds), *Interaction, Conversation and the Development of Language*, London and New York: Wiley.

Gergen, K. (1973), Social psychology as history, *Journal of Personality and Social Psychology*, **26**, 309–320.

Gibson, J. (1917), *Locke's Theory of Knowledge and its Historical Relations*, London and New York: Cambridge University Press, reprinted 1968.

Ginsberg, G. P. (1979), The effective use of role-playing in social psychological research. In Ginsburg, G. P. (ed.), *Emerging Strategies in Social Psychological Research*, Chichester and New York: Wiley.

Goffman, E. (1968), *Stigma*, Harmondsworth: Penguin Books.

Gregg, L. W. (1967), Internal representation of sequential concepts. In Kleinmuntz, B. (ed.), *Concepts and the Structure of Memory*, New York and London: Wiley.

Hamilton, Sir William (1870), *Lectures on Metaphysics and Logic*, Vol. 1, Edinburgh and London: William Blackwood and Sons.

Hamlyn, D. W. (1971), Epistemology and conceptual development. In Mischel, T. (ed.), *Cognitive Psychology and Epistemology*, New York: Academic Press.

Hanson, N. R. (1958), *Patterns of Discovery: An Inquiry into the Conceptual Foundations of Science*, Cambridge: Cambridge University Press.

Harré, R. (1978), Accounts, actions and meanings—the practice of participatory psychology. In Brenner, M., Marsh, P., and Brenner, M. (eds), *The Social Contexts of Method*, London: Croom Helm.

Harré, R. (1979), *Social Being*, Oxford: Basil Blackwell.

Harré, R., and Secord, P. F. (1972), *The Explanation of Social Behaviour*, Oxford: Basil Blackwell.

Healy, A. F. and Miller, G. A. (1970), The verb as the main determinant of sentence meaning, *Psychonomic Science*, **20**, 372.

Hegel, G. W. F. (1842), *Aesthetics: Lectures on Fine Art*, Vol. I, trs. Knox, T. M., Oxford: Clarendon Press, 1975.

Hegel, G. W. F. (1830), *The Encyclopedia of the Philosophical Sciences*, Part I, *The Science of Logic*. In Wallace, W. (trs.), *The Logic of Hegel*, London: Oxford University Press, 1873.

Hegel, G. W. F. (1840) *History of Philosophy*, trss Haldane, E. S., and Simson, F. H., *Lectures on the History of Philosophy*, in 3 vols, London: Kegan Paul, Trench, Trübner and Co., 1892–6; reprinted London: Routledge and Kegan Paul; New York: Humanities Press, 1955 and 1963.

Hegel, G. W. F. (1807), *Phenomenology of Spirit*, trs. Miller, A. V., Oxford: Clarendon Press, 1977.

Hegel, G. W. F. (1837), *The Philosophy of History*, trs. Sibree, J., New York: Dover, 1956

Hegel, G. W. F., (1821), *Philosophy of Right*, ed. & trs. Knox, T. M., London and New York, Oxford University Press, 1952.

Hegel, G. W. F. (1812–16), *Science of Logic*, trs. Miller, A. V., London and New York: George Allen and Unwin, 1969; New York: Humanities Press, 1976.

Heider, F. (1958), *The Psychology of Interpersonal Relations*, New York and London: Wiley.

Heider, F. (1967), On social cognition, *American Psychologist*, **22**, 25–31.

Heider, F., and Simmel, M. (1944), An experimental study of apparent behavior, *American Journal of Psychology*, **57**, 243–259.

Henle, M. (1955), Some effects of motivational processes on cognition, *Psychological Review*, **62**, 423–432.

Henle, M. (1962), On the relation between logic and thinking, *Psychological Review*, **69**, 366–378.

Henle, M., and Michael, M. (1956), The influence of attitudes on syllogistic reasoning, *Journal of Social Psychology*, **44**, 115–127.

Herder, J. G. (1877–1913), *Sämtliche Werke*, ed. Suphon, B., reprinted Hildesheim: Georg Olms, 1967.

Hersen, M., and Barlow, D. H. (1976), *Single Case Experimental Designs: Strategies for Studying Behavior Change in the Individual*, New York: Pergamon Press.

Hume, D. (1779), *Dialogues Concerning Natural Religion*, ed. Pike, N., Indianapolis: Bobbs-Merill, 1970.

Hume, D. (1777), *Enquiries Concerning the Human Understanding and Concerning the Principles of Morals*, ed. Selby-Bigge, L. A., Oxford: Clarendon Press, 1902.

Hume, D. (1757), *The Natural History of Religion*, ed. Colver, A. W., with the *Dialogues Concerning Natural Religion*, ed. Price, J. V., Oxford: Clarendon Press, 1976.

Hume, D. (1739), *A Treatise of Human Nature*, ed. Selby-Bigge, L. A., Oxford: Clarendon Press, 1888.

Hunt, E. B. (1962), *Concept Learning: An Information Processing Problem*, New York, London, and Sydney: Wiley.

Hymes, D. (1971), Competence and performance in linguistic theory. In Huxley, R., and Ingram, E. (eds), *Language Acquisition: Models and Methods*, London and New York: Academic Press.

Jensen, J. (1960a), On functional fixedness. Some critical remarks, Scandinavian Journal of Psychology, **1**, 157–162.

Jensen, J. (1960b), On the *Einstellung* effect in problem solving, *Scandinavian Journal of Psychology*, **1**, 163–168.

Johnson, E. S. (1967), The computer as experimenter, *Behavioral Science*, **12**, 484–489.

Johnson-Laird, P. N. (1975), Models of deduction. In Falmagne, R. J. (ed.), *Reasoning: Representation and Process in Children and Adults*, Hillsdale, NJ: Lawrence Erlbaum Associates.

Johnson-Laird, P. N., and Tagart, J. (1969), How implication is understood, *American Journal of Psychology*, **82**, 367–73.

Jones, O. H. M. (1979), A comparative study of mother–child communication with Down's syndrome and normal infants. In Shaffer, D., and Dunn, J. (eds), *The First Year of Life*, Chichester and New York: Wiley.

Joynson, R. B. (1974), *Psychology and Common Sense*, London and Boston: Routledge and Kegan Paul.

Kahneman, D. (1973), *Attention and Effort*, Englewood Cliffs, NJ: Prentice-Hall.

Kant, I. (1790), *Critique of Judgement*, trs. Meredith, J. C., Oxford: Clarendon Press, 1952.

Kant, I. (1788), *Critique of Practical Reason*, trs. Abbott, T. K., London: Longmans, Green, 1873.

Kant, I. (1781 and 1787), *Critique of Pure Reason*, trs. Smith. N. K., London: Macmillan; New York: St Martin's Press, 1929.

Kant, I. (1800), *Logic*. In *Kant's Werke*, Vol. IX, Berlin und Leipzig: Walter de Grunter, 1923.

212

Katz, J. J., and Fodor, F. A. (1963), The structure of a semantic theory, *Language*, **39**, 170–210.

Keeling, S. V. (1968), *Descartes*, London and New York: Oxford University Press.

Kenny, A. (1968), *Descartes*, New York: Random House.

Kenny, A. (1973), *The Anatomy of the Soul*, Oxford: Basil Blackwell.

Kessler, S. (ed.), (1979), *Genetic Counseling: Psychological Dimensions*, New York: Academic Press.

Kneale, W., and Kneale, M. (1962), *The Development of Logic*, Oxford: Clarendon Press.

Kojève, A. (1969), *Introduction to the Reading of Hegel*, New York and London: Basic Books.

Kordig, C. R. (1971), *The Justification of Scientific Change*, Dordrecht: Reidel.

Kosík, K. (1963), *Dialektika konkrétního*, (Dialectics of the Concrete), Prague: Nakladatelství Československé Akademie Věd.

Kratochwill, T. R. (ed.) (1978), *Single Subject Research*, New York: Academic Press.

Kuhn, T. S. (1962), *The Structure of Scientific Revolutions*, 2nd ed 1970, Chicago: University of Chicago Press.

Kuipers, B. J. (1975), A frame for frames: representing knowledge for recognition. In Bobrow, D. G., and Collins, A. (eds) *Representation and Understanding*, New York and London: Academic Press.

Laing, R. D. (1971), *Self and Others*, Harmondsworth: Penguin Books.

Latané, B., and Darley, J. M. (1970), *The Unresponsive Bystander: Why Doesn't He Help?* New York: Appleton-Century-Crofts.

Lefford, A. (1946), The influence of emotional subject matter on logical reasoning, *Journal of General Psychology*, **34**, 127–151.

Leibniz, G. W. (1714), *Monadology*. In Latta, R. (trs. & ed.), *The Monadology and Other Philosophical Writings*, London: Oxford University Press, 1898.

Leibniz, G. W. (1765), *New Essays Concerning Human Understanding*, trs. Langley, A. G., Chicago and London: Open Court, 1916.

Leibniz, G. W. (1714), *Principles of Nature and Grace*. In Latta, R. (trs. & ed.), *The Monadology and Other Philosophical Writings*, London: Oxford University Press, 1898.

Leontyev, A. A. (1967), *Psikholingvistika*, Leningrad: Nauka.

Levine, L. E., and Hoffman, M. L. (1975), Empathy and cooperation in four-year-olds, *Developmental Psychology*, **11**, 533–534.

Levy, D. M. (1943), *Maternal Overprotection*, New York: Columbia University Press.

Locke, J. (1690), *An Essay Concerning Human Understanding*, ed. Yolton, J. W., 2 Vols, London: Dent; New York: Dutton, 1961.

Locke, J. (1697), *Reply to the Lord Bishop of Worcester*. In *Works of John Locke*, Vol. IV, London: Thomas Tegg *et al*., 1823; reprinted Darmstadt: Scientia Verlag, 1963.

Luria, A. R. (1961), *The Role of Speech in the Regulation of Normal and Abnormal Behaviour*, Oxford and New York: Pergamon Press.

McGuigan, F. J. (1963), The experimenter: a neglected stimulus object, *Psychological Bulletin*, **60**, 421–428.

McGuire, W. J. (1960a), A syllogistic analysis of cognitive relationships. In Rosenberg, M. J., Hovland, C. I., McGuire, W. J., Abelson, R. P., and Brehm, J. W., *Attitude Organization and Change*, New Haven: Yale University Press.

McGuire, W. J. (1960b), Direct and indirect persuasive effects of dissonance-producing messages, *Journal of Abnormal and Social Psychology*, **60**, 354–358.

MacKay, D. M. (1956), The epistemological problem for automata. In Shannon, C. E., and McCarthy, J. (eds), *Automata Studies*, Annals of Mathematics Studies, Number 34.

McNeill, D. (1971), The capacity for the ontogenesis of grammar. In Slobin, D. I. (ed.), *The Ontogenesis of Grammar*, New York and London: Academic Press.

Marková, I., and Farmer, J. (1978), On problems of context and attribution in verbal reasoning, *European Journal of Social Psychology*, **8**, 21–35.

Matalon, B. (1962), Etude génétique de l'implication. In Beth, E. W., Grize, J. B., Martin, R., Matalon, B., Naess, A., and Piaget, J., *Études d'Épistémologie Génétique*, 16. *Implication Formalisation et Logique Naturelle*, Paris: Presses Universitaires de France.

Mates, B. (1965), *Elementary Logic*, New York: Oxford University Press.

Mayo, C. W., and Crockett, W. H. (1964), Cognitive complexity and primacy-recency effects in impression formation, *Journal of Abnormal and Social Psychology*, **68**, 335–338.

Mead, G. H. (1934), *Mind, Self, and Society*, Chicago and London: University of Chicago Press.

Mead, G. H. (1936), *Movements of Thought in the Nineteenth Century*, Chicago and London: University of Chicago Press.

Mead, G. H. (1938), *The Philosophy of the Act*, Chicago and London: University of Chicago Press.

Meyerson, E. (1908), *Identity and Reality*, Paris: F. Alcan, trs. Loewenberg, K., London: George Allen and Unwin; New York: Macmillan, 1930.

Michon, J. A. (1972), Multidimensional and hierarchical analysis of progress in learning. In Gregg, L. W., *Cognition in Learning and Memory*, New York and London: Wiley.

Michòtte, A., (1946), *The Perception of Causality*, Louvain: Editions de l'Institut Supérieur de Philosophie; 2nd edn 1954, Louvain: Publications Universitaires de Louvain, trss Miles, T. R., and Miles, E. M., London: Methuen, 1963.

Miller, A. G. (1972), Role playing: an alternative to deception? A review of the evidence, *American Psychologist*, **27**, 623–636.

Minsky, M. (1975), A framework for representing knowledge. In Winston, P. H. (ed.), *The Psychology of Computer Vision*, New York: McGraw-Hill.

Mixon, D. (1979), Understanding shocking and puzzling conduct. In Ginsburg, G. P. (ed.), *Emerging Strategies in Social Psychological Research*, Chichester and New York: Wiley.

Moray, N. (1969a), *Attention*, London: Hutchinson.

Moray, N. (1969b), *Listening and Attention*, Harmondsworth: Penguin Books.

Morgan, J. J., and Morton, J. T. (1944), The distortion of syllogistic reasoning produced by personal convictions, *Journal of Social Psychology*, **20**, 39–59.

Nagel, E. (1961), *The Structure of Science*, London: Routledge & Kegan Paul.

Neisser, U. (1967), *Cognitive Psychology*, New York: Appleton-Century-Crofts.

Neisser, U. (1976), *Cognition and Reality*, San Francisco: Freeman.

Nelson, K. (1974), Concept, word, and sentence: interrelations in acquisition and development, *Psychological Review*, **81**, 267–285.

Newell, A., Shaw, J. C., and Simon, H. A. (1957), Empirical explorations of the logic theory machine, *Proceedings of the Western Joint Computer Conference*.

Newell, A., Shaw, J. C., and Simon, H. A. (1958), Elements of a theory of human problem-solving, *Psychological Review,* **65**, 151–166.

Newell, A., Shaw, J. C., and Simon, H. A. (1960). Report on a general problem-solving program. In *Proceedings of the International Conference on Information Processing*, Paris: UNESCO House.

Newell, A., and Simon, H. A. (1956), The logic theory machine, *IRE Transactions on Information Theory*, **IT-2** (3), 61–79.

Newell, A., and Simon, H. A. (1963), G.P.S., a program that simulates human thought. In Feigenbam, E. A., and Feldman, J. (eds), *Computers and Thought*, New York and London: McGraw-Hill.

Newell, A., and Simon, H. A. (1972), *Human Problem Solving*, Englewood Cliffs, NJ: Prentice-Hall.

214

Newson, J. (1977), An intersubjective approach to the systematic description of mother–infant interaction. In Schaffer, R. H. (ed.), *Studies in Mother–Infant Interaction*, London and New York: Academic Press.

Newson, J. (1979), The growth of shared understandings between infant and caregiver. In Bullowa, M. (ed.), *Before Speech: The Beginning of Interpersonal Commucation*, Cambridge and New York: Cambridge University Press.

Newton, I. (1730), *Optics*, reprinted London: G. Bell and Sons, 1931; New York: Dover, 1952.

Newton, I., *Mathematical Principles of Natural Philosophy*, 3rd edn, trs. Motte, A., 1729. Rvsd & ed. Cajori, F., Cambridge: Cambridge University Press; Berkeley: University of California Press, 1934.

Nidorf, L. J. (1961), Individual differences in impression formation. Unpublished doctoral dissertation, Clark University. Cited by Rosenkrantz, P. S., and Crockett, W. H. (1965).

Northrop, F. S. C. (1947), *The Logic of the Sciences and Humanities*, Cleveland and New York: The World.

Osherson, D. (1975), Logic and models of logical thinking. In Falmagne, R. J. (ed.), *Reasoning: Representation and Process in Children and Adults*, Hillsdale, N. J.: Lawrence Earlbaum Associates.

Papoušek, H., and Papoušek, M. (1977), Mothering and the cognitive head-start: psychobiological considerations. In Schaffer, H. R. (ed.), *Studies in Mother–Infant Interaction*, London and New York: Academic Press.

Pascal, R. (1953), *The German Sturm and Drang*, Manchester: Manchester University Press.

Pawlby, S. J. (1981), Infant–mother relationships. In Duck, S., and Gilmour, R. (eds), *Personal Relationships*, Vol. 2, London and New York: Academic Press.

Peel, E. A. (1967), A method for investigating children's understanding of certain logical connectives used in binary propositional thinking, *British Journal of Mathematical and Statistical Psychology*, **20**, 81–92.

Petermann, F., and Hehl, F. J. (1979), *Einzelfallanalyse*, München: Urban.

Piaget, J. (1970), *The Principles of Genetic Epistemology*, Paris: Presses Universitaires de France, trs. Mays, W., London: Routledge and Kegan Paul, 1972.

Pico della Mirandola, G., *On the Dignity of Man*, trs. Wallis, C. G., Indianapolis and New York: Bobbs-Merrill, 1965.

Polanyi, M. (1966), *The Tacit Dimension*, Garden City: Doubleday.

Pomponazzi, P. (1516), *On the Immortality of the Soul*. In Cassirer, E., Kristeller, P. O., and Randall, J.H. (1948), *The Renaissance Philosophy of Man*, Chicago and London: Chicago University Press.

Postal, P. M. (1966), Review article. André Martinet, elements of general linguistics, *Foundations of Language*, **2**, 151–186.

Pylyshyn, Z. W. (1980), Computation and cognition: issues in the foundations of cognitive science, *Behavioral and Brain Sciences*, **3**, 111–169.

Raaheim, K. (1960), Problem solving and the ability to find replacements, *Scandinavian Journal of Psychology*, **1**, 14–18.

Raaheim, K. (1962), Problem solving and the awareness of the missing part, *Scandinavian Journal of Psychology*, **3**, 129–131.

Randall, J. H. Jr (1962), *The Career of Philosophy*, Vol. I., New York and London: Columbia University Press.

Revlis, R. (1975), Syllogistic reasoning: logical decisions from a complex data base. In Falmagne, R. J. (ed.), *Reasoning*: Representation and Process in Children and Adults, Hillsdale, N. J.: Lawrence Earlbaum Associates.

Richards, M. P. M. (1971), Social interaction in the first weeks of human life, *Psychiatria, Neurologia, Neurochirurgia*, **74**, 35–42.

Rogers, R. R. (1961), *On Becoming a Person*, Boston: Houghton Mifflin.

Rommetveit, R. (1968), *Words, Meanings, and Messages*, New York and London: Academic Press; Oslo: Universitetsforlaget.

Rommetveit, R. (1971), Words, contexts, and verbal messages. In Carswell, E. A., and Rommetveit, R. (eds), *Social Contexts of Messages*, London and New York: Academic Press.

Rommetveit, R. (1974), *On Message Structure*, New York and London: Wiley.

Rommetveit, R. (1978), On Piagetian cognitive operations, semantic competence, and message structure in adult–child communication. In Marková, I. (ed.), *The Social Context of Language*, Chichester and New York: Wiley.

Rommetveit, R. (1980), On 'meanings' of acts and what is meant by what is said in a pluralistic world. In Brenner, M. (ed.), *The Structure of Action*, Oxford: Blackwell.

Rosenblueth, A., Wiener, N., and Bigelow, J. (1943), Behavior, purpose, and teleology, *Philosophy of Science*, **10**, 18–24.

Rosenkrantz, P. S., and Crockett, W. H. (1965), Some factors influencing the assimilation of disparate information in impression formation, *Journal of Personality and Social Psychology*, **2**, 397–402.

Rubinstein, S. L. (1957), Bitiye i Soznaniye, (Being and Consciousness), Moscow: Izdavatelstvo Akademii Nauk USSR.

Rubinstein, S. L. (1958), *O Myshlenii i Putyach yego Issledovaniya*, (On Thought and Its Investigation), Moscow: Izdavatelstvo Akademii Nauk USSR.

Rubinstein, S. L. (1959), *Principi i Puty i Razvitiya Psikhologii*, (The Principles and Methods of the Development of Psychology), Moscow: Izdavatelstvo Akademii Nauk USSR.

Russell, B. (1917), *Mysticism and Logic, and Other Essays*, reprinted London: George Allen and Unwin, 1963.

Ryan, J. (1974), Early language development: towards a communicational analysis. In Richards, M. P. M. (ed.), *The Integration of the Child into a Social World*, London: Cambridge University Press.

Scaife, M., and Bruner, J. S. (1975), The capacity for joint visual attention in the infant, *Nature*, **253**, 265–266.

Schaffer, H. R. (1974), Early social behaviour and the study of reciprocity, *Bulletin of the British Psychological Society*, **27**, 209–216.

Schaffer, H. R., Collis, G. M., and Parsons, G. (1977), Vocal interchange and visual regard in verbal and pre-verbal children. In Schaffer, H. R. (ed.), *Studies in Mother–Infant Interaction*, London and New York: Academic Press.

Schank, R. C., and Abelson, R. P. (1977), *Scripts, Plans, Goals and Understanding*, Hillsdale, N. J.: Lawrence Erlbaum Associates.

Scheffler, I. (1967), *Science and Subjectivity*, Indianapolis: Bobbs-Merrill.

Schlesinger, I. M. (1971), Production of utterances and language acquisition. In Slobin, D. I. (ed.), *The Ontogenesis of Grammar*, New York and London: Academic Press.

Schuetz, A. (1948), Sartre's theory of the alter ego, *Philosophy and Phenomenological Research*, **9**, 181–199.

Sells, S. B. (1936), The atmosphere effect: an experimental study of reasoning, *Archives of Psychology*, **29**, 3–72.

Sells, S. B., and Koob, H. F. (1937), A classroom demonstration of 'atmosphere effect' in reasoning, *Journal of Educational Psychology*, **28**, 514–518.

Shatz, M., and Gelman, R. (1973), The development of communication skills: modifications in the speech of young children as a function of listener, *Monographs of the Society for Research in Child Development*, **38**, 1–37 (Series No. 152).

Shields, M. M. (1979), Dialogue, monologue and egocentric speech by children in nursery schools. In Garnica, O. K., and King, M. L. (eds), *Language, Children and Society*, Oxford and New York: Pergamon Press.

Shotter, J. (1975), *Images of Man in Psychological Research*, London: Methuen.

Sinclair-de-Zwart, H. (1973), Language acquisition and cognitive development. In

216

Moore, T. E. (ed.), *Cognitive Development and the Acquisition of Language*, New York and London: Academic Press.

Skinner, B. F. (1973), *Beyond Freedom and Dignity*, Harmondsworth: Penguin Books.

Smedslund, J. (1969), Meanings, implications and universals: towards a psychology of man, *Scandinavian Journal of Psychology*, **10**, 1–15.

Smedslund, J. (1970), Circular relation between understanding and logic, *Scandinavian Journal of Psychology*, **11**, 217–219.

Snow, C. E. (1977), The development of conversation between mothers and babies, *Journal of Child Language*, **4**, 1–22.

Strawson, P. F. (1952), *Introduction to Logical Theory*, London: Methuen.

Strawson, P. F. (1966), *The Bounds of Sense*, London: Methuen.

Suzuki, D. T. (1950), *Living by Zen*, London: Rider.

Taplin, J. E. (1971), Reasoning with conditional sentences, *Journals of Verbal Learning and Verbal Behavior*, **10**, 219–225.

Taplin, J. E., and Staudenmayer, H. (1973), Interpretation of abstract conditional sentences in deductive reasoning, *Journal of Verbal Learning and Verbal Behavior*, **12**, 530–542.

Taylor, C. (1964), *The Explanation of Behaviour*, London and Henley: Routledge & Kegan Paul; New York: The Humanities Press.

Taylor, C. (1975), *Hegel*, Cambridge and London: Cambridge University Press.

Tedeschi, J. T. (ed.), (1972), *The Social Influence Processes,* Chicago and New York: Aldine Atherton.

Terris, W., and Milburn, T. W. (1972), Praise, evaluative dependence, and the experimenter as factors in a free-learning task, *Journal of Psychology*, **81**, 183–194.

Thistlethwaite, D. (1950), Attitude and structure as factors in the distortion of reasoning, *Journal of Abnormal and Social Psychology*, **45**, 442–458.

Tolman, E. C. (1932), *Purposive Behavior in Animals and Men*, reprinted New York: Appleton-Century-Crofts, 1967.

Tolman, E. C. (1948), Cognitive maps in rats and men, *Psychological Review*, **55**, 189–208.

Trabasso, T. (1972), Mental operations in language comprehension. In Freedle, R. O., and Carroll, J. B. (eds), *Language Comprehension and the Acquisition of Knowledge*, Washington: Winston.

Trakhtenbrot, B. A. (1957), *Algoritmi i Maschinoe Reschenie Zadatch*, (Algorithms and Machine Problem Solving), Moscow: Fizmatgiz.

Treisman, A. (1960), Contextual cues in selective listening, *Quarterly Journal of Experimental Psychology*, **12**, 242–248.

Trevarthen, C. (1977), Descriptive analyses of infant communicative behaviour. In Schaffer, H. R. (ed.), *Studies in Mother–Infant Interaction*, London and New York: Academic Press.

Trevarthen, C. (1979), Communication and cooperation in early infancy: a description of primary intersubjectivity. In Bullowa, M. (ed.), *Before Speech: The Beginning of Interpersonal Communication*, Cambridge and New York: Cambridge University Press.

Truax, C. B., and Carthuff, R. R. (1967), *Toward Effective Counselling and Psychotherapy: Training and Practice*, Chicago: Aldine.

Truax, C. B., and Mitchell, K. M. (1971), Research on certain therapist interpersonal skills in relation to process and outcome. In Bergin, A. E., and Garfield, S. L. (eds), *Handbook of Psychotherapy and Behavior Change*, New York: Wiley.

Turing, A. M. (1963), Computing machinery and intelligence. In Feigenbaum, E. A., and Feldman, J. (eds), *Computers and Thought*, New York and London: McGraw-Hill.

Turner, M. B. (1967), *Philosophy and the Science of Behavior*, New York: Appleton-Century-Crofts.

Urmson, J. O. (1956), *Philosophical Analysis*, Oxford: Clarendon Press.

Valéry, P. (1948), *Descartes*, London and Toronto: Cassell.

Vygotsky, L. S. (1962), *Thought and Language*, New York: Wiley.

de Waele, J. P., and Harré, R. (1979), Autobiography as a psychological method. In Ginsburg, G. P. (ed.), *Emerging Strategies in Social Psychological Research*, Chichester and New York: Wiley.

Wason, P. C. (1966), Reasoning. In Foss, B. M. (ed.), *New Horizons in Psychology*, Harmondsworth: Penguin Books.

Wason, P. C. (1968), Reasoning about a rule, *Quarterly Journal of Experimental Psychology*, **20**, 273–281.

Wason, P. C., and Johnson-Laird, P. N. (1972), *Psychology of Reasoning: Structure and Content*, London: Batsford.

Wason, P. C., and Shapiro, D. (1972), Natural and contrived experience in a reasoning problem, *Quarterly Journal of Experimental Psychology*, **23**, 63–71.

Watson, G., and Glaser, E. M. (1951), *Watson–Glaser Critical Thinking Appraisal Test*, New York: Harcourt, Brace and World.

Werner, H., and Kaplan, B. (1963), *Symbol Formation*, New York: Wiley.

West, S. G., Gunn, S. P., and Chernicky, P. (1975), Ubiquitous Watergate: an attributional analysis, *Journal of Personality and Social Psychology*, **32**, 55–65.

Whewell, W. (1847), *The Philosophy of the Inductive Sciences*, Vols I and II, reprinted New York and London: Johnson Reprint Corporation, 1967.

White, R. K., Wright, B. A., and Dembo, T. (1948), Studies in adjustment to visible injuries: evaluation of curiosity by the injured, *Journal of Abnormal and Social Psychology*, **43**, 13–28.

Wilkins, M. C. (1928), The effect of changed material on the ability to do formal syllogistic reasoning, *Archives of Psychology*, **102**, 5–83.

Winograd, T. (1975), Frame representations and the declarative-procedural controversy. In Bobrow, D. G., and Collins, A. (eds), *Representation and Understanding*, New York and London: Academic Press.

Wittgenstein, L. (1953), *Philosophical Investigations*, Oxford: Basil Blackwell.

Wittgenstein, L. (1922), *Tractatus Logico-Philosophicus*, trss Pears, D. F., and McGuinness, B. F., London: Routledge and Kegan Paul; New York: The Humanities Press, 1961.

Woodworth, R. S., and Sells, S. B. (1935), An atmosphere effect in formal syllogistic reasoning, *Journal of Experimental Psychology*, **18**, 451–460.

Zaporozhets, A. V. (1948), *Voprosy Psikhologii Rebyanka Doshkol'nogo Vozrasta*, (Problems of the Psychology of the Preschool Child), Moscow and Leningrad: APN RSFSR.

Author Index

Italic numbers refer to the page on which
the reference is listed in full.

Abelson, R.P., 56–58, 79, 85–91, 93, 173,
  205, 215
Abramyan, L.A., 198
Adam, C., 204
Agrippa, 14
Alexander, P., 62, 205
Al-Khawarizmi, 75
Allison, H.E., 52, 205
Alston, W.P., 93, 205
Ancyferova, L.I., 182
Argyle, M., 196, 205
Aristotle, 3, 24, 25, 30, 31, 96, 97, 186,
  205
Aronson, E., 195, 205
Augustine, St., 169, 171
Austin, G.A., 47, 48, 207
Aydin, O., 2, 205

Bannister, D., 195, 205
Barlow, D.H., 202, 211
Barnard, F.M., 141, 205
Bateson, G., 134, 205
Bateson, M.G., 158, 205
Beck, L.J., 16, 205
Begg, I., 32, 206
Belous, V.P., 199, 206
Berdyaev, N., 13, 15, 206
Bergson, H., 90, 206
Berkeley, G., 20, 173
Berlin, I., 103, 141, 204, 206
Bickman, L., 130, 206
Bierwisch, M., 43–45, 49, 206
Bigelow, J., 96, 215
Bilkhugov, S. Yu., 199, 206
Black, J.K., 155, 206
Bobrow, D.G., 55, 206

Boden, M.A., 95, 96, 206
Boole, G., 26, 27, 206
Borke, H., 157, 206
Bourne, L.E., 47, 48, 206
Bower, T.G.R., 89, 206
Bowerman, M., 190, 191, 206
Braithwaite, R.B., 96, 206
Brazelton, T.B., 147, 148, 206
Brenner, M., 194, 195, 206
Brett, G.S., 4, 206
Broadbent, D.E., 35, 68–70, 206
Brown, J., 195, 206
Bruner, J.S., 47, 48, 122, 156, 170, 171,
  207, 215
Brunswik, E., 54, 55, 207
Buber, M., 132, 133, 207
Bucci, W., 32, 207
Bullowa, M., 151, 207
Bungard, W., 194, 195, 206

Cahoon, D.D., 189, 207
Cairns, R.B., 202, 207
Campanella, T., 14
Čapek, K., 123
Carlsmith, J.M., 195, 205
Carthuff, R.R., 160, 161, 216
Cassirer, E., 14, 207, 214
Chapman, J.P., 32, 36, 207
Chapman, L.J., 32, 36, 207
de Charms, R., 195, 207
Chase, W.G., 55, 64–66, 207, 208
Chernicky, P., 217
Cherry, C., 68, 207
Chomsky, N., 43–45, 55, 64, 207
Cicourel, A.V., 155, 207
Clark, E.V., 50, 51, 179, 190, 207

218

Clark, H.H., 55, 64–66, *207, 208*
Coleridge, S.T., 185, *208*
Collins, A.M., 55, 84, 85, 88, *206, 208*
Collis, G.M., 170, *208, 215*
Condillac, E.B. de, 141, 144
Condon, W.S., 146, 148, 200, 201, *208*
Copernicus, N., 80
Copi, I.M., 28, *208*
Coplestone, F., 42, 53, *208*
Crockett, W.H., 165, 166, *208, 213, 215*
Cross, T.G., 151, *208*

Darley, J.M., 130, *212*
Darwin, C., 9, 110, 123, 143, 145, 146, *208*
Dembo, T., 134, *217*
De Morgan, A., 27
Dennett, D.C., 78, 96, *208*
Denny, J.P., 32, *206*
Descartes, R., 4–7, 15–23, 25, 27, 29, 38, 41–46, 53, 60–61, 70, 74, 80–82, 104, 108–110, 112–113, 115, 117, 185, 204, *208, 209*
Deutsch, D., 70, *209*
Deutsch, J., 70, *209*
Devin, J., 159
Duhem, P., 80
Duncker, K., 75, *209*

Eberhard, J.A., 52
Edwards, P., *209*
Einstein, A., 6, 79
Erikson, J.R., 33, 40, *209*
Erwin-Tripp, S., 159, *209*
Estes, W.K., 189, *209*
Evans, J. St. B.T., 4, 39, *209*
Eysenck, H.J., 160, *209*

Farmer, J., 173, *213*
Farr, R.M., 194, *209*
Ficino, M., 14, *209*
Fishman, J., 159, *209*
Fludd, R., 14
Fodor, F.A., 121, *212*
Fodor, J., 4, 5, *209*
Forbes, C.D., 135, *209*
Forehand, G.A., 83, *209*
Forgas, J.P., 197, *209*
Foster, M.B., 98, 99, *209*
Franklin, B., 184
Franks, J.J., 55, *209*
Fransella, F., 195, *205*
Freedman, J.-L., 195, *210*
Frege, G., 27

From, F., 137, 138, *210*

Galilei, G., 3, 80, 81, 188, *210*
Gelman, R., 151, 159, *210, 215*
Gergen, K., 194, 195, *210*
Gibson, J., 61, *210*
Ginsburg, G.P., 195, *210*
Glaser, E.M., 37, *217*
Goffman, E., 135, *210*
Goodnow, J.J., 47, 48, *207*
Green, J.A., 202, *207*
Gregg, L.W., 55, *210*
Gunn, S.P., *217*

Haley, J., 134, *205*
Hamilton, W., 17, *210*
Hamlyn, D.W., 76, 77, 179, *210*
Hanson, N.R., 2, 188, 192, *210*
Harré, R., 92, 93, 193, 195, *210, 217*
Healy, A.F., 173, *210*
Hegel, G.W.F., 6, 7, 11, 20, 45, 53, 98, 101, 103, 106, 108–121, 123–136, 138–140, 144–146, 149–151, 154–155, 162–168, 171, 173–174, 178–179, 181–182, 184–188, 192–193, 201, 203, *210, 211*
Hehl, F.J., 202, *214*
Heidbreder, E., 48
Heider, F., 54, 55, 99, 136, 137, 198, *211*
Henle, M., 29, 35, 37, *211*
Heracleitus, 71
Herder, J.G., 45, 104–107, 140–144, 169–171, 173–174, 184–185, 204, *211*
Hersen, M., 202, *211*
Hoffman, M.L., 157, *212*
Hovland, C.I., 48
Hull, C.L., 48, 189
Hume, D., 4, 20, 62, 63, 82, 88, 91, 92, 106, *211*
Hunt, E.B., 48, *211*
Husserl, E., 7
Hymes, D., 155, *211*

Jackson, D.D., 134, *205*
Jensen, J., 35, *211*
Jevons, W.S., 27
Johnson, E.S., 195, *211*
Johnson-Laird, P.N., 29, 31, 33, 35, 37–39, 55–57, 76–77, *211, 217*
Jones, M.R., 33, 40, *209*
Jones, O.H.M., 148, 149, 202, *211*
Jones, P., 135, *209*
Joynson, R.B., 193, *211*

220

Kafka, F., 178
Kahneman, D., 68, 70, 71, *211*
Kanouse, D.E., 85–88, 173, *205*
Kant, I., 4, 7, 20, 25–27, 31, 47, 52–55, 97–99, 105–106, 109, 127, 166, 173, 178, 186, *211*
Kaplan, B., 171, *217*
Katz, J.J., 121, *212*
Keeling, S.V., 42, *212*
Kenny, A., 17, 41, *212*
Kessler, S., 155, *212*
Klopstock, F.G., 104
Kneale, M., 26, *212*
Kneale, W., 26, *212*
Koch, S., *209*
Kojève, A., 128, 133, *212*
Koob, M.F., 31, *215*
Kordig, C.R., 191, 192, *212*
Kosík, K., 180, *212*
Koslowski, B., 147, 148, *206*
Kratochwill, T.R., 202, *212*
Kuhn, T.S., 2, 3, 5, 6, 8, 9, 40, 79, 124, 188, 192, 193, 195, 204, *212*
Kuipers, B.J., 89, *212*

Laing, R.D., 133, 134, *212*
Latané, B., 130, *212*
Leeper, R., 2, 3
Lefford, A., 37, *212*
Leibniz, G.W., 16, 17, 42, 51, 91, 105, 106, 184, 185, *212*
Leontyev, A.A., 199, *212*
Levine, L.E., 157, *212*
Levy, D.M., 150, *212*
Lewin, K., 189
Locke, J., 18, 20–23, 45–47, 53, 61–63, 66, 70, 91, 109, 141, 173, *212*
Luchins, A.S., 35
Luria, A.R., 198, 199, *212*

MacCorquordale, K., *209*
McGuigan, F.J., 195, *212*
McGuire, W.J., 37, *212*
MacKay, D.M., 68, *212*
McNeill, D., 43, *212*
Mach, E., 62, 173
Main, M., 147, 148, *206*
Mansurov, N.S., 177
Marková, I., 2, 135, 173, *205, 209, 213*
Martsinovskaya, E.N., 198
Matalon, B., 38, *213*
Mates, B., 28, *213*
Mayo, C.W., 166, *213*

Mead, G.H., 80, 106–108, 138–139, 143–145, 153, 155–158, 174, 197, *213*
Meehl, P.E., *209*
Merleau-Ponty, M., 7
Meyerson, E., 89, 193, 194, *213*
Michael, M., 37, *211*
Michon, J.A., 55, *213*
Michotte, A., 197, *213*
Milburn, T.W., 195, *216*
Miller, A.G., 195, *213*
Miller, G.A., 173, *210*
Minsky, M., 88, 89, *213*
Mitchell, K.M., 160, *216*
Mixon, D., 195, *213*
Moray, N., 68, *213*
Morgan, J.J., 37, *213*
Morton, J.T., 37, *213*
Mueller, C.G., *209*

Nagel, E., 95, 96, *213*
Neisser, U., 54, 70–73, 79, *213*
Nelson, K., 171–173, 190, 191, *213*
Newell, A., 55, 67, 75, 76, 83, 84, *213*
Newson, J., 148, 151, 153, 201, 202, *213, 214*
Newton, I., 2, 6, 79, 80, 82, 90, 185, *214*
Nicholas of Cusa, 14
Nidorf, L.J., 166, *214*
Northrop, F.S.C., 4, *214*

Osherson, D., 26, *214*

Papoušek, H., 151, *214*
Papoušek, M., 151, *214*
Parsons, G., 170, *215*
Pascal, R., 184, 185, *214*
Pawlby, S.J., 148, *214*
Peel, E.A., 38, *214*
Petermann, F., 202, *214*
Piaget, J., 40, 76, 77, 91, 157, 179, 199, *214*
Pico Della Mirandola, 14, 15, *214*
Planck, M., 9
Polanyi, M., 55, *214*
Pomponazzi, P., 15, *214*
Postal, P.M., 43, *214*
Priestley, J., 184
Pylyshyn, Z.W., 74, 76, 78, *214*

Quillian, M.R., 84, 85, 88, *208*

Raaheim, K., 35, *214*
Randall, J.H., Jr., 80, *214*
Revlis, R., 31, 35, 56, *214*

Richards, M.P.M., 147, *214*
Robertson, W., 106
Rogers, R.R., 160, *214*
Rommetveit, R., 2, 40, 118–119,
    121–123, 134, 150–151, 158, 161,
    170–172, 180, 198, *215*
Rosenblueth, A., 96, *215*
Rosenkrantz, P.S., 166, *215*
Rousseau, J.J., 121, 141
Rubinstein, S.L., 131, 168–169, 173–178,
    181–183, 200, 202, *215*
Russel, B., 27, 82, 94, *215*
Ryan, J., 151, *215*

Sachs, J., 159
Sander, L.W., 146, *208*
Sartre, J-P., 7, 72
Scaife, M., 170, *215*
Scaliger, J., 42
Schaffer, H.R., 147, 148, 170, *208, 215*
Schank, R.C., 56–58, 79, 89, *215*
Scheffler, I., 188, *215*
Schlesinger, I.M., 43, *215*
Schoenfeld, W.N., *209*
Schuetz, A., 72, *215*
Secord, P.F., 92, 93, 193, 195, *210*
Sells, S.B., 31, 36, *215, 217*
Shapiro, D., 38, *217*
Shatz, M., 151, 159, *210, 215*
Shaw, J.C., 75, 76, 83, 84, *213*
Shea, D.J., 195, *207*
Shields, M.M., 155, *215*
Shotter, J., 193, 195, *215*
Sime, J., 195, *206*
Simmel, M., 136, 198, *211*
Simon, H.A., 55, 67, 75, 76, 83, 84, *213*
Sinclair-de-Zwart, H., 44, *215*
Skinner, B.F., 49, 50, 189, *216*
Smedslund, J., 34, 35, 168, *216*
Smoke, K.L., 48
Snow, C.E., 151–153, *216*
Staudenmayer, H., 39, *216*
Strawson, P.F., 28, 53, *216*
Stuart, J., 135, *209*
Süssmilch, J.P., 141–143
Suzuki, D.T., 3, *216*

Tagart, J., 38, *211*
Tannery, P., 204
Taplin, J.E., 38, 39, *216*
Taylor, C., 96, 97, 103, 105, 112, 116,
    119, 128, 131, 138, 204, *216*
Tedeschi, J.T., 67, *216*
Terris, W., 195, *216*
Thistlethwaite, D., 37, *216*
Thorndike, E.L., 190
Tolman, E.C., 55, 93, 94, 189, 190, *216*
Trabasso, T., 55, *216*
Trakhtenbrot, B.A., 75, *216*
Treisman, A., 70, *216*
Trevarthen, C., 148, 151, 155, *216*
Truax, C.B., 160, 161, *216*
Turing, A.M., 73, 74, *216*
Turner, M.B., 189, 190, *216*

Urmson, J.O., 62, *217*

Valéry, P., 16, *217*
Verplanck, W.S., *209*
Voltaire, E.M.A. de, 106
Vygotsky, L.S., 5, 48, 138, 171, 172, *217*

de Waele, J.P., 195, *217*
Wason, P.C., 29, 32, 33, 37–39, 57, *217*
Watson, G., 37, *217*
Weakland, J., 134, *205*
Weiner, N., 96, *215*
Wellek, R., 180
Werner, H., 171, 172, *217*
West, S.G., 195, *217*
Whewell, W., 3, 4, 21, *217*
White, R.K., 134, *217*
Whitehead, A.N., 82
Wilkins, M.C., 32, 36, *217*
Winograd, T., 83, 89, *217*
Wittgenstein, L., 50, 63–66, 71, 118,
    169–171, *217*
Woodward, R.S., 36, *217*
Wright, B.A., 134, *217*
Wundt, W., 143, 145

Zaporozhets, A.V., 199, *217*
Žukovova, I.M., 175

Subject Index

Absolute, the, 114
abstract *versus* concrete, 139, 154, 164, 171, 201
acts
  disconfirmatory, 133–135
action
  and verbalization, 138
  anticipation of, 158
  as a primitive concept, 95, 136–138
  free, 105
  humanizing nature of, 135–136
  inhibition of, 108
  intentional, 93
  interruption of, 108
  joint, 158
  perception of, 136–137
  priority of consciousness over, 23
  priority of thought over, 23
  purposeful Cartesian conception, 93–95
  social nature of, 145
activity
  development through, 187
  expression by language, 169, 171, 173, 175
  in perception, 71
  in problem-solving, 175–177
  mutuality in, 170–171
  of the will, 60–62
  social nature of, 108
actuality (being-for-itself), 115, 146, 164–165, 186–187
algorithms, 8, 48–49, 74–76, 78, 96, 131
analysis by synthesis, 70
analysis through synthesis, 177, 181–183

anticipation
  in communication, 158
  in decoding, 158–159
apperception
  synthetic unit of, 127
atomism
  logical, 65–66, 71, 82, 86, 88, 110

becoming, 108, 113–115

calculus
  logical, 38–40
causation
  Humean conception, 92–93
  impersonal, 95–96, 98, 99
  personal, 93, 99
certainty, 15–16, 19, 20–23, 60–62, 109
  search for, 15–16, 21, 112, 117–119
  sense-certainty, 117–119
circle returning within itself, 178–180, 181, 182, 201–202
cogito ergo sum, 15–16, 17, 19, 20, 21, 23, 104, 108–109
cognition
  activity of, 70–71
cognitive – purposive theory, 93–94
communicative competence, 148–149, 155–156, 158–159
communication
  asymmetrical, 159–160
  one-way flow, 68–73, 159, 160, 161
  pre-verbal, 153–154, 156, 157, 158
  reciprocal, 153–156, 160–161
  symmetrical, 157–161
  two-way flow, 70–72, 159–161

222

compartmentalization of the mind, 37–38, 39, 162
computer models, 59, 73–74, 77–78, 100
concepts, 47–49, 51–52, 85–86, 88, 118–119, 120–124
  acquisition and formation of, 48–49, 51, 172
  acquisition in a yes-no manner, 172
  'deductive' and 'inductive' evidence for, 86–87
  hierarchical mechanistic model, 85–89
concretization, 154, 201
conditional problems, 32–33, 38
connectives
  logical, 27–29, 38–39, 82
consciousness
  an evolutionary process, 139
  and *Cogito*, 19, 20, 23
  and expression, 108
  and perception, 124–125
  and reflection, 18, 108
  and reflexion, 108
  and self-identity, 18
  and sense-certainty, 117–119, 125
  and understanding, 126–127
  as a static quality, 19, 23
  as revising concepts, 111–112, 192
  Cartesian concept of, 17–20, 23, 108–110
  concepts of, 17
  development of, 154–159, 175
  Hegelian concept of, 106–112, 116, 138–139
  inseparable from thought and reflection, 17–20, 108, 110
  of the child, 139, 154–159
  of the foetus, 19
  of the individual, 143–145
  priority over action, 19, 23
  priority over the world, 16, 17, 20, 21, 109
  projective function of, 180–181
  reflexive function of, 180–181
  relation to reality, 168
  relation to thought, 17–20, 108, 110
  romantic concept of, 107–108
  separation from the world, 16, 17, 19, 20, 24, 25, 109, 184
constructs
  logical, 94
contradiction, 163–166, 168–169, 192–193
  reflexive, 163, 168

conversation
  mother-infant, 151–153
Copernican revolution
  Hegel's epistemology likened to, 173
  Kant's epistemology likened to, 53
counselling, 160–161
creativity, 44–45

decoding
  anticipatory, 158–159
decontextualization, 154, 170–173, 175
deduction, 22–23, 74–75, 117
desire, 128–129, 133
determinism
  principle of, 181
disconfirmation, 133–134
dualism
  Cartesian, 20, 41, 42, 46, 108–110, 138

egocentricity, 157–158
embodiment
  of computer programs, 74, 77–78, 95–96, 131
  of mind, 131, 138
empathy, 107, 130, 133, 154
  ability to empathize, 107, 130, 157–158
empiricism, 4–5, 7, 46–47, 52, 59, 76–77, 109–110, 169–170, 178
encoding
  and anticipatory decoding, 158–159
  as passive, 33–35
  of pictures and facts, 64–66
epistemology
  see knowledge, theory of
explanation
  causal, 92–93, 94–97
  purposive, 93–97
  teleological, 93–97
expressivism, 103–105, 106–108, 110, 138, 184–188
evolutionism, 106, 110, 187

falsity
  positive attitude to, 113–114
filter theory of attention, 68–72
functional fixedness, 35
functional properties of objects, 171–173

games
  function of in child development, 155, 157
General Problem Solver (GPS), 83–84
gestalt psychology, 174
  and alternative conceptual framework, 8–9

224

and the theory-ladenness thesis, 9, 192
gestures,
  conversation of, 143, 156
  modification and adjustment of, 153
  non-significant, 144–145, 150, 153,
    156, 161
  significant, 150, 153

hierarchical structure
  cognition, 83, 88
  decision-trees, 59, 83, 178
  knowledge, 88–89
  layers of knowledge, 83
  machines, 82, 83, 89
  semantic memory, 84–85
  semantic networks, 84–85
humanism, 13–15, 103

I, the, 15–16, 132
ideas
  clear and distinct, 21, 22–23, 38, 42,
    60–61, 109, 117
  innate, 41–43, 45–46, 52, 59
  innate as dispositional, 42, 52, 110
  notion of, 41
  of primary and secondary qualities, 46
  origin of, 41
  relationship to propositions, 63
  relationship to the world, 20, 109
  simple and complex, 46–47, 62
identity
  personal, 18
individual, the
  as egocentric, 104
  relation to society, 144
  relationship with his environment, 187
  Renaissance concept of, 104
individuals
  Hegelian, 117–121, 124–126
information-processing system, 34,
    67–75, 79, 95, 136, 145, 161
intentions, 93, 94
  attribution of, 137
  indication of, 153
  perception of, 138, 153
intersubjectivity, 150–151, 154–161
intuition, 21–23, 117
invariants
  presupposition of, 50, 194
  search for, 89–92

knowing subject (knower), 15–23, 41,
    107–111, 178
  passivity of, 60–62, 70, 73–74, 78–79,
    146

static and predetermined nature of,
    58–59, 96, 146
knowledge
  a posteriori, 45–46, 52
  a priori, 52–53, 55
  adequate, 117
  and certainty, 20–23, 41–47, 60–62,
    117–119
  communicability of, 117–119
  criterion of, external, 8, 110–111
  criterion of, internal, 8, 111
  demonstrative, 24, 28
  fixed by language, 183
  innate, 41–46, 52, 146
  knowledge structure, 57
  material for, 22, 60–63
  modes of, 52–54, 127
  object of, 41, 178
  objective, 20, 24–25, 41, 110–111
  phenomenal, 112–114
  publicity of, 117, 119
  representation of, 83–89
  standard of, 8, 20–23, 31–40,
    110–114
  starting point of, 16, 19, 22–23, 41–47,
    117–119
  storage of, 83–89
  units of, 88
  unmediated, 117
  of the world, 21, 41, 54–55, 108–111,
    178
  of universals, 42–44, 49, 118–127
knowledge, acquisition of, 20–23, 63–74,
    76–77, 78–79, 155, 168–169
  activity of the mind in, 109
  algorithmic nature of, 65, 74–75
  Cartesian account of, 20–23, 60–62,
    74–75, 109–112, 122, 131, 178
  Hegelian account of, 109–114,
    117–128, 131, 169, 178–182
  in a yes–no manner, 52, 178
knowledge, theory of
  based on intuition and deduction,
    22–23, 28
  Cartesian, 1–9, 20–21, 41, 60–62,
    109–110, 111, 127, 128
  Cartesian, Hegelian criticisms of,
    108–113, 122, 127, 131, 173
  epistemology
    empiricistic, 109
  Hegelian, 109–112, 116, 117–129,
    173–174
  incommensurability of Cartesian and
    Hegelian, 116–117
  Kant's, 52–54, 74, 127, 173

layman's, 89
presentational, 20, 62, 173–174
rationalistic, 109
reflexive, 173–174
representational, 46, 61–62, 173–174
social, 135
traditional (*see* Cartesian)

labelling, 50, 170
language
  as a product of reflexion, 142
  as a social activity, 158
  as a system of signs, 141, 144
  as expressing activity, 169, 171, 173, 175
  comprehension of, 84
  data language, 188–190
  deictic use of, 50, 118–119, 170
  development of, 49–51, 149, 170–171
  empiricistic theory of, 46–52, 63–66, 141
  first words of, 49–52, 169–173
  function in child development, 155, 158–159
  learning of, 43–44, 49–52, 169–173, 190–191
  motherese, 151
  natural (or ordinary), 27–29, 63, 89
  origin of, 43–44, 141–143, 144, 169
  picture theory of, 63–66
  private, 50
  rationalistic theory of, 43–45, 141
  relation to ideas, 63
  role of in struggle for recognition, 132
  social nature of, 117–119, 141
language-games, 170, 175
law of contradiction, 164–165, 168–169
law of non-contradiction, 24–25, 164–165
laws of logic
  and human reasoning, 167–169
  Aristotelian, 24–25
  Cartesian, 24–27, 162–165
  formal, 27–29, 162–168
  Hegelian, 163, 166, 167–169, 173–174
  Kantian, 25–26
  reflexive, 168–169
laws of nature, 53, 89, 105
laws of thought
  Cartesian, 24–27, 162–165
  formal, 27, 162–168
  Hegelian, 163, 166, 167–169, 173–174
logic
  and natural language, 27–28
  as a model of reasoning, 29, 31–33, 38–40, 166–169

Aristotelian, 29–33, 168
  formal, 30–31, 33, 38–40, 162
  Hegelian, 163–164, 166–168
  in human thought, 168–169
  propositional, 27–29, 32–33, 38–40
  symbolic, 27–28
  traditional, Hegel's criticisms, 120, 162–163, 166–167, 168
logical atomism, 65–66, 71, 82, 86, 88, 110
logical calculus as a yard-stick, 38–40
logical correctives 27–29, 38–39, 82
logical constructs, 94

machines and mechanisms
  contrasted with organisms, 77–78, 96, 97–100
  hierarchical sub-division of, 82
master and slave, 116, 129–131, 135–136, 149, 159–160
material implication, 27–28, 38
meaning
  acquisition of, 49–52, 150–154, 190–191
  functional similarity in, 190
  meaning potentiality, 121–122
  perceptual similarity in, 190
  shared, 153–154, 156
  of a word, 47–52, 88, 118–119, 121–123
mind
  as a blank sheet or *tabula rasa*, 45–46
  as embodied, 131, 138
  as external to itself, 115
  as giving laws to nature, 53
  as ignorant of things in themselves, 53
  as object for itself, 115
  as ready made, 43–45, 143
  as source of ideas, 41, 42–43
  ascending process of, 117, 124
  activity of, 8, 22, 60–61, 71, 115, 127, 174–175, 185
  analogy of red vision, 53, 55, 74
  becoming of, 115, 116–117, 124
  causality attributed to structure of, 53
  child's mind, computer program of, 73–74
  child's mind, unfolding of, 91, 115, 124
  cognitive structure of, 44, 53
  compartmentalization of, 37–38, 39, 162
  computer program of, 73–77, 83–85
  constitution of, 52–53, 54–55, 83
  creativity of, 45
  disembodied, 74–75, 77–78

distinguished from the self, 115
dynamic, 8, 175
faculties of, 22, 60–62
of the foetus, 19, 44
hierarchical mechanistic model of,
    82–85
ideas as contents of, 20
independent of body, 16–20, 46, 52–55,
    73–75, 108–109, 138
individualistic nature of, 8, 140
innate ideas dispositions of, 42
innateness as a capacity of, 42, 43–44,
    52
innateness rejected, 45–46, 52
intuition and deduction as operations
    of, 23
judgement and will, 22, 60–62
language a product of, 43–45
maturation of, 91, 115, 117, 124
mechanistic model of, 29
modes of, 22, 60–62
organs of, 44, 83
origins of, 143–144, 185
passivity of, 8, 22, 34, 60–62, 66–70,
    109, 185
phenomenal stages of, 115, 116–117
red vision analogy of, 53, 55, 74
representations, internal, 53–59
self, distinguished from, 115
space and time attributed to structure
    of, 53
stages of, 115, 116–117
storage of knowledge in, 83–85
synthesizing activity of, 127
thinking substance, 16, 20
understanding, 22, 60–62, 66–70
will, 22, 60–62
world as inferred from contents of, 20,
    41, 53–55
modus ponens, 33
modus tollens, 33
monads, 16–17, 105
mutual recognition, 129–133, 135–136,
    149–150
mutuality
    as a precondition of self-recognition,
        129–130, 131, 132, 135, 149–150,
        154, 160
    in activity, 170–171
    of control, 160

Nature
    Aristotelian conception of, 186
    as purposive activity, 186–187

laws of, 53, 89, 105
laws of as given by mind, 53
negative rationalism, 40
neutral data, 188–192
neutral data language, 189
neutral observation, 188–193

organisms
    contrasted with machines, 77–78, 96,
        97–100, 186
    must be treated as wholes, 186–187
    relationship to their environment,
        186–187
ostension, 170–171
other-consciousness, 129–132, 149–150,
    154–156, 160–161

particulars, Hegelian, 118–120, 121–125,
    196–197
perception
    as active, 71
personal identity, 18
play
    function in child development, 155–157
potentiality (being-in-itself)
    active unfolding of, 146, 164–165, 187
    and actuality or being-for-itself, 115,
        146, 164, 186–188
    as being-in-itself, 115
    compared to Cartesian potentiality,
        115, 146
problem-solving, 31–35, 38–40, 74–76,
    174–178, 200
programs
    algorithmic, 48–49, 131
    computer, 58–59, 73–74, 75–76,
        77–78, 83–84, 95–96, 100
    of pain, 77–78
propositions
    as picture of facts, 63
    atomic, 63, 65–66, 82
    complex or molecular, 63, 65–66, 82
    deep structure, 64–65
    relation to ideas, 22, 63
    truth-value determined by facts, 63,
        65–66
propositional calculus, 27–28
    as an external standard of correct
        reasoning, 20, 23, 34–35, 40,
        110–111, 162–169
    as representing the world, 162–169
    relation to natural language, 27, 28–29
    use of in psychology, 29, 33–35, 37,
        38–40, 167–169

pseudoconcreteness, 180
pseudo-concepts, 171
purpose, 93–100, 136–138
  as intervening variables, 94
  cognitive-purposive theory of, 93–94
  in Nature, 186–187
  reductionist accounts of, 95–97
purposive action, 93–97, 99–100
purposive activity in Nature, 186–187
purposive systems
  mechanisms v. organisms, 95–100,
    186–187

qualities
  primary and secondary, 46, 81
quantity v. quality, 113–115, 123–124,
  164, 192

rationalism, 7, 21–23, 41–45, 59,
  104–105, 106, 108–110, 178, 184
reaction-time, 65, 84–85, 91
reason v. expression, 104–105
reasoning
  analogical, 36
  conditional, 32–33, 38
  deductive, 26, 28–35, 36–40, 56, 76,
    110, 162–163
  distortion of, 31–32, 36–38
  error, 26, 32, 33, 35, 36, 56
  interfering factors, 31–32, 36–38
  laws of, see laws of thought
  logic as a model of, 24–33, 36, 38–40,
    76, 162–168
  practical, 39, 57–59, 162–169,
    175–178, 182–183
  probabilistic, 36
  propositional, 27–29, 38–40, 76,
    162–164, 166–167
  psychology of, 26–27, 28–29, 31–33,
    34–40, 55–59, 167–168
  pure, 26–27, 31, 39
  syllogistic, 29–33, 35–38, 55–56
  verbal, 36–37
reciprocity, 158
  of gestures, 146–149, 156
recognition, see also self-recognition
  mutual, 129–133, 149–150
  struggle for, 129–133, 135–136, 146,
    149–150
reflection 17–19, 23, 58–59, 108,
  109–110
reflexion, 17, 58, 107–108, 111–112, 142,
  167–169, 174–175
  categories of, 163–165

reflexive identity and contradiction, 168
reflexive laws of thought, 167–169
reflexivity, 141
Renaissance, the, 13–16, 80, 103, 104,
  107–108
representations
  internal, 35, 40, 54–56, 57–59, 63–66,
    74, 95
  of objects, 46–47, 127, 173–174
  of the external world by machines and
    organisms, 195
role-playing, 156–157
romanticism, 45, 103, 106–108, 112, 114,
  135, 138–139

scepticism
  Cartesian, 109–110, 112–113
  Hegelian, 113
science
  as a social activity, 188
self, the
  as individual, 16–17, 104
  Cartesian concept of, 15–20, 132
  expressivist concept of, 104–105,
    107–108
  externalization of, 108
  Hegelian concept of, 127–133,
    135–136, 149–150, 159–160
  its consciousness of objects, 20
  mediaeval concept of, 14, 15
  priority of, 17
  privacy of, 17, 104
  projection into the world, 108
  recognition by others, 124, 129–133,
    135–136, 149–150
  rediscovery of, 13, 16–17, 103
  Renaissance concept of, 14–15, 104,
    107–108
  romantic concept of, 104–105,
    107–108
  unfolding of, 105–106
self-consciousness, 72, 107–108, 116,
  127–132, 135–136, 157
  and other self-consciousnesses,
    129–131, 154–159
  and the importance of the family,
    149–150
  development of, 154–159
  differentiation of, 163
  expressivist, 107–108, 135
  reflective, 108
  reflexive, 107–108, 135
  romantic, 107–108, 135
self-identity, 18, 19

228

self-knowledge, 136, 138
self-recognition, 129–130, 131, 132,
    135–136, 149–150, 154, 160
    at the expense of the other, 130–131,
        154, 159–160
    pathological, 150
self-unfolding, 105–106
semantic components, 49, 52, 191
semantic elements, 52
semantic features, 50–52, 121, 179–180,
    191
semantic feature hypothesis, 50–52, 121,
    179–180
semantic markers, 121, 179
semantic memory, 84–85
semantic networks, 84–85
sense-certainty, 117–119
sentence comprehension, 84–85
social nature of action, 144–145
space
    and time as internal representations,
        52–53
    logical systems as independent of, 23
spatialization of time, 90–91
speech
    regulatory function of, 198
standards
    external, 20–23, 31–40, 110–111, 113
    internal, 20, 111–114
stigma, 135
Sturm and Drang, 104, 184–185
subject
    as epistemologically prior to the object,
        20–21, 41, 109
subjectivity (Cartesian), 16–17, 18, 19, 23
substance
    conscious or thinking, 16–17, 20, 105,
        109
    extended, 20, 42
syllogisms, 29–33, 36–37, 55–56
    hypothetical, 32–33
synchronization, 148
synthetic unity of apperception, 127

teleology, 95–100
theory-ladenness
    of observation, 188–193
    of perception, 2–3, 188, 192
thing-in-itself, 53–55, 127, 179, 181–182
thinking, 15–16, 19, 21–23, 35, 41–43,
    44, 45–46
    logical, 21–23, 24–40, 199–200
thinking thing or substance, 16–17, 20,
    42, 92, 104, 105, 109

thought, 17–19, 22–23
    an active process, 109, 174–177
    and certainty, 21–23, 60–62, 109, 117
    and expression, 108
    and ideas, 41
    faculties or modes of, 60–62
    impossible without language, 142, 177,
        198–199
    in the foetus, 19, 44
    inseparable from consciousness, 17–20,
        108, 110
    laws of, 24–27, 162–169, 173–174
    reflective, 17–19, 23, 58–59, 108
    reflexive, 17, 58, 107–108, 142,
        167–169, 174–175
    relation to action, 23, 174–176, 199
    the mind identified with, 16–17, 20, 42,
        92, 104, 105, 109
time
    and space as internal representations,
        52–53
    Cartesian conception of, 91
    elimination of in physics and
        psychology, 89–92
    logical systems as independent of, 23
    spatialization of, 90–91
timelessness, 89–91
truth, 16, 21–23, 42, 60–62, 65, 112–114
    and consciousness, 17–20
    and error, 60
    appearance of, 117–119
    approach to, 111–114, 116, 117, 126,
        178–182, 201–202
    as a finished product, 19, 22, 112–113,
        163, 166–167
    as a reflexive process, 108, 163–169,
        174, 178–182
    certain and static elements of, 22
    empiricist theory of, 45–46, 52, 61–62,
        188–192
    Hegelian theory of, 108, 111–114,
        126–127, 163–169, 174, 178–182
    identified with certainty, 21–23, 60–62,
        117
    intuitive, 21–23, 109, 124
    lower stages as phenomena, 113–114,
        117
    journey towards, 111–114, 116, 117,
        126, 178–182, 201–202
    mediated, 109–110, 124–125, 174
    not a finished product, 19, 112–113,
        178–182, 201–202
    rationalist theory of, 21–23, 41–45, 52,
        178

representational theory of, 46, 173–174
search after, 15–16, 21, 60, 126
truth-functional connectives, 27–29,
    38–39, 82
truth-functional language, 27–29, 38–39,
    63
truth-tables, 28, 33, 38
truth-values, 28, 38, 63, 110
turn-taking, 156, 158, 160
  in conversation, 151–153

understanding, the, 20–23, 40–42, 45–47,
    52–55, 60–62, 126–129
  activity of, 109, 127–129, 135–138
  passivity of, 60–62, 79, 109, 117
universal validity
  Kantian, 52–53
  Piagetian, 91
universals
  Cartesian, 42, 43–44, 46, 49, 51, 120,
    196
  Hegelian, 118–126, 132, 196, 203
  relation to particulars, 118–120,

121–125, 139, 196–197
  unity with particulars, 120–121,
    196–197
universality
  empirical, 52
  strict, 52–53, 55

verbs
  as the first words of language, 169, 173
  function of, 85–88, 90, 93, 173

world
  as essentially contradictory, 163–165
  as essentially non-contradictory, 24–25
  as inferred from the contents of the
    mind, 20, 41, 53–55, 108–110
  as unknown and impenetrable, 20,
    92–93
world-in-itself, 16–17, 19–20, 41, 53–55,
    92–93, 108–110
world-for-consciousness, 111–112, 139
world-of-consciousness, 19–20, 41,
    52–55, 108–110, 139